Law, Ethi...
Limits of ...

Sheffield Hallam University
Learning and IT Services
Collegiate Learning Centre
Collegiate Crescent Campus
Sheffield   S10 2BP

Sheffield Hallam University
Learning and Information Services
Withdrawn From Stock

102 074 246 1

ONE WEEK
LOAN

This book is due for return on or before the last date shown below.

A conflict ...
patient. Th...
treat or not...
ment featu...
nent examp...
Schiavo in ...
2005, the ...
alongside a...
or through ...

Richard ...
frequently ...
require. H...
issues at st...
mise' here, ...
edence. He...
system of ...
courts to re...

Providin...
adults alike...
this book ...
informing ...

Richard H...
of the Cent...
tions inclu...
(Routledge...
Medical Eth...
clinical eth...
Palliative C...

Sheffield Hallam
Learning and Inform...
Withdrawn Fr...

D1375634

Biomedical Law and Ethics Library

Series Editor: Sheila A.M. McLean

Scientific and clinical advances, social and political developments and the impact of healthcare on our lives raise profound ethical and legal questions. Medical law and ethics have become central to our understanding of these problems, and are important tools for the analysis and resolution of problems – real or imagined.

In this series, scholars at the forefront of biomedical law and ethics contribute to the debates in this area, with accessible, thought-provoking, and sometimes controversial ideas. Each book in the series develops an independent hypothesis and argues cogently for a particular position. One of the major contributions of this series is the extent to which both law and ethics are utilised in the content of the books, and the shape of the series itself.

The books in this series are analytical, with a key target audience of lawyers, doctors, nurses and the intelligent lay public.

Available titles:

Human Fertilisation and Embryology (2006)
Reproducing Regulation
Kirsty Horsey & Hazel Biggs

Intention and Causation in Medical Non-Killing (2006)
The Impact of Criminal Law Concepts on Euthanasia and Assisted Suicide
Glenys Williams

Impairment and Disability (2007)
Law and Ethics at the Beginning and End of Life
Sheila McLean & Laura Williamson

Bioethics and the Humanities (2007)
Attitudes and Perceptions
Robin Downie & Jane Macnaughton

Defending the Genetic Supermarket (2007)
The Law and Ethics of Selecting the Next Generation
Colin Gavaghan

The Harm Paradox (2007)
Tort Law and the Unwanted Child in an Era of Choice
Nicolette Priaulx

Assisted Dying (2007)
Reflections on the Need for Law Reform
Sheila McLean

Medicine, Malpractice and Misapprehensions (2007)
Vivienne Harpwood

Euthanasia, Ethics and the Law (2007)
From Conflict to Compromise
Richard Huxtable

Best Interests of the Child in Healthcare (2007)
Sarah Elliston

Values in Medicine (2008)
The Realities of Clinical Practice
Donald Evans

Autonomy, Consent and the Law (2009)
Sheila McLean

Healthcare Research Ethics and Law (2009)
Regulation, Review and Responsibility
Hazel Biggs

The Body in Bioethics (2009)
Alastair V. Campbell

Genomic Negligence (2011)
An Interest in Autonomy as the Basis for Novel Negligence Claims
Generated by Genetic Technology
Victoria Chico

Health Professionals and Trust
The Cure for Healthcare Law and Policy
Mark Henaghan

Medical Ethics in China
A Transcultural Interpretation
Jing-Bao Nie

Law, Ethics and Compromise at the Limits of Life
To Treat or not to Treat?
Richard Huxtable

Forthcoming titles include:

Abortion Law and Policy
An Equal Opportunity Perspective
Kerry Petersen

Bioethics
Methods, Theories, Scopes
Marcus Düwell

Birth, Harm and the Role of Distributive Justice
Burdens, Blessings, Need and Desert
Alasdair Maclean

The Jurisprudence of Pregnancy
Concepts of Conflict, Persons and Property
Mary Ford

About the Series Editor
Professor Sheila McLean is International Bar Association Professor of Law and
Ethics in Medicine and Director of the Institute of Law and Ethics in Medicine
at the University of Glasgow.

Law, Ethics and Compromise at the Limits of Life

To treat or not to treat?

Richard Huxtable

Routledge
Taylor & Francis Group

LONDON AND NEW YORK

First published 2013
by Routledge
2 Park Square, Milton Park, Abingdon, Oxon OX14 4RN

Simultaneously published in the USA and Canada
by Routledge
711 Third Avenue, New York, NY 10017

Routledge is an imprint of the Taylor & Francis Group, an informa business

© 2013 Richard Huxtable

The right of Richard Huxtable to be identified as author of this work
has been asserted by him in accordance with sections 77 and 78 of
the Copyright, Designs and Patents Act 1988.

All rights reserved. No part of this book may be reprinted or
reproduced or utilised in any form or by any electronic,
mechanical, or other means, now known or hereafter
invented, including photocopying and recording, or in any
information storage or retrieval system, without permission in
writing from the publishers.

Trademark notice: Product or corporate names may be trademarks or
registered trademarks, and are used only for identification and
explanation without intent to infringe.

British Library Cataloguing in Publication Data

A catalogue record for this book is available from the British Library

Library of Congress Cataloging in Publication Data
Huxtable, Richard.
  Law, ethics and compromise at the limits of life: to treat or not to
treat? / Richard Huxtable.
    p. cm. — (Biomedical law and ethics library)
  ISBN 978-0-415-49279-9 (hardback) — ISBN 978-0-415-
  49280-5 (pbk.) — ISBN 978-0-203-09844-8 (e-book)
  1. Terminal care—Law and legislation—England.   I. Title.
  KD3410.E88H89 2013
  344.4203'2175—dc23

                                                    2012008492

ISBN: 978–0–415–49279–9 (hbk)
ISBN: 978–0–415–49280–5 (pbk)
ISBN: 978–0–203–09844–8 (ebk)

Typeset in Garamond
by RefineCatch Limited, Bungay, Suffolk

MIX
Paper from
responsible sources
FSC® C004839
www.fsc.org

Printed and bound by CPI Group (UK) Ltd, Croydon, CR0 4YY

For Ted and Tom

Contents

Acknowledgements   xiii
List of abbreviations   xv
Table of reported cases   xvii

Introduction   1

1   Judging law and ethics at the limits of life   11

   1.1 Conflicts in the clinic: the case of David Glass 11
   1.2 Judging law: rationality and the rule of law 14
      1.2.1 Judging law from within 14
      1.2.2 Criteria for rational law 16
      1.2.3 Fuller and the rule of law 18
      1.2.4 Taking stock: criteria for judging law 21
   1.3 Judging ethics 22
      1.3.1 Judging ethics from within (law): immanent
         critique 22
      1.3.2 Judging ethics from outside (law): judgments,
         principles and theories 25
   1.4 Conclusion: (not) just law 29

2   Law at the limits of life: children, welfare and
   best interests   33

   2.1 Conflicts in the clinic: the case of Charlotte Wyatt 33
   2.2 Best interests, welfare and the law 36
      2.2.1 Criminal beginnings? 37
      2.2.2 Civil proceedings? 39
   2.3 Conclusion: in the child's best interests? 49

3   **Law at the limits of life: adults, incapacity and precedent autonomy**   51

    3.1 Conflicts in the clinic: the case of Terri Schiavo 51
    3.2 Best interests, incapacity and precedent autonomy 54
        3.2.1 Best interests and the persistent vegetative state 55
        3.2.2 Best interests beyond the persistent vegetative state 62
        3.2.3 Advance directives 65
        3.2.4 Lasting powers of attorney 71
    3.3 Conclusion: autonomy or welfare? 72

4   **The limits of law at the limits of life: to treat or not to treat?**   75

    4.1 Conflicts in the clinic: to treat or not to treat? 75
    4.2 Taking exception to exceptions: a duty to treat? 76
    4.3 In the patient's best interests? 80
        4.3.1 Treating like cases alike? 80
        4.3.2 Objective rule(s)? 84
        4.3.3 Know-ability and perform-ability? 85
    4.4 Respecting autonomy? 90
    4.5 Subjective judgments? From law to ethics at the limits of life 95
    4.6 Conclusion: problems painting unicorns with Odysseus 101

5   **Calculating the value of life at the limits of life**   103

    5.1 Looking for values in English law 103
    5.2 The value of life in English law 104
    5.3 Calculating the value of life 109
        5.3.1 The intrinsic value of life: the disutility of futility? 109
        5.3.2 The instrumental value of life: worthless lives? 114
        5.3.3 The self-determined value of life: autonomy unbound? 116
    5.4 Subjective judgments or objective judgments? 120
    5.5 Conclusion: beyond conflict? 122

6   **A case for compromise at the limits of life**   123

    6.1 Beyond conflict in the clinic: towards compromise 123
    6.2 Contemplating compromise 125
    6.3 Criticising compromise 127
    6.4 Cause to compromise: six reasons to compromise 132
    6.5 Constructing compromise: three virtues of compromising 135
    6.6 Conclusion: compromise in theory and practice 140

7   Crafting compromise: courts or clinical ethics committees?   143

   7.1 Conflicts in the clinic revisited: to treat or not to treat? 143

   7.2 Viewing values in the court 144

      7.2.1 For the courts as vehicles of values 145

      7.2.2 Against the courts as vehicles of values 146

      7.2.3 Law and ethics in the courts and beyond 148

   7.3 Viewing values in clinical ethics support 153

      7.3.1 For the ethics support of clinical ethics support 153

      7.3.2 Against the ethics support of clinical ethics support 159

   7.4 Conclusion: compromise in court or clinical ethics committee? 163

8   Committees, courts and compromise at the limits of life   165

   8.1 Reconstructing clinical ethics support 165

   8.2 The products of clinical ethics consultation: issuing consistent guidance 166

   8.3 The processes of clinical ethics consultation: observing due process 168

   8.4 Expertise in clinical ethics consultation: exhibiting ethical expertise 172

   8.5 Conclusion: clinical ethics committees, courts and compromise 177

Bibliography   183

Index   199

Acknowledgements

This book has been written in various locations and its arguments tested before a variety of audiences, which has helped to enrich both the process of writing and (hopefully) the resulting product. I am particularly grateful to the Wellcome Trust, whose award of a small research grant made the project possible, and to the Ethox Centre at the University of Oxford, whose conferment of a Caroline Miles Visiting Scholarship enabled me to transform the possible into the actual. Thanks too to my colleagues at the Centre for Ethics in Medicine in Bristol for their ongoing support, and to those who helped cover some of my teaching duties while I was writing.

I am also indebted to the diverse audiences who have provided me with feedback on the arguments as they have developed. Special thanks must go to: the staff and students who have attended research seminars in Bristol and Oxford; clinicians and other members of clinical ethics committees who participated in conferences organised in Lincoln and in the Royal Society of Medicine in London; the audiences at Medicine Unboxed 2011 in Cheltenham and at the Bath Royal Literary and Scientific Institution; and to the members of the public, clinicians, philosophers and lawyers who attended conferences in Munich and in Rovereto.

Although the usual caveat applies, there are certain individuals who made a direct contribution, and to whom I am especially grateful. Thanks, then, to Fred Cram, who provided some research assistance, and to Giles Birchley, Zuzana Deans, Ruth Horn and José Miola, who each commented on parts of the manuscript; thank you all for bringing your distinctive skills to bear, and thereby improving on my own efforts. Of course, I owe my greatest debt of gratitude to Genevieve: confidante, comedienne and cajoler; sounding board and, all-too-often, the sound of sense, who unfailingly helps me to stay on target, here as elsewhere. Thanks for everything.

Finally, I thank Jordan Publishing Ltd, Taylor and Francis, Cambridge University Press and my co-authors for permitting me (in Chapters 1, 2 and 6, respectively) to reproduce and rework elements of: Huxtable, R. and Forbes, K. (2004) 'Glass v UK: Maternal instinct vs. medical opinion', *Child and Family Law Quarterly*, 16(3): 339–54; Jackson, L. and Huxtable, R. (2005) 'The doctor-parent relationship: As fragile as *Glass?*', *Journal of Social Welfare and Family Law*, 27(3–4): 369–81; Huxtable, R. (2012) 'Euthanasia excused: Between prohibition and permission', in A. Alghrani, R. Bennett and S. Ost (eds) *The Criminal Law and Bioethical Conflict: Walking the Tightrope*, Cambridge: Cambridge University Press.

List of abbreviations

ACT	Association for Children's Palliative Care
ANH	Artificial nutrition and hydration
BBC	British Broadcasting Corporation
BMA	British Medical Association
CANH	Clinically assisted nutrition and hydration
CEC	Clinical ethics committee
CPAP	Continuous positive airway pressure
CPR	Cardiopulmonary resuscitation
CPS	Crown Prosecution Service
DNAR	Do not attempt resuscitation
DNR	Do not resuscitate
DPP	Director of Public Prosecutions
fMRI	Functional magnetic resonance imaging
GMC	General Medical Council
GP	General Practitioner
ITU	Intensive treatment unit
J	Justice
LCJ	Lord Chief Justice
LJ	Lady/Lord Justice
LPA	Lasting power of attorney
MCS	Minimally conscious state
MR	Master of the Rolls
MS	Multiple sclerosis
NCPC	National Council of Palliative Care
NHS	National Health Service
P	President of the Family Division of the High Court
PEG	Percutaneous endoscopic gastrostomy
PVS	Permanent/persistent vegetative state
QC	Queen's Counsel
RCN	Royal College of Nursing
RCPCH	Royal College of Paediatrics and Child Health
TPN	Total parenteral nutrition
VS	Vegetative state

Table of reported cases

England and Wales

A Hospital v SW [2007] EWHC 425. 61
A National Health Service Trust v D [2000] 2 FLR 677. . . . . .44, 98, 106, 108
Airedale NHS Trust v Bland [1993] 2 WLR 316. . . . . 45, 51, 55–57, 58,
64, 66, 71, 75–76, 77–78, 79, 82–83,
87, 94, 98, 103, 104, 105, 107,
108, 111, 113, 114, 115, 124,
131, 145, 146, 150, 151, 158
An NHS Trust v A and SA [2005] EWCA Civ 1145 . . . . .62–63, 83
An NHS Trust v D [2005] EWHC 2439. . . . . .61, 108
An NHS Trust v J [2006] All ER (D) 73 (Dec) 61
An NHS Trust v MB [2006] EWHC 507 . . . . 46–47, 80, 82, 84, 87, 88, 89,
90, 97, 99, 100, 124, 146, 179
AVS v A NHS Foundation Trust and B PCT [2011] EWCA Civ 7 72

B NHS Trust v J [2006] EWHC 3152 . . . . .54, 58, 61, 73
Bolam v Friern Hospital Management Committee
[1957] 1 WLR 582. . . . . .56, 58, 78, 98, 100, 161, 170
Burke v United Kingdom (Application No 19807/06) 70

Chester v Afshar [2004] 3 WLR 927 90
Council of Civil Service Unions (CCSU) v Minister for the Civil Service
[1985] AC 374 24

Frenchay NHS Trust v S [1994] 1 WLR 601 . . . . .57, 82, 83

Gibbins v Proctor (1918) 12 Cr App Rep 134. .38, 76, 77
Glass v UK [2004] 1 FCR 553 . . . . .11–14, 45, 98
Glass v United Kingdom (Admissibility) (61827/00) (2003)
37 EHRR CD66 (ECtHR). 14

HE v A Hospital NHS Trust [2003] 2 FLR 408 . . . . .67, 90, 93, 128
Hedley Byrne and Co Ltd v Heller and Partners Ltd [1964]
AC 465 11

In re MB (medical treatment) [1997] 2 FLR 426 . . . . .65, 66
In the Matter of SA [2005] EWHC 2942. 101

National Health Service Trust v D [2000] 2 FLR 677 . . . . .44, 98, 106, 108
NHS Trust A v H [2001] 2 FLR 501. . . . . .59, 158
NHS Trust A v M; NHS Trust B v H [2001] 2 WLR 942 . . . . .58, 108, 158
NHS Trust v A (a child) [2007] EWHC 1696. . . . . .47–48, 81, 82, 100, 107
NHS Trust v I [2003] EWHC 2243 . . . . .59, 108
NHS Trust v T (adult patient: refusal of medical treatment) [2005]
   1 All ER 387. . . . . .68, 69, 93

Portsmouth Hospitals NHS Trust v Wyatt (Costs) [2006] EWCA
   Civ 529. 36
Portsmouth NHS Trust (No 1) v Wyatt [2005] EWHC 117. 34
Portsmouth NHS Trust v W [2005] EWHC 2293. 36
Portsmouth NHS Trust v Wyatt [2004]
   1 FLR 21. . . . . .33, 34, 46, 165

R (on the application of Burke) v General Medical Council [2005]
   2 WLR 431. . . . . .69, 158
R (on the application of Burke) v General Medical
   Council [2005] 3 WLR 1132 . . . . .69, 85, 91, 93, 94–95, 108, 145
R (on the application of Pretty) v DPP [2002]
   1 FLR 268. . . . . .79, 118, 146, 147
R (on the application of Purdy) v DPP [2009]
   UKHL 45 . . . . .79, 91
R v Adomako [1995] AC 789. 77
R v Arthur (1981) 12 BMLR 1 . . . . .38–39, 49, 78–79, 80, 89, 96
R v Bingley Magistrates' Court ex p Morrow
   [1995] Med L Rev 86 . . . . .39, 56
R v Brown et al [1993] 2 WLR 556. 105
R v Cambridge Health Authority ex p B [1995] 2 All ER 129. 42
R v Collins and Ashworth Hospital Authority ex p Brady [2000]
   Lloyd's Rep Med 355. 92
R v Davies, Wild and Hodgson [2000] WL 1084485
   (CA (Crim Div)). 13
R v Evans [2009] EWCA Crim 650 77
R v G and Another [2003] 1 AC 1034. 28
R v Howe [1987] 1 All ER 771 . . . . .24, 25
R v Instan [1893] 1 QB 450 145
R v Portsmouth Hospital NHS Trust ex p Glass [1999]
   2 FLR 905. . . . . .13, 23, 43, 75, 89
R v Smith [1979] Crim LR 251. 76
R v Stone and Dobinson [1977] QB 354 . . . . .38, 77
Re A (children) (conjoined twins: medical treatment)
   [2000] 4 All ER 961. . . . . 23, 44–45, 81, 86, 88, 89,
                                    97, 105, 106, 108, 123,
                               146, 147, 150, 158, 163
Re A (male sterilisation) [2000] 1 FLR 549. . . . . .78, 80, 98
Re A [1992] 3 Med LR 303 112
Re AK (medical treatment: consent) [2001] 1 FLR 129 . . . . .67, 93, 108
Re AVS v A NHS Foundation Trust [2010] EWHC 2746. 72
Re B (a child)(medical treatment) [2008] EWHC 1996 . . . . .48–49, 50, 89
Re B (a minor)(wardship: jurisdiction) [1988] AC 199. .86
Re B (a minor)(wardship: medical treatment) [1981] 1 WLR 1421 . . . . 38, 79–80,
                                               100, 106

Re B (adult: refusal of medical treatment) [2002] 2 All ER 449 . . . . . 66, 92, 108, 117, 122, 146, 158

Re C (a baby) [1996] 2 FLR 43 . . . . 42, 86

Re C (a minor)(wardship: medical treatment) [1990] Fam 26 . . . . 40, 41, 84,

Re C (adult patient: restriction of publicity after death) [1996] 1 FCR 605 57

Re C (adult: refusal of treatment) [1994] 1 WLR 290 . . . . 66, 93

Re C (medical treatment) [1998] 1 FLR 384 . . . . 43, 82, 113

Re C [2010] EWHC 3448 61–62

Re D (medical treatment) [1998] 1 FLR 411 . . . . 58, 83, 107

Re D (medical treatment: mentally disabled patient) [1998] 2 FLR 22 62

Re E (a minor)(wardship: medical treatment) [1993]
1 FLR 386 90

Re F (mental patient: sterilisation) [1990] 2 AC 1 . . . . 56, 71, 85, 98

Re G (2002) 65 BMLR 6 59

Re G (adult patient: publicity) [1995] 2 FLR 528 57

Re G (persistent vegetative state) [1995] 2 FCR 46 57

Re H (a patient) [1998] 2 FLR 36 . . . . 58, 83

Re J (a minor)(wardship: medical treatment)
[1991] 1 FLR 366 . . . . 41, 42, 62, 80, 106, 115, 125

Re J (a minor)(wardship: medical treatment) [1992] 2 FLR 165 . . . . 42, 80, 99

Re JT (adult: refusal of medical treatment) [1998] 1 FLR 48 66

Re K (a child)(withdrawal of treatment) [2006] EWHC 1007 106

Re L (a child)(medical treatment: benefit) [2004]
EWHC 2713 . . . . 45–46, 87, 98, 106

Re OT [2009] EWHC 633 . . . . 49, 108, 171

Re R (adult: medical treatment) [1996] 2 FLR 99 . . . . 62, 83, 87

Re SL (adult patient)(medical treatment) [2000] 2 FCR 452 82

Re T (a minor)(wardship: medical treatment) [1997] 1 All ER 906 . . . . 43, 81, 88

Re T (adult: refusal of medical treatment) [1992] 4 All ER 649 . . . . 66, 92, 117

Re W (adult: refusal of medical treatment) [2002] EWHC 901 118

Re Wyatt (a child)(medical treatment: continuation of order) [2005]
EWHC 693 34

Re Wyatt [2006] EWHC 319 36

Re Z (local authority: duty) [2005] 1 WLR 959 79

Royal Wolverhampton Hospitals NHS Trust v B [2000]
2 FCR 76 43–44

Swindon and Marlborough NHS Trust v S [1995]
Med L Rev 84 57

Trust A, Trust B, Dr V v Mr M [2005] EWHC 807 . . . . 59–60, 150, 163

W Healthcare NHS Trust v KH [2005] 1 WLR 834 . . . . 68, 93

W v M and S and A NHS Primary Care Trust [2011]
EWHC 2443 . . . . 59, 63–64, 82, 83, 92, 93–94, 124, 179, 181

Wyatt v Portsmouth Hospital NHS Trust
[2005] EWCA Civ 1181 . . . . 33–36, 50, 80, 81, 87, 88, 98

New Zealand

Re G [1996] NZFLR 362 159–159

Auckland Area Health Board v Attorney-General [1993]
1 NZLR 235 159

USA

Bush v Schiavo, 885 So 2d 321, 324 (Fla 2004) 54

Cruzan v Director, Missouri Department of Health, 497 US 261 (1990) 55

In re Browning, 568 So 2d 4 (Fla 1990) 52
In re Conservatorship of Torres, 357 NW2d 332 (Minn 1984) 158
*In re Guardianship of Theresa Marie Schiavo, Incapacitated. Robert Schindler
  and Mary Schindler, Appellants, v Michael Schiavo, as Guardian of the
  person of Theresa Marie Schiavo, Appellee; and Michael Schiavo, as
  Guardian of the person of Theresa Marie Schiavo, Appellant, v
  Robert Schindler and Mary Schindler, Appellees.* Case Numbers:
  2D00-1269, 2D01-1836 and 2D01-1891 53
In re Quinlan, (1976) NJ 355 A 2d 647 . . . . .54–55, 87, 103–104, 158, 177
In re Schiavo, 90-2908GD-003 (Fla Cir Ct,
  Pinellas Co, 11 February 2000) 52
In re Schiavo, 90-2908GB-003 (Fla Cir Ct, Pinellas Co,
  22 November 2002) 53
In re Guardianship of Theresa Marie Schiavo, Incapacitated,
  File No 90-2908GD-003 53
*In re Guardianship of Theresa Marie Schiavo, Incapacitated.
  Michael Schiavo, as Guardian of the person of Theresa Marie Schiavo,
  Petitioner, v Robert Schindler and Mary Schindler, Respondents,*
  File No 90-2908-GD-003 54

Re AC, 573 A2d 1235 (DC 1990) 143
Re Colyer, 660 P 2d 738 (1983) 158
Re Superintendent of Family and Child Service and Dawson (1983)
  145 DLR (3d) 610 42
Re Weberlist, (1974) 360 NYS 2d 783 42

Schindler v Schiavo, 792 So 2d 551, 557 (Fla Dist Ct App 2001) 52
Schindler v Schiavo, 851 So 2d 182, 187 (Fla Dist Ct App 2003) 53
Superintendent of Belchertown State School v Saikewicz, 373 Mass
  728, 370 NE 2d 417 (1977) 87

Introduction

A conflict arises in the clinic about whether life-supporting treatment should be provided to a patient who is not capable of indicating her wishes. The family and other loved ones of the patient want treatment to be given, but the doctors and their colleagues do not think this would be appropriate. Elsewhere on the ward, the family of another incompetent patient is opposed to treatment, which the team wishes to provide. The emphasis in contemporary health care is on health professionals working in partnership with patients and their families, with a view to securing consensus.[1] Yet, conflicts continue to arise and the dilemmas can be especially acute when the treatment in question is capable of prolonging life. The question inevitably arises: to treat or not to treat?

The National Council for Palliative Care (NCPC) describes a not uncommon case:

> Mr W, aged 59, has end-stage multiple sclerosis. Confined to bed over the last 2 years, he has a suprapubic catheter, and fixed flexion contractures of his knees. His pressure areas are intact, and he has been superbly cared for by his wife until she could no longer get him to swallow even water. His MS has caused progressive cognitive impairment over the last 2 years such that he is now unable to recognise family members. He is unable to speak or communicate even his basic needs. He moans when turned in bed . . .
>
> His GP has admitted Mr W into hospital to have a PEG feeding tube fitted, as he is aware of another GP who was taken to court for not 'force-feeding' a patient. His wife and daughter oppose the fitting of a feeding tube, saying, 'He's had enough'. One of the staff nurses on hospital ward says, 'You can't just let him starve to death'.[2]

There is a plethora of guidance available to guide the GP, the nurse and, indeed, Mr W's family. The professionals can draw on decades of material

---

1 eg General Medical Council 2010: para 47.
2 National Council for Palliative Care 2007: 19.

developed by such organisations as the Royal College of Nursing (RCN), the British Medical Association (BMA) and the General Medical Council (GMC).[3] The family, meanwhile, might find support in documents issued by charities, such as the NCPC.[4] All of these sources will provide useful steers, highlighting such issues as the need to serve a patient such as Mr W's best interests and to involve him and his loved ones in decision-making.

The messages are broadly the same, regardless of the age of the patient – whether he or she is an adult, a young person or an infant. Of course, if the patient is a young child and thus not capable of indicating her wishes, there is an obvious person with a good claim to involvement in the decision: her parent, or parents. Here too professional guidance, such as that issued by the Royal College of Paediatrics and Child Health (RCPCH), promotes a decision-making partnership between parents and professionals.[5] As the charity Association for Children's Palliative Care (ACT) puts it: 'Usually the best decisions and best outcomes are those where the parents and professionals can reach agreement'.[6]

But what if agreement cannot be reached? Can an answer to the dilemma be gleaned from any of this guidance? Whilst undoubtedly useful in highlighting the salient issues, any such guidance – by itself – is unlikely to provide *a*, let alone *the*, solution. The concepts which litter these documents introduce a multitude of ethical considerations, which give rise to further questions. What is to count as the course that serves the patient's best interests? Should decisions err on the side of prolonging life or on the side of prolonging only lives of sufficiently good 'quality'? What significance should be attached to any indications coming from the incompetent patient, particularly where these have been stated in advance of capacity being lost? And whose opinion should ultimately carry most weight when deciding on whether or not to terminate life-support? Although different documents might emphasise different features, there will remain areas of contention such that none is likely to provide definitive answers to these questions, nor to the overarching question: to treat or not to treat?

In this book, I set out to look for an answer to that question, focusing in particular on what guidance is available from the law, primarily in England and Wales. The book is a companion to my *Euthanasia, Ethics and the Law*.[7] It examines an issue only briefly considered in that volume, the withdrawal and withholding of life-support from incapacitated patients, that is, those currently incapable of expressing their wishes about such

---

3 eg British Medical Association 2007; British Medical Association, the Resuscitation Council (UK) and the Royal College of Nursing 2007; General Medical Council 2010.
4 eg National Council for Palliative Care 2007.
5 eg Royal College of Paediatrics and Child Health 2004: 15–16.
6 Association for Children's Palliative Care 2001: 8.
7 Huxtable 2007.

treatment.[8] The book follows a similar path to its predecessor, in first detailing numerous ethical dilemmas within and beneath the legal position that obtains in England and Wales, then defending the ethical compromise the law seeks to achieve between multiple values, before finally showing how enhanced scrutiny of these values would help with decision-making in this area. Knowledge of the prequel is not required, but readers of that book will see how my thinking has evolved, particularly in relation to compromise over ethical conflict. While that book addressed the criminal law dimensions of a range of decisions involving the end(ing) of life,[9] the present text is more overtly located in the civil law, and specifically the medical law governing decision-making in health care at the end of life.[10]

Chapter 1 begins with a widely-reported example of the type of conflict with which the book is concerned, in which the family of 12-year-old David Glass strongly contested the judgments of his doctors. Before looking in detail at the perceived rights and wrongs of this case, this chapter considers what parties like these can legitimately expect of the law when such a situation arises. Fundamentally, the legal endeavour involves the use of rules to guide people's behaviour. Flowing from (and thus intrinsic to) this endeavour are certain norms, which particular laws must observe if they are to count as law — and if they are to achieve their fundamental goal.

Following Roger Brownsword, these norms can be described as criteria of legal rationality.[11] There are three sets of requirements. First, law in a particular jurisdiction must be formally rational, which essentially means its rules must be consistent. Secondly, law must be instrumentally rational, such that it is capable of guiding action. Not only should the specific legal interventions chosen be capable of doing their job, but also, more generally, there must be rules, which can be known and which are capable of being followed. Finally, there is the question of substantive rationality, which holds that the substance of the particular rules should be legitimate. Quite what counts as a legitimate substance is, of course, a considerable question. In medical law, and thus in cases including that of David Glass, the substance is bound to have a

---

8 The patients under consideration in this book are to be considered alive (in legal terms), that is, their brainstems still function at the point at which the removal or denial of life support is contemplated. For discussion of the legal meaning of 'death' and the dis/continuation of treatment after a patient has been declared dead see Woodcock and Wheeler 2010.

9 Although I do consider the issue (in Chapter 5), it is not my intention here to examine in detail whether withdrawing and withholding treatment involve the (positive) end(ing) of life.

10 However, I acknowledge that the book might best occupy John Coggon's (2010a) narrower category 'end-of-life law', and I am also mindful that leading commentators have recently queried the nature — and even the very existence — of 'medical law' (Brazier and Glover 2000; Montgomery 2006: 208; Veitch 2007).

11 eg Brownsword 1996.

substantial moral component. It is possible to identify the moral commitments adopted in a particular legal system, through an immanent critique, by
which values are revealed and the extent to which they are consistently
observed in law is gauged. However, such a critique will not reveal whether
these are the right values. In order to steer law towards the ethically right
resolution of a contested case, we need further criteria for judging the available moral positions. As we see at the close of Chapter 1, criteria are available
for assessing moral judgments, principles and theories, which can help law in
its task, since they too emphasise the need to guide action. These criteria thus
emphasise the need for clarity, consistency, critical reflection and simplicity
(in articulation and application) when issuing moral guidance, which must
again be capable of achievement in the real world. In sum, rationality, and
particularly consistency, will be essential if there is to be successful guidance
for the family members and professionals caring for David Glass.

Equipped with a critical framework for assessing the particular rules that
may be brought to bear in a case like David Glass's, Chapters 2 and 3 then
describe, in some detail, the law pertaining to the withholding and withdrawing of life-supporting treatment from incapacitated patients. Proceeding
chronologically, each chapter aims to provide as comprehensive an account as
possible of the pertinent statutory provisions and rulings. Chapter 2 focuses
on children, in particular critically ill infants; Chapter 3 then turns to adults.
Each chapter again opens with a prominent case, which illustrates the main
controversies and concepts.

Chapter 2 thus begins with the case of seriously disabled newborn Charlotte
Wyatt, which went before the courts on more than 10 occasions. The paramount concern in such cases is the best interests of the child, as judged from
the assumed point of view of the child. The cases reveal that when the denial
of life-support is in issue, the judges are alert to the need to prolong life, but
they recognise also that treatment might sometimes be deemed 'futile' and,
indeed, that some lives might even be judged 'intolerable'. They strive to
reach these difficult decisions by drawing up a balance sheet, listing factors for
and against treatment in the individual case.

A similar approach – and, indeed, the same underlying standard – can be
found in the law pertaining to incapacitated adults, which is described in
Chapter 3. However, other factors may have a bearing on the outcome for
these patients, particularly exercises of precedent autonomy, by which, in
advance of losing capacity, a patient seeks to govern for an incompetent future
by conferring a lasting power of attorney or executing an advance directive.
The conflicts that can surround assessments of best interests and advance exercises of autonomy are illustrated in the American case of Terri Schiavo, over
whose care her parents and husband came into repeated conflict. The chapter
then describes how these issues have been addressed in English law, beginning
with patients who – like Terri Schiavo – have been diagnosed as being in a
vegetative state, such that their higher brain no longer functions, but they are
(legally and clinically) deemed to be alive. A substantial body of rulings has

developed, in which the judges (who must have the final say here[12]) have decided that clinically assisted (or 'artificial') nutrition and hydration need not be supplied to such patients where to do so is not in their best interests.

The best interests standard has also been applied to other patients lacking capacity, from whom life-sustaining measures have been removed; indeed, this standard underpins the Mental Capacity Act 2005, which came into force in 2007. In these cases similar approaches to those taken in relation to children can be detected, including the judges' use of a balance sheet of pros and cons. However, the groups of cases more obviously diverge in the greater weight purportedly attached to the older patient's prior wishes. The 2005 Act now governs advance exercises of autonomy, according to which an adult might set down instructions (in a specified form and fashion) or appoint a surrogate to decide on her behalf. Importantly, the surrogate decision-maker is still bound by the obligation to serve the incompetent patient's best interests.

Having set out what the current law apparently is in relation to patients both young and old, Chapter 4 proceeds to ask whether this body of law measures up to the demands described in Chapter 1. The short answer is that it does not. For one thing, the rulings from the civil courts that authorise the withdrawal of life-support from incapacitated patients do not sit comfortably alongside established precedents from the criminal courts, which point to a duty to take care of such individuals. Even focusing on the civil courts' attempts to serve the best interests of such patients does not restore rationality to the law, since we encounter different approaches to comparable cases and a dearth of objective rules. What rules there are appear unclear and unpredictable, such that it will be difficult for professionals, patients and their families to know or act upon what the law purports to require. Similar problems attend the law's attempts to provide for advance exercises of autonomy: had the mythical Greek hero Odysseus been subject to English law, he could scarcely have predicted whether his crew would have been required to honour his advance directive and thus leave him bound to the mast as they sailed past the Sirens.[13]

In the absence of a predictable legal steer, the fate of Odysseus – as well as others who have made no such provision for an incapacitated future – seems to depend on the subjective judgments of those empowered to make the final decision. Patients and their families have some such powers; health care professionals (doctors in particular) seem to be more influential; but judges are ultimately in control, and their approaches to the legal answer in a given case will be guided by more than 'mere' law, since they will be imbued with ethical import. Whether their resultant answers are sufficiently ethical thus becomes the central concern of Chapter 5.

---

12 As we will see in Chapter 3, such cases are required to come before the courts.
13 Homer *The Odyssey* XII; see also Morgan 1994.

Chapter 5 begins with an immanent critique of the law we have surveyed, which reveals three accounts of the ethical value of life embedded in the various rulings and statutory provisions. These accounts respectively hold that life has: first, an intrinsic value, such that it should not intentionally be ended; secondly, an instrumental value, such that it is only valuable (and worth protecting) insofar as it is a life of sufficiently good quality; and, thirdly, a self-determined value, according to which the value of life is a matter for the individual (who may therefore decide that its end has come). These calculations of the value of life are obviously at odds with each other and, as we saw in Chapter 1, an immanent critique can only take us so far; it cannot, alone, tell us which (if any) of these accounts is best. Unfortunately, on applying the criteria for judging such accounts from Chapter 1, we find that none of these positions makes a sufficient case for its priority over matters of life and death; although they all reveal something morally important, they also all fail to provide the clarity and consistency required of ethical edicts in the law.

Given that widespread consensus is unlikely but no conquering concept can be found, how are we to decide whether or not to treat the incapacitated patient when the parties involved in his or her care are not agreed? In Chapter 6 I suggest that the answer lies in compromise, specifically in the process for achieving *principled compromise*. This may not be a popular proposal, given the affront to integrity and moral responsibility it seems to entail, but I argue that such concerns are misplaced. Defenders of ethical pluralism, who hold that moral conflict is unavoidable in practice and in principle, help us to see the wisdom in remaining open to a variety of ethical solutions to a particular dilemma, including one which might split the difference between disputants. I do not suggest that compromise is the answer to all ethical woes; however, I do argue that compromise can be entirely defensible when certain conditions are present. Embarking on the process of principled compromise will be particularly indicated in situations of considerable complexity and uncertainty, where it is impossible to honour every competing value, but where a decision is unavoidable. These sorts of conditions are amply met in the cases with which this book is concerned. In such situations, the disputing parties would do well to come together around the compromise table, where – with the assistance of a third party – they can negotiate their way to a resolution. Such negotiation will then need to observe three ground rules if it is to count as principled: it must be conducted in a reflective, reliable and respectful manner.

Equipped with the principles of 'principled' compromise, we then need to work out how best to meet these requirements in practice. Chapter 7 contemplates two particular contenders: the courts and clinical ethics committees (CECs). The courts initially look well qualified for the work: they have the terminology and (in some judges at least) a track record for addressing the ethical dimensions of the cases before them; they have the authority to impose decisions on warring parties; and they are characteristically concerned with procedural rigour. However, as the previous chapters disclosed, the courts do not always issue consistent guidance; they are more often ethics-resistant than ethics-alert; and they are adversarial in nature, which suggests they will not be entirely fitting forums for securing a peaceful resolution. The 'de-moralisation' of recent legal judgments stands out as a particular concern.[14]

Although other means of achieving dispute resolution are available, I propose that we look to the growing numbers of CECs in the UK in an effort to 're-moralise' the law. Ethical appraisal is, after all, central to the work of CECs. They also, like the courts, aim to guide action, by providing advice in ethically complex situations; however, unlike the courts, they are concerned with providing support, rather than adjudicating between adversaries. It may not be surprising, then, that even the judges have expressed support for such groups. However, these groups have also come under recent attack.[15] There are three particularly problematic issues that undermine the CEC's potential to satisfy the ground rules of principled compromise. First, there is reason to doubt their function and accordingly their domain and expertise: are they able to claim any real expertise in ethics? Secondly, the guidance they issue is not necessarily consistent, but neither is it (merely?) advisory: advice might easily be seen as instruction, which troubles some commentators because the CEC then starts to resemble the court.[16] This might not be so problematic were it not for the third difficulty, which concerns the apparent lack of due process in clinical ethics support and thus attention to those issues we surveyed in Chapter 1.

On the one hand, the courts look process-heavy but ethics-light; on the other, ethics committees claim to be ethics-heavy but they are certainly process-light. This leads me to argue, in Chapter 8, that the way forward can be charted by combining the best of both worlds. In order for ethics committees to deliver on their potential they need to attend to their products, processes and purported expertise. This means, first, that the committees should aspire to issuing consistent guidance, which will at least mean a (procedural) commitment to issuing guidance consistently. Secondly, and developing from this recommendation, complaints about due process deserve serious consideration, which will require careful thought regarding the members, meetings and monitoring of CECs. Thirdly, and perhaps most controversially for some readers, committees should be prepared to acquire and exhibit ethical expertise. Although I will otherwise use the words 'ethics' and 'morals' interchangeably through this book, I should here clarify that I do not mean that CECs should acquire and exhibit moral expertise, in the sense of proclaiming definitively on matters of right and wrong. Rather, I mean merely to propose that CECs should be capable of reflecting critically on such matters, following the careful steer (and education) provided by a moral philosopher. The

14 See especially Montgomery 2006.
15 See especially McLean 2007b, 2008, 2009a.
16 eg McLean 2007b, 2008, 2009a.

committee should therefore be prepared to use a pluralistic ethical framework, in which different values can be identified, which they can then subject to critical attention. The moral philosopher will help the group to navigate through choppy ethical waters, but he or she will not assume the role of captain; instead, the group as a whole will decide on the direction to be taken.[17]

Where the committee's advice is accepted and the parties decide to proceed accordingly, then a principled resolution has been reached. However, when this does not occur, and one side continues to dispute the appropriate course, then the courts must remain available as the final arbiters, to issue binding decisions. By combining them like this, we might ensure that each forum best delivers on its potential. When they are called upon, the courts should be open to receiving a committee's deliberations on the values at stake; in this way, their own work might be 're-moralised'. And, by attending to their processes, clinical ethics support can better exhibit the necessary procedural virtues (and safeguards). At the book's conclusion I illustrate how this combination of roles might work in practice, by returning to the case of Mr W, which was described at the outset.

And so, at the end, we find no single answer to the question 'to treat or not to treat?', but instead a process for selecting an answer from the plurality of opposing principles which purport to prevail in the particular circumstances. If this means that the endeavour has failed, then the failure should be seen as a noble one, since we should have come to appreciate when and how to achieve principled compromise in situations in which more than one value appears capable of being our guide.

There is undoubtedly merit in studying further the meaning and limits of principled compromise; more detail is also needed on how best to combine the work of clinical ethics committees with that of the courts. For now, however, I hope to have provided some insight into various emerging and overlapping themes, including: the 'internal morality' of 'practices' like law, clinical ethics support and principled compromising; the resolution of conflicts in the clinic which arise at the limits of life; developments in both medicine and the law concerning patients who (apparently) lack capacity; ensuring that law does not avoid its ethical commitments; and ensuring that ethics committees do not shirk their procedural obligations.

Although the book is designed to be read as one sustained argument, some parts are likely to appeal more to particular audiences, given the breadth of the issues covered: clinicians and students of law and bioethics who are seeking to find out about the law should look to Chapters 2 and 3 for an overview of the main legal principles and judgments; legal scholars with an interest in jurisprudential concerns might favour Chapters 1 and 6; more

---

17 See Zoloth-Dorfman and Rubin 1997.

philosophically-inclined bioethicists and clinical ethicists could look to Chapters 5, 7 and 8; and critical medical lawyers might be particularly drawn to the arguments in Chapter 4. Whichever aspects (if any) might most appeal, I hope all readers will find something of interest in what follows.

Richard Huxtable

Bristol, February 2012

1 Judging law and ethics at the limits of life

The common law is tolerant of much illogicality, especially on the surface;
but no system of law can be workable if it has not got logic at the root of it.
Hedley Byrne and Co Ltd v Heller and Partners Ltd [1964] AC 465
at 516 (Lord Devlin)

1.1 Conflicts in the clinic: the case of David Glass

David Glass was born in 1986 with hydrocephalus, spastic quadriplegia, learning difficulties and no ability either to walk or talk.[1] His family, in particular his mother Carol, provided him with 24-hour care. Having become particularly unwell in July 1998, he was admitted to St Mary's Hospital, Portsmouth, where an operation to alleviate an upper respiratory tract obstruction was undertaken. Post-operative complications, including infections, led to David being placed on a ventilator. The health care team advised David's family that he was dying and that further intensive care was inappropriate. Although the family members were not satisfied with this judgment,[2] they twice declined the team's offer to arrange an independent second opinion.

In the event, David was well enough by the end of July to be moved from intensive care to the paediatric ward. Around this time, the possibility of using morphine to relieve David's distress was explored, to which his mother objected. David was discharged in early September but was readmitted on a number of occasions for treatment for respiratory tract infections. The use of morphine was again discussed when David was hospitalised on 8 September; Mrs Glass remained firmly opposed to this and she also instructed that efforts should be made to resuscitate her son in the event of cardiac arrest.

One of the doctors recorded that he thought an outside view should be sought, perhaps from the courts. David's GP also contacted the team, noting the family's concern that David would be 'helped on his way' with morphine.[3]

---

1 Huxtable and Forbes 2004.
2 Although a contemporaneous note drawn up by the clinicians disputes this.
3 *Glass v UK* [2004] 1 FCR 553 para 12.

Other notes taken by the doctors that day and the next suggest that Mrs Glass accepted that intubation would be inappropriate (although oxygen would be offered) and, as the Official Solicitor had advised,[4] that morphine could be used to relieve David's distress even without her consent. One of the team, Dr Hallet, noted Mrs Glass's opposition to 'euthanasia' and explained that this was not the team's intention; he recorded that Mrs Glass agreed with the use of morphine if it was needed to control pain.[5] Satisfied that agreement had been reached, Dr Hallet concluded that 'involvement of the court may not be necessary'.[6]

In October, David's condition again deteriorated, necessitating readmission. By 20 October, the doctors felt that David was 'dying from his lung disease'.[7] Mrs Glass and her family disputed this view, and objected to the proposed use of diamorphine (which is a more soluble and potent opioid than morphine). Once more the doctors recorded that 'the use of Morphine is *not* euthanasia – it is to relieve [David's] distress'.[8] By this time, the police had become involved; an officer advised the family that any attempt to remove David would result in arrest and that they themselves would be removed if they attempted to interfere with the administration of diamorphine. The dose of the analgesic was also disputed (1 mg per hour, which the family argued was an adult dose), but the doctors replied that David had built up tolerance to opioids and that the dose was appropriate given his weight. Security guards then intervened and threatened to eject the family after they attempted to prevent the doctors from entering David's room. Around this time, a 'Do Not Resuscitate' (DNR) order was placed in David's notes, without Mrs Glass's knowledge.[9] The doctors also recorded that the diamorphine was achieving its intended purpose, although the dose was reduced following further objections.

The next day Mrs Glass was alarmed at David's deterioration and demanded that the diamorphine be stopped. Dr Walker was willing to do this provided that the family did not attempt to revive David, and thus disturb his current 'peace'.[10] A fistfight broke out between some family members and two of the doctors, during which time Mrs Glass apparently 'resuscitated' her son.[11]

---

4 The Official Solicitor may act for those who lack the capacity to represent themselves: http://www.courtfunds.gov.uk/os/offsol.htm (accessed 18 December 2011).

5 *Glass v UK* [2004] 1 FCR 553 para 17.

6 ibid.

7 ibid para 21.

8 ibid para 5 (emphasis in original).

9 In current medical practice, it is more accurate to refer to (not) *attempting* resuscitation and hence DNAR (and sometimes DNACPR) orders: see British Medical Association, the Resuscitation Council (UK) and the Royal College of Nursing 2007.

10 *Glass v UK* [2004] 1 FCR 553 para 29.

11 ibid para 31. However, it looks more likely that Mrs Glass 'roused' (rather than 'resuscitated') her son after she removed the diamorphine drip. See Huxtable and Forbes 2004: 349.

The police intervened, and they – along with a mother visiting another patient – were also assaulted. All but one of the patients on the ward had to be evacuated.

The day after these incredible incidents, David's condition had improved sufficiently that, after arrangements were made for home care (albeit incomplete arrangements, according to Mrs Glass), he was discharged. In a letter in November 1998, the Portsmouth Trust notified the family that it could no longer offer treatment to David and, given the disagreements, explained that any future care should be provided in Southampton General Hospital.

Unsurprisingly, this difficult situation generated a flurry of legal activity. The criminal law was brought to bear, which resulted in some of the Glass family being convicted of assault and imprisoned (although their sentences were reduced on appeal).[12] The Crown Prosecution Service meanwhile found insufficient evidence to charge the doctors with attempted murder, conspiracy to murder, or any offences against the person. The General Medical Council also declined to find the doctors guilty of unprofessional behaviour; Mrs Glass had alleged that the doctors assaulted David in administering 'heroin' without parental or judicial approval.[13] Efforts to invoke the civil law of tort, albeit this time against Mrs Glass, also failed, as the trust was unable to prove trespass to the person.

Mrs Glass also looked to administrative law for a remedy, by seeking judicial review of the Trust's decisions in relation to David's care. Scott Baker J rejected the case, finding that this was an inappropriate legal mechanism for assessing a situation that no longer obtained (as the Portsmouth Trust no longer provided David's care) and that any prospective advice would be worthless as it would rest on speculation and might inhibit future treatment. On appeal,[14] Woolf MR felt it unnecessary to worry about which legal mechanism was employed in a case such as this. However, he also ruled that the numerous 'questions of judgment involved' prevented the court from making any decision in advance of the situation which might materialise.[15] He nevertheless reiterated Scott Baker J's advice that the courts would be available if needed.

On 5 June 2000, David and Mrs Glass brought an action to the European Court of Human Rights, complaining that their rights under the European Convention on Human Rights had been breached. They specifically claimed violations of Articles 2 (the right to life), 6 (the right to a fair trial), 8 (the right to respect for private and family life), 13 (the right to an effective remedy) and 14 (freedom from discrimination in the enjoyment of the Convention rights). The Court admitted the case for a full hearing, albeit only

---

12 *R v Davies, Wild and Hodgson* [2000] WL 1084485 (CA (Crim Div)).
13 *Glass v UK* [2004] 1 FCR 553 para 42.
14 *R v Portsmouth Hospitals NHS Trust ex p Glass* [1999] 2 FLR 905.
15 ibid para 40.

on the basis of those claims pertaining to Article 8.[16] At this hearing, the Court unanimously ruled that the right had been violated. Although Judge Casadevall felt that the non-consensual DNR order should also have been considered, the majority of the judges focused on the use of diamorphine: in the face of Mrs Glass's 'firm opposition', this amounted to an interference with David's 'right to respect for his private life, and in particular his right to physical integrity'.[17] The doctors had legitimately sought to serve David's interests; it was clear also that they had not intended to hasten his death; but it was the Trust that fell short of its obligations, in failing to refer the matter to the High Court, particularly in the face of the doctors' comments to this effect. The Trust could not have anticipated the fracas but it certainly could have obtained an emergency hearing. In addition to costs incurred, damages of €10,000 were awarded jointly to David and his mother.

1.2 Judging law: rationality and the rule of law

Did the law respond appropriately to the dilemmas in David Glass's case? Or, more accurately, were the responses of the various legal officials and bodies (such as the prosecutors and judges), and the statements and principles of law on which they relied, appropriate to this case? And how are we to judge that which is appropriate and inappropriate here? The temptation to delve directly into the substantive issues posed by David Glass's case is great; indeed, it is probably the standard approach in a book like this. However, I think it worth breaking with convention and postponing this enquiry until later chapters in favour of first developing a set of criteria for judging whether (any) law is 'good' or 'bad'.

1.2.1 Judging law from within

In order to assess how law fares with the dilemmas arising in David Glass's care, we first need to find some ground rules for judging law. More than a moment's reflection on this task is merited, since the ground rules are often too readily assumed in the campaign to criticise the old and craft the new.

Distinctions emerge depending upon the *standpoint* from which one views law, and the *substance* with which one fills the criteria for judging law. Starting with the standpoint, one might view law from elsewhere, that is, from some external perspective, such as might be offered by ethical theory.[18] This will often be entirely appropriate, certainly in a case like David's, but we need also to be satisfied that we are judging law on its own terms, that is, from within,

---

16 *Glass v United Kingdom (Admissibility)* (61827/00) (2003) 37 EHRR CD66 (ECtHR).
17 ibid para 70.
18 'Might be' since, as we will see, some contend that law and morality should not (and even cannot) be separated.

mindful of that which law is capable of achieving and, indeed, that which it is not. In the words of Alastair MacIntyre, we want to get within the practice known as 'law', where 'a practice' can be understood as:

> . . . any coherent and complex form of socially established cooperative human activity through which goods internal to that form of activity are realized in the course of trying to achieve those standards of excellence which are appropriate to, and partially definitive of, that form of activity, with the result that human powers to achieve excellence, and human conceptions of the ends and goods involved, are systematically extended.[19]

It is also important to consider whether the criteria against which we will judge law are substantive or formal (content-free) in nature. Ongoing disputes between natural lawyers and legal positivists over whether law is a moral enterprise illustrate some of the differences between the two. Members of the former group tend to believe that law is committed to a particular moral substance, whilst the latter deny any necessary relationship between law and morality.[20] Of course, the particular moral content in question is bound to attract criticism from those who cleave to competing accounts of morality.

There are evidently difficulties with the four options for judging law generated by these two sets of distinctions (internal-substantive, external-formal, and so on). To my mind, there is most merit in starting with the view from within law and on criteria that do not presume to impose any content on law. By taking this approach, we leave open important questions about the validity of legal rules as judged from substantive, external standpoints, whilst also being able to say something about the success (or otherwise) of law in a particular area.

Of course, in order to develop such criteria, we need to be clear about what is meant by 'the law'. Here, it is advisable to start with law in a *conceptual* sense, thus ignoring the particularities of specific legal systems, such as the one within which David Glass, his family and his doctors found themselves.[21] Inconveniently, the conceptual core of law is contested. However, probably the best candidate for getting this debate off the starting blocks is Lon Fuller's claim that the legal endeavour is 'the enterprise of subjecting human conduct to the governance of rules'.[22] Not for nothing is a leading legal primer entitled *How to Do Things with Rules*, in which the authors define a rule as 'a general

---

19 MacIntyre 2007: 187.
20 The natural law position, which can be traced back to such thinkers as Aristotle and Aquinas, finds contemporary (albeit diverse) expression in the work of Finnis (1986), Beyleveld and Brownsword (1994) and Simmonds (2007); legal positivists include Bentham, Austin, Kelsen and Hart, as well as more recent defenders including Kramer (1998).
21 ie the legal system in England and Wales, which is the main focus of this book.
22 Fuller 1969: 96.

norm mandating or guiding conduct or action in a given type of situation'.[23] Lawyers are specialists in 'rule-handling', although (as the authors rightly admit) lawyers are not alone in this; indeed, rather than dilute Fuller's definition, this admission may simply require us to acknowledge that there is more to (and captured by) 'law' than is often allowed. But, regardless of how far its domain extends, the question remains: what are the standards we might legitimately expect of law?

1.2.2 Criteria for rational law

Roger Brownsword, sometimes writing with Deryck Beyleveld and others, adopts Fuller's concept of law since he thinks it provides us with a suitably neutral candidate for further debate, which does not beg any of the questions usually at stake in jurisprudential disputes about the necessary connection between law and morality.[24] From this starting point, Brownsword argues that certain principles of 'rationality' flow from the concept of law.[25] 'Rationality' itself permits of a variety of interpretations but Nozick nudges us in the direction in which Brownsword is heading:

> To term something rational is to make an evaluation: its reasons are good ones (of a certain sort), and it meets the standards (of a certain sort) that it should meet. These standards . . . may vary from area to area, context to context, time to time . . .[26]

Focusing on the legal context, Brownsword sees Fuller's concept of law as implicitly connecting law to (practical) rationality: law is all about the regulation of human actions; rationality points the way to the 'best' actions; so, by definition, law ought to be rational.[27] Brownsword accordingly derives three criteria for judging particular laws and legal systems: *formal* rationality (or 'internal rationality'); *instrumental* rationality (or 'system rationality'), which is divisible into *generic* and *specific* forms; and *substantive* rationality (or 'norm rationality').

Formal rationality insists that legal doctrine should not be contradictory, that is, '*within a particular legal system* there should not be competing ground rules'.[28] Mere tensions between legal doctrines will not suffice, since Brownsword is here concerned with upholding the logical principle of

---

23 Twining and Miers 1991: 131.
24 Brownsword and Beyleveld 1994: 120.
25 cf Weber 1968.
26 Nozick 1993: 98.
27 Brownsword 1996.
28 Adams and Brownsword 1995: 10 (emphasis in original).

non-contradiction.[29] Where the material facts of two cases are indistinguishable but the legal officials adjudicate differently would be such a failure; so, if David Glass's case were to be resolved in a manner quite at odds with a ruling in a directly comparable case, the law in question could be criticised for formal irrationality. Reconciliation might be possible in some cases and, in any event, explicit contradictions are likely to be exceptional. Yet, formal rationality also forbids 'less obvious contradictions screened from view by traditional compartments and categories'.[30] The erection of traditional legal divisions (for example, contract and tort) and categories (for example, negligent acts and negligent statements) will not suffice to secure consistency.

Understood in its generic sense, *instrumental* rationality demands that law be capable of guiding action. From this seemingly uncontroversial opening,[31] Brownsword then proceeds to stipulate that this requires particular laws to observe what Fuller called the 'inner morality of law'.[32] There are eight requirements to satisfy: legal rules should be general (ie there must be rules, rather than, say, specific edicts), promulgated, prospective, clear, non-contradictory,[33] and relatively constant; legal rules should not require the impossible; and there should be congruence between the rules as officially declared and the rules as administered.

Brownsword sees these requirements as essentially procedural or formal, that is, lacking any substantive impingement.[34] This is clearest in the case of promulgation – legal rules might have any content, provided they are publicised. Neither is law obliged to have any particular content by the requirements of clarity, congruence, constancy and non-contradiction, although, with these, some reference to the content of other rules might be needed in order to establish that rationality is maintained. Meanwhile, says Brownsword, generality, prospectivity, and possibility of compliance might have some substantive impingement, but they do not commit law to what Fuller might term the governance of some 'external' morality.

As the label implies, specific instrumental rationality moves from the general requirements that must be obeyed by any legal rule aiming to guide action to the appropriateness of particular legal interventions in specific situations.[35]

---

29 Beyleveld and Brownsword 1991: 55.
30 Brownsword 1996: 152.
31 See Beyleveld and Brownsword 1991: 52.
32 Fuller 1969: 33–94.
33 Instrumental rationality repeats this requirement associated with formal rationality, since it emphasises that law must be capable of guiding action. Contradictory law obviously cannot do so and neither can unclear nor frequently fluctuating legal rules. Thus, although they are not pertinent in terms of formal rationality, instrumental rationality will be alert to doctrinal tensions which cloud the legal picture.
34 eg Brownsword 1993: 251–53.
35 See Brownsword 1993: 255–56.

Here, the efficacy of steps taken to secure particular purposes is the central concern, and attention may be focused on the particular branch of law employed to achieve particular ends. For example, if the purpose is to prohibit, then the right tools and techniques should be chosen to achieve this, which might involve criminal law, private law or some other branch(es) entirely. Socio-legal enquiries into any 'gaps' between declared rules and official practices will help gauge the extent to which law succeeds in its endeavours. Moreover, Brownsword contends that the generic and specific requirements 'must work together as a set of necessary and sufficient conditions for effective law'.[36]

Brownsword's criteria so far appear readily applicable to any legal system, with any set of legal rules, with any substance. However, with his third criterion Brownsword questions the very legitimacy of the substance of such rules: does the law conform to some given justifying end or principle? For him, only when it does so can law be viewed as fully rational, and thus fully defensible. Candidate theories abound,[37] and Brownsword favours a distinctive moral perspective, based on the work of rationalist philosopher Alan Gewirth.[38] Gewirth claims to have derived the definitive moral principle, instructing us to respect the freedom and well being of moral agents, from non-moral premises (essentially the fact of agency itself). This argument, albeit with some modifications,[39] is seen by Brownsword as the necessary cornerstone of practical (and thus legal) rationality, since to espouse any other criteria would be irrational. In other words, in the final analysis of David Glass's case, Brownsword would insist that the particular answers given by the legal officials must accord with those generated by this rationalist moral philosophy.

1.2.3 Fuller and the rule of law

Brownsword's final criterion is probably the most controversial aspect of his framework for judging law. It is a matter to which I shall return. In the meantime, it is worth reflecting on – and, where appropriate, revising – the preceding criteria, which otherwise seem to offer a fruitful starting place for judging law on its own terms.

The next stop on this journey is the 'Rule of Law',[40] as conceptualised by noted theorists including Dicey and Jennings, all the way up to Beale, Raz, Finnis, Rawls and Dworkin.[41] Although no agreed definition exists, it is

---

36   Brownsword 1997: 32.
37   Brownsword 1996: 143.
38   Gewirth 1978.
39   Beyleveld and Brownsword 2001.
40   To avoid any confusion with particular rules of law, 'Rule of Law' is used: cf Finnis 1986: 270; Radin 1989.
41   Beale 1935; Raz 1977, 1990: especially 357–60; Finnis 1986: 266–74, 289; Rawls 1972: especially 235–43; Dworkin 1985: especially 11–16.

commonly accepted that the rule of law conveys the sovereignty of law over human agents; as Aristotle put it, 'the rule of law, not of men [sic]'.[42] Law therefore prescribes and proscribes the behaviour of citizens whilst also protecting them, by ensuring that the government acts according to law – hence Fuller saw his insistence on congruence between the law as stated and applied as 'the very essence of the Rule of Law'.[43]

The connections between the rule of law and Brownsword's criteria for rational law are strong. The aforementioned scholars have issued requirements that are strikingly similar to those described by Fuller.[44] Thus, we are told that there must be rules, and that these must be promulgated, prospective, clear, consistent, constant and possible of performance. The requisite fit between the rules as stated and administered is also present. Additional requirements do occasionally feature, notably in Raz's account: he requires the judiciary to be independent from the executive and the courts to be both accessible and capable of reviewing the implementation of other rules. Raz is also not alone in seeking 'due process' and in insisting that the dictates of natural justice (such as openness and fairness) be observed.

With the reference to justice comes the suspicion that these principles might commit law to some particular content, such as might be imposed by external moral standards. Certainly, as Dworkin, Craig and Radin each recognise, there are accounts of the rule of law that adopt such a *substantive* (or 'rights') conception, in which the rule of law embodies tenets of a particular external morality. However, they also point out the existence of *formal* ('rule-book') conceptions, in which no judgment is passed on the content of the rules themselves.[45]

For his part, Fuller explicitly conceded that his principles were formal or procedural in nature.[46] Although resident in the natural law camp, in which law and morality are necessarily related, Fuller distanced himself from questions of 'ultimate ends' and dubbed his area of study *eunomics*, in order to convey his interest in 'the best working laws in view of the particular ends of a given society'.[47] The content of those ends was not his concern; indeed, his principles could be 'indifferent toward the substantive aims of law' and could 'serve a variety of such aims with equal efficacy'.[48] But Fuller did insist, especially in his exchanges with HLA Hart (which find their modern

---

42   Aristotle 1962: Book III, 10: 1286a9.
43   Fuller 1969: 209.
44   It is notable that, although Fuller did not attribute his eight principles to any secure point of reference (cf Morrison 1997: 389), he edited the volume containing Beale's thesis prior to the publication of *The Morality of Law*.
45   Dworkin 1985: 11; Radin 1989: 783; Craig 1997: 467.
46   Fuller 1969: 184.
47   d'Entrèves 1970: 149.
48   Fuller 1969: 153.

expression in the work of Simmonds and Kramer[49]), that his principles were not *merely* the procedural, amoral principles of 'good legal craftsmanship'.[50] Hart famously drew an analogy with poisoning: as a craft with a purpose, this activity might reveal 'internal principles', but these could not properly constitute a 'morality'.

In short, Fuller wanted to impart something *substantive* about the nature of law. He found Hart's critique incomprehensible,[51] countering that an immoral regime might find it more efficacious to violate the precepts,[52] but he notoriously failed to mount a more positive case for the moral character of the principles he espoused.[53] Fuller does refer to the principles as a 'morality of aspiration', to be treated as collective ideals, such that violation of one principle might necessitate a (remedying) violation of another,[54] but this arguably adds little. More revealing is the way he appears to mount a contingent case for the morality of his framework, since it allegedly 'affects and limits the substantive aims that can be achieved through law', and provides the ground rules for social coexistence.[55] Critics nevertheless detect a missing step in this argument, not least a compelling account of the ends of humanity and their relationship with law.[56]

Some accounts of the rule of law do make the contended moral connection more explicit: for example, Finnis derives the principles from particular 'natural laws'[57]; in other words, from substantive moral requirements, which 'human' laws must in turn obey. Other theorists offer alternative values, such as liberty (for Rawls[58]) or freedom and justice (for Dworkin[59]), and even those who appear less willing to accept the imposition of the principles from 'external' sources (like Beale and, initially at least, Raz[60]) are willing to acknowledge that the rule of law can help safeguard morality in the law. As such, the principles appear capable of securing moral ends, or at least preventing intrusions on such important values as individual freedom (autonomy, dignity) and the ethics of the community (justice, social stability).[61]

---

49 Simmonds 2007; Kramer 1998.
50 Hart 1965: 1286.
51 Fuller 1969: 201.
52 ibid: 200–204.
53 Summers 1984: 37.
54 Fuller 1969: 5–6, 910.
55 ibid: 184; see also ibid: 186, 205.
56 eg Morrison 1997: 390–91.
57 Finnis 1986: 289.
58 Rawls 1972: 239–43.
59 Dworkin 1985: especially 164–66.
60 See Beale 1935: 351, 353; Raz 1977: 198, 204–205, 207–210.
61 See Finnis 1986: 272–74; Rawls 1972: 239–40; Raz 1977: 204–205, 207–208; Beale 1935: 351, 353.

1.2.4 *Taking stock: criteria for judging law*

So which is it to be? Do principles like those advanced by Brownsword and Fuller commit law to some sort of moral mission or not? Brownsword (writing with Adams) concludes that they do: 'The principles are not just about order, they are about just order'.[62] But it seems reasonable to suggest that Hart had an equally good case for claiming that the principles, at least as presented by Fuller, were 'just about order'. Tellingly, Craig has detected, in Raz's recent work, a 'middle way' between the formal and substantive accounts of the rule of law, in which a particular moral position (emphasising democracy and civil rights) is both presupposed and implied by the rule of law.[63] Perhaps, then, the best answer is to say that both accounts are plausible and that neither obliterates the other.

Whichever conclusion one reaches, given that there are compelling grounds for detecting both formal and substantive dimensions to the various criteria for judging law, perhaps few will dispute the *necessity* of observing the relevant principles (albeit we might have to disagree about *why* we see this as necessary). Brownsword's terminology will be adopted here since his account arguably fares best in distilling and systematising the essence of the rule of law, whilst also separating out the most overtly external, substantive judgments from the other principles.

Thus, we might focus on *formal* rationality if we are concerned with consistency in the law, at least in the sense that contradictory laws will effectively cancel one another out, with the result that the law will say nothing about a practice about which it purports to say something.[64] *Instrumental* rationality, meanwhile, considers how effective the particular laws or rules are in achieving their intended ends. Radin helpfully adds that Fuller's *desiderata*, which Brownsword adopts, effectively boil down to two principles: first, there must be rules and, secondly, the rules must be capable of being followed.[65] The second of these principles, Radin continues, then divides into 'know-ability' and 'perform-ability', where the first requires the rules to be promulgated, congruent, non-contradictory, clear and constant, while the second insists that the rules must be prospective, possible of performance and, again, not contradictory or incongruent.

Brownsword has a strong case for claiming that observance of these requirements is necessary if law is to achieve its fundamental goal of guiding human action through rules. But are these criteria *sufficient* for the attainment of that goal? Here, at least one new criterion can usefully be added to the

---

62 Adams and Brownsword 1992: 20.
63 Craig 1997: 484–85; cf. Raz 1990: especially 359–60.
64 In contrast, Fuller argues that contradictory rules do not 'kill one another off' in the manner of contradictory logical statements: Fuller 1969: 65, 69.
65 Radin 1989.

requirements of instrumental rationality: the avoidance of *legal fictions*. Such a manoeuvre 'often involves extending an existing rule or concept well beyond its scope, but with the pretense [sic] that the case at hand really falls within existing precedent'.[66] Remarkably, despite Fuller himself once devoting an entire book to the topic,[67] the concept has been rather neglected of late[68] and does not tend to feature in discussions about the rule of law. Its inclusion here is warranted, however, since a legal fiction can scarcely guide those who wish to observe the law. Of course, the subterfuge of the legal fiction also has moral connotations; it appears, then, that consideration of what Brownsword calls 'substantive rationality' can be put off no longer.

1.3 Judging ethics

We began with a bare concept of law, according to which the legal enterprise involves subjecting human conduct to the governance of rules. From this flowed certain principles of rationality, specifically requirements of formal and instrumental rationality, which law (in a particular legal system) must satisfy if it is to be effective in achieving its goal of guiding action. But are the laws in question (and, indeed, any and all laws) required to have any particular substance? Is there some substantive goal which law should be pursuing? A useful way into contemplating these issues is to begin with the particular legal system that is under review.

1.3.1 *Judging ethics from within (law): immanent critique*

When we apply the criteria of rationality to a particular legal system, we will encounter the norms which that legal system espouses. In other words, the requirements of law as a matter of principle are tools which can assist us in excavating the principles to which a particular legal system, as a matter of fact, clings. As Brownsword earlier suggested, these principles might come from a variety of domains; business law, for example, is likely to require some consideration of the principles of economics. Medical law too might benefit from such reference; however, medical law more frequently and distinctively (albeit not exclusively) has cause to contemplate its underlying ethical commitments.[69] The judges might state that 'this is a court of law, not of morals', but this rings hollow when principles such as the sanctity of human life provide the focal point in cases of life or death (including the one from

---

66 Summers 1982: 149–50; see further Olivier 1975.
67 Fuller 1967.
68 Harmon 1990: 1–2.
69 Assuming, that is, that we can define and confine 'medical law'. See eg Brazier and Glover 2000; cf Veitch 2007.

which the quotation is drawn).[70] However, as we shall see, this is scarcely the only value to which the judges refer. In its consideration of David Glass's situation, the Court of Appeal made reference to the following principles:

(1) the sanctity of life;
(2) the non-interference by the courts in areas of clinical judgment in the treatment of patients . . . where this can be avoided . . .;
(3) the refusal of the courts to dictate appropriate treatment to a medical practitioner . . . subject to the power which the courts always have to take decisions in relation to the child's best interests. In doing so, the court takes fully into account the attitude of medical practitioners.
(4) that treatment without consent save in an emergency is trespass to the person . . .;
(5) that the courts will interfere to protect the interests of a minor or a person under a disability.[71]

However, as Lord Woolf MR was only too aware, such principles will not always or obviously point in one direction: 'The difficulty in this area is that there are conflicting principles involved. The principles of law are clearly established, but how you apply those principles to particular facts is often very difficult to anticipate'.[72] At this juncture, a more critical inquiry into such norms is invited. Here, an *immanent critique* can assist us in comparing how a set of laws would look if it sincerely and consistently observed the norms it claims as its own with how it in fact looks.

Pearson and Salter have described the immanent critique of law as: 'the effort to turn the normative standards that a legal ideology employs back upon the institutional procedures and actions which are supposed to embody these standards'.[73] For them, the critique involves four stages. First, the critic identifies the major internal norms of the object of study.[74] Secondly, the critic examines these claims, extracting and analysing any internal discrepancies, tensions and contradictions.[75] Thirdly, the critic describes the empirical reality entailed by the norms and compares this with the actual reality that obtains.[76] Finally, the critic will map out the practical (reform) implications of the critique.[77]

---

70 *Re A (Children) (Conjoined Twins: Medical Treatment)* [2000] 4 All ER 961 at 969 (Ward LJ).
71 *R v Portsmouth Hospitals NHS Trust ex p Glass* [1999] 2 FLR 905 at 908D–G (Lord Woolf MR).
72 ibid at 911B.
73 Pearson and Salter 1999: 484.
74 ibid: 489–90.
75 ibid: 491.
76 ibid: 491, 495.
77 ibid: 493.

For Pearson and Salter, immanent critique can occur at many levels in the realm of law, be they textual or rhetorical; as Fuller put it, 'the Word and the Deed' both count.[78] Like Fuller and, especially, Brownsword, immanent critique has a rationalistic preoccupation with the interplay between these different expressions of law: the critic assumes that consistency is preferable to inconsistency, a presumption that she imputes to the object of study (or else she could simply 'shrug off' inconsistencies as irrelevant and immaterial).[79] Notably this very preoccupation is, in fact, present in English law and associated scholarship: judges make reference to serving – or failing – the dictates of logic,[80] and 'black letter' lawyers strive to convey rationality, while critical and post-modern scholars condemn (as 'logonomocentrism') the presentation of law as a coherent and unified body of principles, subject to and justified by reason.[81]

Whether law is in fact rational is one thing; what Brownsword has shown is that it ought to be, since this is written into the very nature of law. Pearson and Salter similarly distinguish immanent critique from one that makes its assessment by reference to external values, since the latter '*superimposes* the normative standards of the legal scholar upon the "target" of legal critique'.[82] They do acknowledge a continuum, and suggest that neither extreme is entirely desirable since a fully external critique might miss its (legal) target, while a fully internal critique might lose its critical edge.[83] Nevertheless, the immanent critique takes as its starting point the view from within a particular legal system.

Brownsword's framework therefore appears well equipped to facilitate an immanent critique, thereby enabling the discovery of the actual norms of the legal system under review, which can then be compared and contrasted with other norms and with particular rules and practices. Indeed, Anthony Bradney's analysis of the concept of duress in family law implicitly relies upon this feature of Brownsword's model. Briefly citing Brownsword's notion of formal rationality, Bradney perceives different accounts of the concept within

---

78 Fuller 1968: 8. As Fuller recognised, his requirement that there be congruence 'between official action and the law' was 'most complex' (Fuller 1969: 81). The courts occupy the 'crossover point' (Fuller 1968: 11), because they both apply *and* make the law, but deciding when 'word' becomes 'deed' is complicated. However, for our purposes, we need not determine when one becomes the other, since any conflict between the two might be judged irrational, either in formal terms (a clash of 'words') or in instrumental terms (a gap between the 'word' and the 'deed').

79 Pearson and Salter 1999: 499–500.

80 In addition to the quotation with which this chapter opened see *R v Howe* [1987] 1 All ER 771 at 780E–F; *Council of Civil Service Unions (CCSU) v Minister for the Civil Service* [1985] AC 374 at 410–411 (Lord Diplock).

81 Balkin 1992: 746; see also eg Norrie 1993.

82 Pearson and Salter 1999: 484, emphasis in original.

83 Pearson and Salter 1999: 494, 495, 498–99.

and between family law, criminal law and contract law, such that the courts 'commit the simple but strict logical error of saying both P and not-P at the same time'.[84] For Bradney, the underlying inconsistent regard for individualistic arguments undermines the law's legitimacy; in short, a formal legal irrationality conceals a deeper ethical conflict.

If they were to respond to Bradney, Pearson and Salter would apparently say that the way forward is implicit in the immanent critique.[85] Here, however, I must depart from their arguments. If, as Bradney detects, the critique only shows us P and not-P as our options, then there is no self-evident reason for preferring P to not-P (or, of course, vice versa). In other words, we need some reasons for choosing between them, which the immanent critique alone cannot provide: it only shows us the crossroads; it does not tell us which road to take.

1.3.2 *Judging ethics from outside (law): judgments, principles and theories*

'Consistency and logic, though inherently desirable, are not always prime characteristics of a penal code based like the common law on custom and precedent. Law so based is not an exact science.'[86] So said Lord Hailsham in the course of a 1987 ruling, but Brownsword has constructed a persuasive case for saying that there are some scientific principles to which law should aspire. Can the same be said of moral theory? Lansing Pollock thinks so: 'there are rational criteria for evaluating moral theories which are similar to the ones used in judging the adequacy of scientific theories'.[87] With this, Pollock offers us the map with which we can plot our onward journey from the crossroads to which the immanent critique has brought us.

Pollock begins with two questions: What reasons do we have to be moral? And what must we do to be moral?[88] The first of these questions requires a defence of the moral point of view. Mindful that this is a profound philosophical question, I will nevertheless side with Pollock in observing that successful social living provides reason enough, albeit one that is unlikely to persuade the sceptic who sees no need for the relevant rules to apply to her, provided that everyone else complies. In response to this, Pollock points to universalisability: the sceptic and the saint are both social beings and so they

---

84 ibid 496.
85 ibid.
86 *R v Howe* [1987] 1 All ER 771 at 780E–F.
87 Pollock 1988: 229.
88 Gewirth (the source of Brownsword's preferred moral theory) calls the first of these the authoritative question; the second question seems then to cover what Gewirth dubs the distributive question (whose interests other than our own should we consider?) and the substantive question (which interests should be protected or promoted?): Gewirth 1978: 3.

should both be obliged to observe the rules that underpin social existence. However, echoing our earlier discussions, Pollock acknowledges that the universalisability requirement is only a formal requirement based on consistency, which says nothing of the substance of the rules needed to guarantee successful social living. It is here that our attention turns to the second question and to the illuminating work of Tom Regan.

Regan usefully distinguishes between moral judgments, principles and theories, where each builds on the last, such that a judgment might be about what to do in an individual case, whilst principles might be seen as more general statements that seek to systematise these judgments, and theories strive to unify the various principles.[89] Starting with judgments, Regan describes five conditions that would be met by the ideal moral judgment and for which we should therefore strive, even if (as fallible humans) our efforts are destined to fall short of the ideal. This ideal moral judgment is clear, informed, rational, impartial and considered.

Conceptual clarity is the first criterion, since without knowing what we are discussing, we cannot be confident in our judgments; similarly, and secondly, we need accurate information about the real world as it pertains to the moral matter at hand. The judgment must also be rational, in that it observes the logical principle of non-contradiction, such that any judgment should be consistent with the remainder of our moral beliefs. Regan next wants us to ward against 'extreme, unquestioning partiality; otherwise we shall run the risk of having our judgment clouded by bigotry and prejudice'.[90] He sees this as tied to the formal principle of justice, such that like cases should be treated alike.[91] Rationality also features in his final criterion, which Elmore Leonard would summarise as: 'be cool'.[92] Here, Regan points out that a considered moral judgment will be less attainable in an emotionally volatile state.

Regan addresses these requirements to moral agents, which he describes as those who can reach their decision on the basis of impartial reasons (thus excluding, for example, young children). However, the judgment reached by this agent will not suffice unless or until it is based upon a valid or true moral principle. Here too Regan claims there 'are criteria for rationally evaluating and choosing between competing ethical principles'.[93] A moral principle will therefore be consistent, adequate in scope, precise and conform to our (reflective) intuitions.

---

89 Regan 2004.
90 Regan 2004: 128.
91 Echoing our earlier discussion, Regan distinguishes this concept of justice from a more substantive concept, which would furnish the grounds for discerning the dis/similarity of individuals: Regan 2004: 128.
92 Leonard 2000.
93 Regan 2004: 130. He does acknowledge that what follows is incomplete, although he strives to provide as persuasive a case for the necessity of the conditions as he can.

'Consistency concerns the *possible conjoint* truth of two or more statements';[94] so, for example, the statements 'Attempting to resuscitate David Glass is right' and 'Attempting to resuscitate David Glass is wrong (not right)' cannot simultaneously be true.[95] A valid moral principle must be consistent – and must not imply contradictory judgments such as these – or else it will be incapable of achieving its aim 'to provide rational guidance in the determination of what is right and wrong'.[96] The need for 'practical guidance' also requires the principle to have a sufficiently wide scope in a myriad of real-world circumstances.[97] Yet, precision is also essential – at least, as Aristotle has it, 'so far as the nature of the subject admits'.[98]

A principle's conformity with our moral intuitions is, as Regan acknowledges, the most controversial of his criteria. Regan is here careful to distinguish between *pre-reflective* intuitions, which predate our detailed consideration of a situation, and *reflective* intuitions, our considered beliefs, which reflect moral judgments that have been arrived at along the lines he earlier described. Yet even these latter beliefs might sometimes come into conflict with a moral principle. On such occasions, Regan joins Rawls (and others[99]) in seeking 'reflective equilibrium' between the two.[100] This might mean we must abandon a principle that conflicts with too many of our considered beliefs; alternatively, we might group our beliefs together to formulate a principle that distils their common essence. Regan does anticipate (and receive) criticism here, to which he often responds by redirecting the critic towards his interest in *reflective* (as opposed to pre-reflective) intuitions.[101]

Regan finally arrives at ethical theory, which 'seeks to bring maximum order to ethical thinking'.[102] Candidate theories abound, for example, from utilitarian and deontological thinkers, who respectively focus upon achieving the best outcomes and doing one's duty. What are the rational criteria for evaluating and then choosing between such theories? First, says Regan, the theory should satisfy the requirements associated with moral principles, that is, the theory should be consistent, adequate in scope and precision, and meet our reflective intuitions. Secondly, the best theory will comply with the

---

94 Regan 2004: 131.
95 As noted above, in current medical practice, it is better to talk of *attempting* resuscitation: see British Medical Association, the Resuscitation Council (UK) and the Royal College of Nursing 2007.
96 Regan 2004: 131.
97 ibid.
98 Aristotle 1954: 3.
99 eg Beauchamp and Childress 2001; Ives and Draper 2009. See also Chapter 8 section 8.4.
100 Rawls 1972.
101 See Regan 2004: especially 136–40.
102 ibid 140.

principle of simplicity (or parsimony).[103] If, say, two theories fare comparably when judged against the first set of criteria, then the victor should be that which requires the fewest principles and, particularly, 'the fewest unproved (and perhaps unprovable) assumptions'.[104] So, he concludes, the best moral theory:

> (1) systematizes the maximum number of our considered beliefs, thereby having maximum scope; (2) systematizes them in a coherent fashion, thereby achieving consistency; (3) does this without compromising the degree of precision it is reasonable to expect and require of any moral principle(s); and (4) satisfies these other criteria of evaluation while making the fewest possible assumptions necessary to do so, thereby meeting the criterion of simplicity.[105]

The prima facie plausibility of Regan's scheme is reinforced by its strong echoes in Pollock's account (in which no direct reference is made to Regan). Pollock therefore insists that the moral theory should have explanatory power, simplicity, coherence and (what might be dubbed) empirical plausibility. The insistence on explanatory power resembles Regan's twin interests in sufficient scope and precision. It is Pollock, meanwhile, who introduces greater subtlety into the notion of simplicity, as he detects two levels: simplicity of *structure*, with the ideal moral inquiry perhaps resulting in a single general principle; and simplicity of *application*, such that the theory issues clear moral guidance.[106] Again, however, it is possible to detect these themes in, for example, Regan's references to precision and his overarching concern with action-guidance. Indeed, where the two explicitly agree is in their insistence on coherence or consistency: as Pollock states, a moral theory which issues contradictory prescriptions 'will obviously fail as an action-guide'.[107] Finally, Pollock wants the theory to fit the real world: 'The assumptions of a moral theory should at least be consistent with what is known about human nature and society'.[108] 'In the real world, logical possibility without the check of plausibility is a worthless guide to action' is how Lamb has put this.[109] The idea brings to mind Kant's requirement that 'ought implies can' and, although there are shades of this idea in Regan's account (at least when he discusses the need for informed moral judgments), Pollock helpfully brings them to the fore.

103 ibid 146.
104 ibid 147.
105 ibid 149.
106 Pollock 1988: 232.
107 ibid.
108 ibid: 233.
109 Lamb 1992: 32. Cf Lord Steyn's comment: 'The surest test of a new legal rule is not whether it satisfies a team of logicians but how it performs in the real world' in *R v G and Another* [2003] 1 AC 1034 at para 57.

These criteria for evaluating moral judgments, principles and theories provide a moral map, which should enable us to move on from any crossroads exposed by an immanent critique. Their promise lies not only in their connection with the real world (with which particular laws necessarily must engage) but also in their derivation from the goal of action guidance, which, following Fuller, has been seen as a central feature of law throughout this discussion. Preoccupation with that goal should help explain why both here and, notably, in Regan's writing, moral approaches not primarily concerned with action (like virtue ethics, which is primarily interested in character) have tended not to feature. Whether, and in what ways, character-based ethical approaches interact with action-focused morality is a debate for others.[110] The focus here is squarely upon achieving action guidance, specifically through rules. Equally, I am alert to the controversy that surrounds appeals to rationality and logic, particularly in light of feminist critiques.[111] Although it will surely not suffice, the best I can say here is that the concept of rationality employed so far is minimal in content and, importantly, substantial moral appraisal of the state of the world (at least as expressed in its particular laws) has not yet been attempted. There should therefore remain plenty of scope for people of radically different perceptual, conceptual and ethical commitments to bring their perspectives to bear.[112] Moreover, although this might lead us directly into controversial territory, I would hope that a sufficiently robust case has been made for upholding the principle of non-contradiction in law. Simply put, I would wager that none of us wants a legal system that issues flatly contradictory instructions.[113] From this most simple of principles has evolved much of the framework for judging law and, in turn, judging ethical theory, which has been presented here.

1.4 Conclusion: (not) just law

Regan and Pollock have essentially given us an 'internal morality' of morality, and this is unsurprising given their shared concern, with Fuller, with guiding action.[114] We began, also with Fuller, with a basic concept of law, according

---

110 eg Campbell 2003.

111 Falmagne and Marjori 2002.

112 Albeit, if law is to fulfil its function of guiding action via rules, then any ethical perspectives reflected in the law will also need to contribute to this end and accordingly be judged against criteria such as those outlined by Regan and Pollock. This might mean that some perspectives will lose out.

113 Or, indeed, would label such a system 'law'. And it is not only law that requires logic to function: it seems this underpins any and every human interaction. Some have therefore argued that anthropology – and by extension any efforts by one human to enter into discussion with another – must presuppose a commitment to the principle of non-contradiction. See eg Hollis 1970; Lukes 1970.

114 It will not escape notice that I have not directly touched on the related but distinct debates about the 'internal morality of medicine'. See Veatch and Miller 2001.

to which the legal enterprise essentially involves using rules to guide human conduct. From this flowed certain principles of rationality to which law in a particular system, if it is to be effective as law, must subscribe. The first requirement, formal rationality, simply insists that law must be consistent: fundamental norms should not directly compete, and similar cases should be dealt with similarly. The second requirement, instrumental rationality, requires the particular rules to be capable of achieving the goal of law, that is, action guidance. Generally, there must therefore be rules and these must be known and capable of being acted upon; official practices that do not measure up to the stated rules, unclear edicts and the use of legal fictions resulting in misshapen legal categories all fail to reach the standards which might legitimately be expected of law. So too the specific legal measures invoked to respond to a particular phenomenon should be capable of achieving the desired response.

When we measure particular laws against these standards associated with law as a concept we will inevitably encounter the more substantive principles to which that legal system is apparently committed. An immanent critique of what these principles do and should entail will help determine the extent to which the system is as committed to these principles as it purports. But here we arrive at a crossroads: should the legal system make necessary adjustments in order to preserve a particular principle or should it be supplanted by some other principle or principles? Here we need to consider substantive questions of rationality, which, considering medical law in particular, is very likely to require some engagement with ethical theory. The ethical theories, principles and judgements made in, or underlying, the particular legal system are themselves amenable to rational assessment. Such thinking, at least as it is expressed in law, must also be capable of guiding action. Individual judgements should therefore aspire to being conceptually clear, informed, rational, impartial and considered. At the next level, ethical principles should be consistent, adequate in scope and precision, and conform to our (reflective, considered) intuitions. And any overarching theory should not only comply with that which we require of ethical principles, it should also have sufficient simplicity in structure and application, and be capable of working in (and with) the real world.

Equipped with this framework for judging a legal system and, by extension, its purported ethical commitments, we can now set to work assessing the adequacy of the laws to which David Glass, his family and his doctors were subject. The legal system in question, England and Wales, has witnessed much activity of late in relation to cases like David's, and not only in those concerning children and young people, but also in relation to adults who lack the capacity to decide for themselves at the relevant time how they should (or should not) be treated. Although the specific legal frameworks for dealing with each group of patients are different, some common themes do emerge when addressing the incompetent patient. In the next two chapters we will encounter different answers to two fundamental questions: On what basis should a decision about the treatment (or non-treatment) of an incapable patient be made? And who should be entitled to take such a decision? Chapters 2 and 3 will, like the present one, open with a case of conflict in the clinic, which illustrates the main areas of controversy and complexity associated with these questions.

After plotting the main features of the legal landscape, I will then use the criteria developed in this chapter to demonstrate (in Chapter 4) some of the ways in which the law that governs the limits of life in cases like David Glass's is itself limited – and I will also show (in Chapter 5) how the ethical approaches associated with such cases are also far from perfect. We will not rest at the crossroads for too long, since a way forward will be proposed, in Chapters 6, 7 and 8. But before we get there we first need to see how English law is, indeed, at an ethical crossroads when it is faced with the fundamental question: to treat or not to treat?

2 Law at the limits of life

Children, welfare and best interests

> The judge must decide what is in the child's best interests. In making that decision, the welfare of the child is paramount, and the judge must look at the question from the assumed point of view of the patient. There is a strong presumption in favour of a course of action which will prolong life, but that presumption is not irrebuttable. The term 'best interests' encompasses medical, emotional, and all other welfare issues. The court must conduct a balancing exercise in which all the relevant factors are weighed and a helpful way of undertaking this exercise is to draw up a balance sheet.
>
> *Wyatt v Portsmouth Hospital NHS Trust* [2005] EWCA Civ 1181 at para 87 (Wall LJ)[1]

2.1 Conflicts in the clinic: the case of Charlotte Wyatt

Charlotte Wyatt was born on 21 October 2003, three months prematurely. She was brain damaged and had severe problems with her lungs, heart and kidneys. In the first 10 months of her life, Charlotte had to be resuscitated three times. The medical opinion was that she would be unlikely to see or hear, would not develop neurologically and that her existence was, to her, intolerable. By September 2004, she was almost completely reliant on a head box, which supplied her with oxygen, in order to survive. Portsmouth NHS Trust, which was responsible for Charlotte's care, approached Hedley J in the High Court for a declaration to the effect that it would be lawful to withhold artificial ventilation should Charlotte suffer a fourth crisis. Charlotte's parents, who were hoping for a 'miracle born of divine intervention',[2] contested the application, arguing that she should be given the chance of life (perhaps even the chance to return home) and they made their position known in the national media.

At the first hearing in October 2004, Hedley J ordered that it would be lawful, in her best interests, for the paediatricians to decline to intubate and

---

1 Case references omitted.
2 *Portsmouth NHS Trust v Wyatt* [2004] 1 FLR 21, hereafter *Wyatt (No 1)* para 14.

ventilate Charlotte, although CPAP (continuous positive airway pressure) could be administered in order to keep her airways open and ease her breathing, unless this caused her visible distress.[3]

A few months later Hedley J was asked to stay these declarations, in view of perceived improvements in Charlotte's condition.[4] Her reliance on the head box, for example, had slightly declined and she could spend periods outside of the box, albeit with the support of a face mask. Yet, despite such improvements, Hedley J felt that the orders could remain. He recorded the court's 'delight' at Charlotte's improvements and emphasised the strong presumption in favour of preserving life.[5] However, the doctors' duty was still to act in the best interests of the child 'as and when any crisis might arise' and Charlotte's condition implied that she would be unlikely to 'survive such aggressive or invasive treatment'.[6] Indeed, he was concerned that the removal of the orders might encourage 'wholly false expectations'.[7]

The doctors did not expect Charlotte to survive the winter, and yet in April 2005 Hedley J was observing: 'in dealing with a child you can rarely be certain. Children do not stand still; they develop or regress'.[8] Charlotte certainly seemed to have developed well: her oxygen requirements had further declined and she had become increasingly responsive to her environment and stimuli. But, as the judge put it, 'her neurological condition remains about as bad as it could be'.[9] Medical experts still maintained that Charlotte would not be able to withstand invasive efforts to deal with a respiratory crisis, given her severe chronic lung disease coupled now with malnutrition, which resulted from 'her low tolerance of food'.[10]

Hedley J was again persuaded that artificial ventilation should not be offered. The chances of such 'futile aggressive treatment' restoring her to her current condition seemed slim and would most likely either threaten her chance of a peaceful death or return her to an 'intolerable' existence.[11] He decided that an anticipatory declaration could be made, given the intractable (and seemingly 'volatile') nature of the disagreement between the parents and the health care team,[12] and the fact that the nature of the crisis was 'fairly precisely anticipated'.[13] He felt his declarations should nevertheless remain

---

3 *Wyatt (No 1)*.

4 *Portsmouth NHS Trust (No 1) v Wyatt* [2005] EWHC 117, hereafter *Wyatt (No 2)*.

5 *Wyatt (No 2)* para 16.

6 ibid para 19.

7 ibid.

8 *Re Wyatt (a child) (medical treatment: continuation of order)* [2005] EWHC 693, hereafter *Wyatt (No 3)* para 3.

9 ibid para 6.

10 ibid.

11 ibid para 16.

12 ibid para 18.

13 ibid para 21.

subject to review and, if or when the crisis came, it would remain the doctors' decision, in consultation with the Wyatts, to determine what ought or ought not to be done.

Charlotte was still alive in September 2005, when her parents went before the Court of Appeal, in which Hedley J's decisions were upheld.[14] Delivering the judgment of the court, Wall LJ undertook an exhaustive examination of the law pertaining to best interests, including that concerning incompetent adult patients, with the aim of providing guidelines for future judges that were 'as clear and as simple as is consistent with the serious issues which they engage'.[15] He felt it was 'nearly always a matter of regret' when cases like the present one had 'to be conducted in a courtroom, rather than a hospital or a consulting room'.[16] When that happens, however, the test is indeed the best interests of the child. This test involves examining the issues 'from the assumed point of view of the patient' and working from the (rebuttable) presumption that life should be preserved.[17] Medical, emotional and other welfare issues are included in the consideration and the court should undertake a balancing exercise, which might involve drawing up a 'balance sheet' of harms and benefits.[18] Like Hedley J, the Court of Appeal felt that the notion of 'intolerability', whilst a 'valuable guide' to making the assessment, 'should not be seen either as a gloss on or a supplementary guide to best interests'.[19]

Each case had to be decided on its specific facts and, turning to this particular case, Wall LJ felt that Hedley J had proceeded appropriately in issuing 'permissive, not mandatory' declarations, which were amenable to review, and he noted that the Trust was also keeping its decision not to reventilate Charlotte under review and that this would be 'discussed with her parents before it is implemented'.[20] Wall LJ discouraged any belief that 'open-ended' declarations should be sought or that the court should be viewed as a 'general advice centre' since it is 'not the function of the court to oversee the treatment plan for a gravely ill child. That function is for the doctors in consultation with the child's parents ... The court's function is to make a particular decision on a particular issue'.[21] Although he disapproved of the Wyatts' occasionally 'less than helpful' conduct (such as reporting the doctors to the police), he recognised the strain they were under and was encouraged by the news that their relationship with the Trust was improving. He hoped, then, that a treatment plan could be agreed at the next hearing.[22]

---

14 *Wyatt v Portsmouth Hospital NHS Trust* [2005] EWCA Civ 1181, hereafter *Wyatt (No 4)*.
15 ibid para 85.
16 ibid para 86.
17 ibid para 87.
18 ibid paras 87, 89.
19 ibid para 91.
20 ibid para 114.
21 ibid para 117.
22 ibid para 119.

The case thus returned to Hedley J, with the trust now seeking a declaration to the effect that the doctors would have the final say in the event of a further dispute with the Wyatts. Hedley J felt that a 'novel' declaration of this sort was not required.[23] A doctor is obliged to act in the best interests of the patient, working 'in partnership with the parents'.[24] There may be occasions when parents and doctors disagree, on reasonable grounds, and in such situations the final decision might rightly be left with the parents.[25] Yet, clinical judgment can comprise an intellectual dimension and a 'professional conscience, intuition or hunch',[26] and the clinician cannot be compelled to act contrary to his or her conscience (although another professional might not be so troubled and might thus be willing to act). This, thought Hedley J, provided sufficient protection for Charlotte's doctors.

Four months later the case was back before Hedley J for another (and, for our purposes, final[27]) hearing.[28] Charlotte had been able to return home for visits but her condition had now deteriorated considerably: she had developed a cough and was apparently suffering from a viral infection. Intubation and ventilation looked likely to be the only available intervention if her condition continued to decline, and her parents (who had by now separated) felt that this would lead her to recover, although the doctors unanimously felt it would be futile and contrary to her best interests. Hedley J issued another 'permissive and not mandatory' declaration that 'at the moment the decision arises to be taken the medical authorities are required to use their best judgment in Charlotte's best interests as to whether they desist' from intubation and ventilation.[29] By the end of 2009, Charlotte had reportedly been out of hospital for two years and living in foster care, where she was learning to walk.[30]

2.2 Best interests, welfare and the law

Charlotte Wyatt's case, whilst remarkable, is but one in a substantial body of jurisprudence, which has its roots in the criminal law and yet which has grown to occupy a distinct field of medical (or, more broadly, health care) law, gaining sustenance from family law, tort law and human rights law along the way. The central question in cases like Charlotte's is whether life-sustaining measures can be withdrawn or withheld from a patient incapable (currently or

---

23 *Portsmouth NHS Trust v W* [2005] EWHC 2293, hereafter *Wyatt (No 5)* para 40.
24 ibid para 29.
25 ibid para 31.
26 ibid para 36.
27 See also for example *Portsmouth Hospital NHS Trust v Wyatt (costs)* [2006] EWCA Civ 529. Bridgeman (2010: 187) says the case came 'before the court on at least 11 occasions'.
28 *Re Wyatt* [2006] EWHC 319, hereafter *Wyatt (No 6)*.
29 ibid para 15.
30 Levin 2009; Smyth 2009: 13. No further information appears to be publically available after this time.

perhaps ever) of expressing their views on the matter. Distinct jurisdictions are available, depending on whether the patient in question is an adult or child, and the judges have also developed specific bodies of case law, relative (for example) to the disorder with which the patient is afflicted. Particularly notable are those rulings pertaining to the more severe disorders of consciousness, specifically the persistent vegetative state (PVS).[31] Yet, despite the existence of such distinctions, the standard which is used to determine the outcome in all of these cases is essentially the same: the decision turns on the 'best interests' or welfare of the patient.[32] It is instructive, therefore, to consider in some detail how the courts have interpreted and applied this standard across a range of cases in which the denial of pills, tubes and even cups and spoons is in issue. We start, in this chapter, with those rulings concerning critically ill minors, which extend from newborns like Charlotte Wyatt to older children and adolescents like David Glass, whose case opened the previous chapter.

2.2.1 *Criminal beginnings?*

The law that governs Charlotte's case can be traced back to reports, many emerging in the 1970s, that treatment was routinely being withdrawn or withheld from severely disabled neonates. In 1973, R.S. Duff and A.G.M. Campbell reported that 43 of the last 299 consecutive deaths in the special-care nursery in which they worked were as a result of the denial of treatment.[33] As they summarised in 1980:

> All of the 43 babies were afflicted severely by one or a combination of conditions: congenital anomalies, prematurity, birth injuries, and assorted acquired maladies. Even with maximal, heroic treatment, most had a very poor chance of survival beyond a few hours or days. Thus, treatment, often abusive and always expensive, also seemed futile. In addition, all were believed to have a bleak or hopeless outlook regarding quality of life. These facts coupled with concerns about financial and other family burdens prompted parents, physicians, nurses, social workers, clergymen, and others involved in deciding care to view treatment as imprudent. As we knew was common practice, life was preferred to the end for most and death was accepted for a few. There were some inescapable feelings of doubt about the decisions in both cases.[34]

Duff and Campbell were not alone: for example, other professionals revealed that 23 of 24 babies at one centre had been sedated and denied food, with the

---

31 See Chapter 3 section 3.2.1
32 Although the position is more complex when the patient is an adult: see Chapter 3.
33 Duff and Campbell 1973.
34 Duff and Campbell 1980: 20.

result that all were 'pushed into death',[35] while an unnamed paediatrician wrote in *The Lancet* of offering parents 'some help in hastening the end of a life'.[36]

The issues first came before the courts in 1981, when, in *Re B (a minor) (wardship: medical treatment)* [1981] 1 WLR 1421, the Court of Appeal considered the future of Alexandra (B), a newborn with Down's syndrome and an intestinal obstruction. Surgery could remedy the obstruction, but it would otherwise prove fatal. Although there was some disagreement among her doctors, Alexandra's parents believed that the operation should not be performed. Ewbank J concurred, but his decision was reversed by Templeman LJ, who felt that the judge had been overly concerned with the parents' wishes, when his duty was to consider the child's best interests. Authorising the operation, Templeman LJ stated that the court must:

> . . . decide whether the life of this child is demonstrably going to be so awful that in effect the child must be condemned to die, or whether the life of this child is still so imponderable that it would be wrong for her to be condemned to die.[37]

Alexandra was likely to be severely mentally and physically disabled, but (as Templeman LJ regrettably put it) she would not be a 'cabbage'.[38] He left open the possibility that a different conclusion could be reached where 'severe proved damage' meant the child's life was 'bound to be full of pain and suffering'.[39]

Following the ruling, Glanville Williams, the renowned criminal law scholar, speculated that a murder charge might result from any case not fitting Templeman LJ's exception.[40] Certainly, there was prior precedent which confirmed that failure to fulfil a duty to care for a dependent could result in a homicide conviction.[41] Indeed, investigations were mounted in response to concerns expressed by special interest groups such as the Society for the Protection of Unborn Children and Life about the practices of doctors, including Drs Garrow and Jolly.[42] However, it was ultimately to be Dr Leonard Arthur who came before a court.

R v Arthur (1981) 12 BMLR 1 involved a paediatrician who had prescribed an appetite suppressant (dihydrocodeine) and ordered 'nursing care only' for a

---

35 Linacre Centre 1982: 18.
36 A Children's Physician 1979: 1123.
37 *Re B (a minor)(wardship: medical treatment)* [1981] 1 WLR 1421 at 1424.
38 ibid 1423.
39 ibid 1424.
40 Williams 1981: 9.
41 *Gibbins v Proctor* (1918) 12 Cr App Rep 134; *R v Stone & Dobinson* [1977] QB 354, discussed in Chapter 4 section 4.2.
42 See *The Guardian* 1978; Timmins 1981: 1.

newborn rejected by his parents. John Pearson – who, unlike Alexandra, had been born with apparently 'uncomplicated' Down's syndrome – died 69 hours later. When evidence emerged suggesting that the baby might have died from natural causes, the charge was reduced from murder to attempted murder. The prosecution alleged that the case notes and treatment chart, along with the administration of the appetite suppressant, evidenced an attempt to kill. The defence contended that this was a (passive) 'holding operation', revocable if John's mother changed her mind. Furthermore, it was claimed that the administration of the drug was not evidence of an intention to kill: it had been directed at the relief of distress.

Summing-up, Farquharson J noted that selective non-treatment was 'accepted by modern paediatric thought',[43] and he made repeated references to Arthur's good character and 'noble motives'.[44] But, he admitted, '[t]here is no special law in this country that places doctors in a separate category and gives them extra protection over the rest of us'.[45] He saw the law as distinguishing between, on the one side, unlawful practices such as murder and, on the other, lawful practices including administering analgesics (even if death might result) and refraining from sustaining the life of a child with an 'irreversible handicap'. It was for the jury to decide where Arthur's case fell; if Arthur's conduct amounted to a 'holding operation', 'then he would not be guilty'.[46] After deliberating for only 124 minutes, the jury returned to acquit Arthur. The Attorney General saw no need to refer the case to the Court of Appeal, since he perceived no conflict with established principles of homicide law,[47] and the Director of Public Prosecutions announced that no similar prosecutions were being considered.[48]

2.2.2 Civil proceedings?

Dr Arthur's trial was effectively the last time that such a case would be heard in the criminal courts.[49] Taking their prompts from *Re B*, the civil courts led

---

43 *R v Arthur* (1981) 12 BMLR 1 at 14.

44 ibid at 3, 4, 7, 8, 23.

45 ibid at 5.

46 ibid at 5–6.

47 19 *Hansard* HC Official Report (Sixth Series) written answers cols 348–49 (8 March 1982). As we will see in Chapter 4 section 4.3.3, commentators are divided over the accuracy of these statements and the continuing relevance of *Arthur* as a precedent.

48 Osman, Ferriman and Timmins 1981: 1.

49 As we will see in Chapter 3 section 3.2.1, a Reverend Morrow later failed in his attempt to initiate proceedings against doctors who withdrew life-support from a patient in a PVS: *R v Bingley Magistrates' Court ex p Morrow* [1995] Med L Rev 86. Police investigations which did not appear to lead to proceedings are reported by eg Fenton (1995) and *The Guardian* (2000). However, as I have described elsewhere, there have been proceedings brought against laypersons: see Huxtable 2007: 68–77, 126–28.

the way thereafter, starting with *Re C (a minor)(wardship: medical treatment)* [1990] Fam 26. C, who was four months old, was hydrocephalic, blind and probably deaf, with severe cerebral palsy of all four limbs. Without sedation she cried as if in pain. Medical opinion was unanimous that there was no chance of improvement. On the central issue, the Court of Appeal agreed with Ward J that treatment could be withheld from C, since treatment was not in her best interests. C's best interests, as understood in the light of *Re B*, were the paramount consideration. However, Ward J had 'failed to express himself with his usual felicity' when he gave leave 'to treat the minor to die'; this 'misleading phrase' was removed, as were references to the specific treatments that might be withheld (such as naso-gastric feeding and antibiotics).[50]

In C's case, the courts exercised their inherent (or wardship) jurisdiction, which meant that C was made a ward of court. Many of C's successors followed the same course, despite the fact that the year in which C's fate was determined – 1989 – also brought the Children Act. This Act sought to provide a comprehensive framework for tackling a multitude of issues pertaining to children, including medical treatment. Central to the Act is the welfare principle, according to which the welfare of the child 'shall be the court's paramount consideration', and the court shall have particular regard for (inter alia): the ascertainable wishes and feelings of the child concerned (considered in the light of his or her age and understanding); the child's physical, emotional and educational needs; age, sex, background and any characteristics which the court considers relevant; any harm the child has suffered or is at risk of suffering; and how capable the parents and other relevant parties are of meeting the child's needs.[51] The Act empowers a court to make a variety of orders, such as the 'specific issue order',[52] in circumstances where 'it considers that doing so would be better for the child than making no order at all'.[53] The Act also introduces the notion of 'parental responsibility', which encompasses 'all the rights, duties, powers, responsibilities and authority which by law a parent of a child has in relation to the child and his property'.[54] It is the person with such responsibility who may, for example, consent to medical treatment on behalf of a minor.

The 1989 Act therefore promised a new approach to cases like C's, which could (and perhaps should) supplant the wardship route. When a child is made a ward of court, then no important step can be taken in the child's life without the consent of the court.[55] In C's case such ongoing judicial oversight

---

50 *Re C (a minor)(wardship: medical treatment)* [1990] Fam 26 at 35 (Lord Donaldson MR).
51 Children Act 1989 s 1(1)(3).
52 ibid under s 8.
53 ibid s 1(5).
54 ibid s 3(1).
55 See the Family Procedure Rules 2010 ch 12 pt 5; Practice Direction 12D – Inherent Jurisdiction (Including Wardship) Proceedings.

might have been entirely appropriate, since she had actually been made a ward before her medical condition was known, when social workers expressed concern over C's parents' inability adequately to care for her.[56] Whether this was necessary in all subsequent cases is open to question, but in any event, the next – now leading – case also originated in the inherent jurisdiction.[57]

Whereas effort (which some saw as excessive[58]) had been expended to present C's condition as terminal, the severely disabled five-month-old in *Re J (a minor)(wardship: medical treatment)* [1991] 1 FLR 366 could not be described as such. For the first time, the court appeared prepared to say that it was inappropriate to seek to extend a life of considerable disability and suffering, albeit one that was not imminently due to end. The diagnoses and prognosis for J were extremely poor: although he would and could experience pain, J had sustained severe brain damage at birth, which would result in spastic quadriplegia. He experienced fits and difficulty in breathing unaided, and he would be blind, unable to sit up, hold his head up or speak.

Scott Baker J decided that, provided it was deemed appropriate at the time, artificial ventilation could be withheld if J again endured the convulsions which would ordinarily prompt attempts at resuscitation. The Official Solicitor appealed, making the 'absolute' submission that this decision contravened the sanctity of human life,[59] and the 'qualified' submission that, in any event, J's case fell on the life-saving side of the test articulated in *Re B*.

Dismissing the appeal, Lord Donaldson MR and colleagues noted that, where the child was a ward, it was for the doctors and the court (rather than the parents) to reach decisions together, although reference would be made to the parents' views. Whilst there was a strong presumption in favour of prolonging life, this was rebuttable: instead, it was the best interests of the child that provided the key. According to Taylor LJ:

> I consider the correct approach is for the court to judge the quality of life the child would have to endure if given the treatment and decide whether in all the circumstances such a life would be so afflicted as to be intolerable to that child. I say 'to that child' because the test should not be whether the life would be tolerable to the decider. The test must be whether the child in question, if capable of exercising sound judgment, would consider the life tolerable.[60]

---

56 *Re C (a minor)(wardship: medical treatment)* [1990] Fam 26 at 31.
57 The patient in question, J, was reportedly made a ward for reasons 'extraneous' to the case at hand: *Re J (a minor)(wardship: medical treatment)* [1991] 1 FLR 366 at 368H.
58 Roberts 1990: 221.
59 He allowed for two exceptions: the terminally ill minor, like the child in *Re C*, and the child whose faculties were completely destroyed.
60 *Re J (a minor)(wardship: medical treatment)* [1991] 1 FLR 366 at 383H–384A.

The latter sentiment, which Lord Donaldson MR shared, appeared to import a 'substituted judgment' test into the calculation of a young patient's best interests.[61] In making the final calculation, his Lordship did not feel bound to treat the *Re B* test as 'a quasi-statutory yardstick',[62] but he recognised that a balancing exercise was required, in which (for example) the child's prospects for development and pain were weighed against any suffering the child might endure in the event of treatment. As Taylor LJ explained, 'the court never sanctions steps to terminate life . . . The court is concerned only with the circumstances in which steps should not be taken to prolong life'.[63]

What the court apparently cannot do is *dictate* that steps be taken to prolong the patient's life. *Re J (a minor)(wardship: medical treatment)* [1992] 2 FLR 165 involved another profoundly disabled ward, aged 16 months. Waite J had directed the Health Authority to provide J with life-saving measures, including artificial ventilation, but the Court of Appeal held that no one – including the judges – could order a medical professional to treat a patient contrary to their clinical judgement that such treatment was not in the patient's best interests. The court was (and remains) wary of instructing the Health Authority about how it should allocate its resources.[64] In short, a court might authorise treatment, but it cannot require its provision.

After a period in which some well publicised cases narrowly avoided the courts,[65] the High Court was next called on in the case of *Re C (a baby)* [1996] 2 FLR 43. Brown P decided that continued ventilation was not in the best interests of the severely brain damaged three-month-old patient, whose death would immediately result from the withdrawal of ventilation. 'It is almost a living death. She is not in a coma as medically defined; she has a very low awareness of anything, if at all', explained the judge.[66] Everyone (eventually) supported the application and Brown P commended the use of the wardship jurisdiction in such cases, to relieve the parents and doctors of the 'grave responsibility' for deciding.[67] Yet, he added, there was no formula dictating which situations should come before the court, as 'each case must be considered on its merits'.[68] Ian Kennedy noted the progression since *Re B*: 'the sadness and regret are still there, but the court no longer felt the need to explore the law'.[69]

---

61 Lord Donaldson MR cited with approval the judgment of McKenzie J in the British Columbia case of *Re Superintendent of Family and Child Service and Dawson* (1983) 145 DLR (3d) 610 (at 620), which supported the subjective test stated by Asch J in the New York State decision of *Re Weberlist* (1974) 360 NYS 2d 783 (at 787).
62 *R v Portsmouth Hospital NHS Trust ex p Glass* [1999] 2 FLR 905 at 938F–G.
63 *Re J (a minor)(wardship: medical treatment)* [1991] 1 FLR 366 at 381E.
64 *R v Cambridge Health Authority ex p B* [1995] 2 All ER 129.
65 See Hinchliffe 1996: 1580.
66 *Re C (a baby)* [1996] 2 FLR 43 at 44C.
67 ibid 46.
68 ibid.
69 Kennedy 1997: 102.

However, there was considerably more exploration of the rulings to date in *Re T (a minor)(wardship: medical treatment)* [1997] 1 All ER 906, in which the Court of Appeal declined to overrule a mother's refusal to consent to a life-saving liver transplant for her two-year-old son. Connell J had deemed the mother's refusal unreasonable, which was the wrong approach according to the appellate court. The views of the parents – who, in the present case, 'were trained as health care professionals and are both experienced in the care of young sick children'[70] – were to be included in the balancing exercise by which a child's best interests are determined.

In the next case, *Re C (medical treatment)* [1998] 1 FLR 384, the parents of 16-month-old C failed to persuade the court that their opinion should carry the same weight as that of T's parents. C had spinal muscular atrophy and was expected to die in two months. His Orthodox Jewish parents opposed the withdrawal of artificial ventilation because 'life should always be preserved' and failure to prevent C's death would 'be punished by God'.[71] Granting the declaration, Brown P acknowledged that the sanctity of life was 'vitally important' but he confirmed that C's welfare was the paramount consideration.[72]

The potential for diverse and conflicting interpretations of a child's welfare was even more apparent in the next set of proceedings, which marked the first occasion on which David Glass's care came before the courts. Echoing guidance (then) recently issued by the Ethics Advisory Committee of the Royal College of Paediatrics and Child Health,[73] Lord Woolf MR made a plea for discussion and consensus.[74] Rather less helpfully, as we saw in Chapter 1, Woolf MR declined to issue an anticipatory declaration as he felt this would be 'fraught with danger', given the unpredictability of the situation.[75] He felt it sufficient to say that guiding (albeit conflicting) principles were available, as were the courts if they were needed.[76]

Although David Glass's case would later come before the Strasbourg judges, the English courts were next needed in *Royal Wolverhampton Hospitals NHS Trust v B* [2000] 2 FCR 76, which concerned Emily, who had been born 16 weeks prematurely with a range of significant problems, including chronic lung disease. As her condition deteriorated over a few months, doctors believed that her death was inevitable and that the artificial ventilation that she was receiving would serve no long term purpose and would only prolong her

70 *Re T (a minor)(wardship: medical treatment)* [1997] 1 All ER 906 at 908E–F (Butler-Sloss LJ).
71 *Re C (medical treatment)* [1998] 1 FLR 384 at 389A–B (Brown P).
72 ibid at 390H (Brown P).
73 See Royal College of Paediatrics and Child Health 1997: 19–20.
74 *R v Portsmouth Hospitals NHS Trust ex p Glass* [1999] 2 FLR 905 at 910H.
75 ibid at 910G.
76 ibid at 908.

suffering. Emily's parents contested this view and opposed the recommendation. The Trust made an emergency application to the High Court, seeking a direction which would allow Emily to be treated by the doctors in what they judged to be her best interests. The Official Solicitor, on Emily's behalf, objected that this came too close to intruding on the doctors' clinical expertise. Bodey J recognised the merits of the Official Solicitor's objection but decided, in view of the breakdown in trust between the parents and the professionals, to issue the Trust with a permissive order (regardless of whether this was strictly required), which empowered the clinicians to treat Emily in her best interests as they judged them.

The order sought by the Trust was also granted in the case of *A National Health Service Trust v D* [2000] 2 FLR 677. Cazalet J ruled, against the wishes of the parents, that a 19-month-old boy with a life expectancy of a few weeks should neither be ventilated nor receive any life-sustaining measures in the event of a crisis, although he should continue to receive palliative care. Counsel on both sides had made reference to the European Convention on Human Rights, which was shortly to enter English law via the Human Rights Act 1998. Cazalet J saw nothing in the Convention or its associated jurisprudence to suggest that English law was contrary to Article 2, the right to life, and he further opined that his decision protected 'the right to die with dignity' afforded by Article 3, the right to be free from inhuman or degrading treatment.[77]

Human rights considerations featured little in the (otherwise lengthy) judgments of the Court of Appeal in the next notable case, *Re A (children) (conjoined twins: medical treatment)* [2000] 4 All ER 961. Something of a departure from the cases to date (in more than one sense), the ruling merits consideration for what it reveals of the judges' approaches to questions of life and death. 'Jodie' and 'Mary' (or, as it was later revealed, Gracie and Rosie) were ischiopagus tetrapus conjoined twins, which meant they were joined from the umbilicus to the sacrum, with the lower ends of their spines and spinal cords fused. Jodie was the stronger twin: her heart and lungs supplied blood to Mary, whose own heart and lungs did not function. The prognosis was that, without separation, both twins would die within 6 to 24 months of their birth, as Jodie's organs would not be able to withstand the strain of supporting Mary. If separated, however, Mary would be certain to die, but Jodie could be expected to live a life of normal duration largely free from disability.

A couple of weeks after their birth, Johnson J authorised the separation of the twins, despite their Roman Catholic parents' refusal to consent.[78] Johnson J drew an analogy with the provision of life-supporting treatment: the withdrawal of Jodie's blood supply was comparable to the withdrawal of artificial

---

77 *A National Health Service Trust v D* [2000] 2 FLR 677 at 695D.
78 Unreported. See Burnet 2001.

nutrition and hydration from a patient in a PVS.[79] Such an 'omission' could be sanctioned where this accorded with the patient's best interests: here, the operation would not only be in Jodie's best interests, it would also be in Mary's best interests, as the continuation of her life would bring her nothing but pain.

The Court of Appeal upheld the result but rejected Johnson J's reasoning. The issues were largely divided into those pertaining to family law and those concerning the criminal law. Accepting that they were dealing with two legal persons, the majority of the judges conceded that separation would not necessarily be *in* Mary's interests but they unanimously concluded that the best interests balance fell in favour of saving Jodie. In terms of the criminal law, and in stark contrast to Johnson J, separation was to be seen as a positive act, which would amount to murder. This was justified, however, either on the basis of a private defence of Jodie (according to Ward LJ) or necessity (according to Brooke LJ in particular). The sisters were separated in a 20-hour procedure, in which (as predicted) Mary died.

Although it featured little in the judges' reasoning, the Human Rights Act 1998 came into force less than two weeks after the decision in *Re A*. In any event, the next case necessarily viewed the issues through the human rights prism, since it came before the European Court of Human Rights. This was, again, the case of David Glass.[80] In stark contrast to most of the rulings outlined here, on this occasion the Court shared the family's perspective. In administering diamorphine against the express wishes of his mother and in failing adequately to address her dispute with the doctors, the Strasbourg Court found the Trust to be in violation of David's 'right to respect for his private life, and in particular his right to physical integrity'.[81]

A flurry of cases was predicted in the wake of this apparent challenge to the orthodox approach, according to which the judges tended to defer to medical opinion.[82] The High Court did indeed soon have to consider a situation which proved nearly as contentious as David's, and this too was a case we have already encountered, since it involved the plight of Charlotte Wyatt. And as Hedley J embarked on what would prove to be a lengthy consideration of which treatment would (or would not) be appropriate for Charlotte, in *Re L (a child) (medical treatment: benefit)* [2004] EWHC 2713 the President of the Family Division contemplated the fate of Luke Winston-Jones, again in open court and under the media's scrutiny.

Luke was born on 30 January 2004 and was diagnosed with trisonomy 18 ('Edward's syndrome'), a genetic disorder which caused him to suffer from multiple heart defects, chronic respiratory failure, gastroesophageal reflux,

---

79 See *Airedale NHS Trust v Bland* [1993] 2 WLR 316, described in Chapter 3 section 3.2.1.
80 See Chapter 1, section 1.1.
81 *Glass v UK* [2004] 1 FCR 553 para 70.
82 Huxtable and Forbes 2004.

severe developmental delay, epilepsy and hypertonia. In hospital since his birth, Luke had endured numerous cardiac and respiratory arrests and lesser episodes of desaturation on a near-daily basis. He also had difficulty in feeding through a naso-gastric tube and required escalating amounts of oxygen. The medical team sought a declaration, which Luke's mother opposed, that it would be lawful to withhold mechanical ventilation. The agreed medical opinion was that babies in this condition had a short life-span and that only palliative (not curative) measures were appropriate; boys seldom lived for more than one year and, at the time at which the case came to court, Luke was nearly nine months old.

Granting a declaration, Butler-Sloss P explicitly endorsed the approach taken by Hedley J in relation to Charlotte Wyatt.[83] Like him, she acknowledged the strong presumption in favour of life, but found there to be 'no obligation on the medical profession to give treatment which would be futile'.[84] She similarly emphasised that the focus was on the child's best interests, broadly construed, rather than 'intolerability', although she admitted that 'the latter may be encompassed in the former'.[85] Applying these ideas to Luke, Butler-Sloss P noted that he would be unlikely to benefit from intubation and ventilation; indeed, he would be likely to suffer cardiac arrest. Even if he did survive, his quality of life would diminish since, confined to a ventilator, he would be denied the close physical relationship he now had with his mother.[86] However, the judge agreed with Luke's mother that cardiac massage, which had been successful on two previous occasions, should remain an option – although its use would ultimately 'depend on the clinical judgement of the treating doctors'.[87]

Two weeks after the ruling, Luke succumbed to his disorder. Despite claims by his parents that the doctors had unlawfully withheld adrenaline and 'dismantled' breathing equipment that might have saved their son, the coroner concluded that the doctors could have done nothing more. Luke's death was recorded as having occurred naturally, through cardiac arrest.[88]

The outcome of *An NHS Trust v MB* [2006] EWHC 507 marked something of a departure, not least from the two earlier rulings named *Re C*, which were both distinguished. Like C in 1998, 18-month-old M had been born with a severe form of spinal muscular atrophy; the condition was progressive, degenerative and would prove fatal, although it could not be predicted whether death would be soon and sudden or within the next few years. M's cognitive functioning and suffering were difficult to assess but, in the words

---

83   In *Wyatt (No 1)*.
84   ibid para 12.
85   ibid.
86   ibid para 25.
87   ibid para 30.
88   Jenkins 2005.

of the judge, the doctors believed 'the quality of life for M is now so low and that the burdens of living are now so great that it is unethical (the word "cruel" has been used) to continue artificially to keep him alive'.[89] Although the parents objected, the trust sought permission to withdraw the ventilation on which M relied.

As Holman J put it:

> So far as I am aware, no court has yet been asked to approve that, against the will of the child's parents, life support may be withdrawn or discontinued, with the predictable, inevitable and immediate death of a conscious child with sensory awareness and assumed normal cognition and no reliable evidence of any significant brain damage.[90]

Re C from 1996 had involved a child with little or no awareness and the parents had supported the application; *Re C* from 1998, whilst concerning a child with the same condition as M, involved the cessation of ventilation on which the child only intermittently relied, again with the parents' support. In Holman J's opinion, M continued to enjoy some benefits; he had 'age appropriate cognition, and does continue to have a relationship of value to him with his family, and does continue to gain other pleasures from touch, sight and sound'; although not susceptible to 'mathematical' quantification, these benefits outweighed 'all the routine discomfort, distress and pain that the doctors describe'.[91] However, Holman J did recognise that a limit might be reached, as M approached death. As such, whilst he declined to authorise the withdrawal of ventilation, he accepted that life-saving measures beyond this (like cardiopulmonary resuscitation (CPR)) did not need to be offered, unless the doctors felt this appropriate at the relevant moment.

In reaching his decision, Holman J had noted the views of M's father, a practising Muslim who believed 'that it is not right for people to choose whether another person should live or die'.[92] Holman J nevertheless (respectfully) stated that this was 'irrelevant' to the 'objective balancing' of M's interests.[93] Holman J repeated this notion in *NHS Trust v A (a child)* [2007] EWHC 1696, when he authorised a bone marrow transplant for A, notwithstanding A's parents' argument that A had suffered enough through treatment, that she should enjoy a reasonable quality of life for what time she had left, and that God had the ability to cure her of the genetic defect from which she suffered (haemophagocytic lymphohistiocytosis). Leaving 'entirely out of

---

89 *An NHS Trust v MB* [2006] EWHC 507 para 10.
90 ibid para 11.
91 ibid paras 101, 102.
92 ibid para 49.
93 ibid.

account any possibility of a miraculous cure',[94] the judge found that the balance tipped in favour of the transplant, since this would grant the child a 50 per cent prospect of a full, 'normal' life ('even though infertile'[95]), as opposed to a certain death before reaching 18 months.

Shortly prior to this case, the President of the Family Division had considered the plight of another child with an inherited condition, congenital myotonic dystrophy, a neuromuscular disorder causing chronic muscle weakness. He decided, in *Re K (a child)(withdrawal of treatment)* [2006] EWHC 1007, that the medical staff could remove from K's abdomen the intravenous line providing her with nutrition (total parenteral nutrition (TPN)) and begin palliative care. Aged five-and-half months, K was judged unlikely to survive to one year. The consultant neonatologist situated K somewhere between the 'no chance' and 'no purpose' situations outlined in the guidance from the Royal College of Paediatrics and Child Health, which was now in its second edition.[96] Treatment could, accordingly, either be considered futile and burdensome, or otherwise contrary to the child's best interests, because (for example) 'the child may develop or already have such a degree of irreversible impairment that it would be unreasonable to expect them to bear it'.[97] No one opposed the declaration sought; Potter P concluded 'that it would not only be a mercy, but it is in her best interests, to cease to provide TPN while she is still clinically stable, so that she may die in peace and over a comparatively short space of time'.[98] Whilst several articles of the European Convention on Human Rights were engaged, Potter P noted that these did nothing to detract from the established principles of domestic law as they applied here.

L, the child at the centre of *Re B (a child) (medical treatment)* [2008] EWHC 1996, had a marginally better prognosis than K, although she was considered unlikely to reach the age of five. The precise inherited metabolic condition from which L (who was in foster care) suffered had not been diagnosed, but it encompassed severe mental and physical disabilities, and did not appear amenable to treatment. The clinicians were concerned that L would gradually deteriorate; in the event of a crisis developing (such as pneumonia, for example), they wanted the freedom to withhold intensive resuscitation measures, including CPR or intubation for the purposes of ventilation.

Coleridge J, granting the declaration, acknowledged the clinicians' wish to determine when 'enough is enough; that she should not be subjected to any further futile prolongation of her life in circumstances where the end is only being postponed by a short time'.[99] Although (to his knowledge)

---

94 *NHS Trust v A (a child)* [2007] EWHC 1696 para 68.
95 ibid para 70.
96 Royal College of Paediatrics and Child Health 2004: 10–11.
97 ibid 29.
98 ibid 57.
99 *Re B (a child) (medical treatment)* [2008] EWHC 1996 para 18.

unprecedented, Coleridge J appended to his order a report, prepared jointly by the four experts in the case, in the hope that this might prove useful guidance to anyone caring for L in the future. Indeed, he considered this a potentially useful addition to any future case concerning 'a sick child, or a sick patient, where the medical definitions and situations which may arise in emergencies are not necessarily capable of complete contemplation'.[100]

An emergency – or, more accurately, a series of crises – precipitated the next case, *Re OT* [2009] EWHC 633, which concerned nine-month-old T. T was suffering from a genetic condition and had been hospitalised and entirely dependent upon a ventilator from the age of three weeks. He had borne brainstem damage, a metabolic stroke, inflammation causing calcification in his brain and atrophy of his brain and brainstem. T endured fits, was unable to breathe unaided, could not suck or swallow and had to be fed via a nasogastric tube; he also intermittently required oxygen treatment. Although his parents wanted him to have all available treatments, the medical staff felt that T was distressed and that long-term care was not in his best interests.

In an emergency application, the Trust sought authorisation to withdraw artificial ventilation from T and withhold further invasive treatment, in favour of palliative care. Following the parents' objections, the Trust further sought assurance that its personnel were at liberty to provide T with such treatment and care that would involve for him the least pain and distress and the greatest dignity. The Trust pointed to the unanimity of the treating doctors and the experts regarding T's condition and prognosis. Arguing that T would get better and should be treated, his parents complained that their human rights had been violated, since an emergency hearing should not have been sought and they should have been provided with more time to present their case.

Parker J granted the declarations sought. An emergency application itself did not signal a breach of human rights[101] and, in this case, the parents had had ample time to seek alternative medical opinions. Furthermore, whilst Article 2 of the Human Rights Act 1998, the right to life, 'imposes a positive obligation to give life sustaining treatment, where responsible medical opinion is of the view that such treatment is in the best interests of the patient it does not impose an absolute obligation to treat if such would be futile'.[102] In the latter situation, which was the case here, neither Article 2 nor Article 8 (the right to respect for private and family life) is contravened.

2.3 Conclusion: in the child's best interests?

The judges have travelled a considerable distance since Dr Leonard Arthur's alleged failure to care for John Pearson first required them to consider whether

100 ibid para 4.
101 *Re OT* [2009] EWHC 633 para 79.
102 ibid para 97.

there might be limits to the duty to provide life-supporting treatment to seriously ill infants. Since the conclusion of that trial the civil courts have largely assumed jurisdiction over these cases of life-or-death. Charlotte Wyatt's case exemplifies not only how contested and complicated these hearings can be, but also how difficult it can be to reach an answer to the question: to treat or not to treat?

Certain principles nevertheless emerge, which merit reiteration. The best interests or welfare of the child is central to the jurisprudence pertaining to both the inherent jurisdiction and the Children Act 1989. This is, indeed, the paramount consideration for the court and, by extension, all those responsible for the care of the child, be they professionals, parents or other proxies. A decision about whether to initiate or terminate life-support must be examined from the assumed viewpoint of the child in question. There is a strong presumption in favour of life, but this can be rebutted where, for example, the courts consider continued or fresh intervention to be 'futile'. References have been made to the child's perceived quality of life and, particularly, to its perceived 'intolerability', although the judges emphasise that no such guide to the child's best interests can supplant the primary focus – which is indeed on the best interests of that child. This principle is seen as encompassing cultural, familial and spiritual dimensions. It therefore comprises more than the medical indications that have seemed to dominate in many cases – albeit with notable exceptions like those of T, from whom a liver transplant was withheld, and David Glass, to whose mother the Trust should apparently have listened more attentively. When such cases come before a court, the judge nowadays conducts a balancing exercise, plotting the factors for and against a particular outcome. The judge may append additional guidance for the future,[103] and may propose different courses for different developments, although he or she apparently will never stipulate that a team must treat, contrary to their clinical judgment.

Although the welfare principle dominates, there are a number of subordinate principles which can further help to guide the various parties concerned with the care of a critically ill child. This chapter opened with an excerpt from a speech by Wall LJ, in which he outlined the main issues; later in that speech, his Lordship called for 'caution in the application to children of factors relevant to the treatment of adults, although some general statements of principle plainly apply to both'.[104] This requires us to consider how the courts approach patients who have reached majority but who also (somewhat akin to infants) lack the capacity currently to direct their medical treatment. We turn, then, to adults, in Chapter 3.

---

103 See *Re B (a child) (medical treatment)* [2008] EWHC 1996.
104 *Wyatt v Portsmouth Hospital NHS Trust* [2005] EWCA Civ 1181 para 90 (Wall LJ).

3 Law at the limits of life

Adults, incapacity and precedent autonomy

> [T]he principle of self-determination requires that respect must be given to the wishes of the patient, so that if an adult patient of sound mind refuses, however unreasonably, to consent to treatment or care by which his life would or might be prolonged, the doctors responsible for his care must give effect to his wishes, even though they do not consider it to be in his best interests to do so . . . To this extent, the principle of the sanctity of human life must yield to the principle of self-determination . . . and . . . the doctors' duty to act in the best interests of his patient must likewise be qualified . . . Moreover the same principle applies where the patient's refusal to give his consent has been expressed at an earlier date, before he became unconscious or otherwise incapable of communicating it . . .
>
> *Airedale NHS Trust v Bland* [1993] 2 WLR 316 at 367F–G (Lord Goff)

3.1 Conflicts in the clinic: the case of Terri Schiavo

English law has encompassed a variety of complex situations concerning the treatment of – and removal of treatment from – incapacitated adult patients. However, the world's attention was most recently captured by a case from another jurisdiction, in which the conflicts were particularly acute. The case, concerning Terri Schiavo, provides a useful starting point, since it illuminates the main areas of legal (and ethical) contention that can arise, including in our jurisdiction.

On 25 February 1990, Mrs Schiavo, who was 26 years old, collapsed in her home in Florida, suffering severe hypoxia (deprivation of oxygen) for some minutes. She had been dieting and may have been bulimic: her husband Michael later won a malpractice lawsuit against the obstetrician treating his wife's infertility who had failed to diagnose bulimia as its cause. On arrival at hospital, Mrs Schiavo was intubated and ventilated. Given her inability to swallow, a percutaneous endoscopic gastrostomy (PEG) tube was also subsequently sited.

Four months after the injury, Mrs Schiavo was judged incompetent and Michael was appointed her legal guardian, to which his wife's parents, Mary and Robert Schindler, did not object. Terri had not appointed a surrogate decision-maker (proxy or attorney) and neither had she formally executed an advance directive indicating her views should she lose the capacity to make treatment decisions for herself.

Within a year of the injury, Terri Schiavo was diagnosed as being in a persistent vegetative state (PVS). PVS is a disorder of consciousness in which the patient is wakeful but unconscious. The condition tends to be labelled as permanent when it has persisted for more than one year, although other terms have recently been proposed, such as 'post-coma unresponsiveness' and 'unresponsive wakefulness syndrome'.[1]

The family worked with each other and with a range of health professionals – including physical, speech and occupational therapists – in an effort to rehabilitate Mrs Schiavo, but to no substantial effect. After his wife contracted a urinary tract infection, Michael requested a 'do not resuscitate' order,[2] seemingly having concluded that his wife's condition would never improve and that further treatment or intervention was no longer warranted. The Schindlers resisted this conclusion; from here the relationship they had once enjoyed with their son-in-law deteriorated considerably.

In stark opposition to his in-laws, Mr Schiavo felt that the nutrition and hydration being provided to Terri by tube should be stopped. Around this time, he voluntarily relinquished his guardianship role, preferring that the court provide an independent judgment as to what should happen.[3] In January 2000, a hearing was held to determine Mrs Schiavo's condition and, in the absence of a specific advance directive executed by the patient herself, to determine what her wishes would have been with regard to life-prolonging treatment. Both sides presented witnesses, with Mrs Schiavo's parents arguing that their daughter had been a Roman Catholic, who would have shared the Church's opposition to the withdrawal of treatment, on the basis that this could be interpreted as 'euthanasia'. Michael argued that his wife had made verbal statements to the effect that she would not want her life continued in this condition. Having confirmed that Mrs Schiavo was in a PVS, the judge preferred Michael's view, and ordered that the PEG tube be withdrawn.[4] In what became known as *Schiavo I*, the Florida Appeal Court confirmed this decision:[5] in line with Florida law, it found there was 'clear and convincing evidence'[6] that Mrs Schiavo would choose 'a natural death' over continued treatment.

1   National Health and Medical Research Council 2004; Laureys et al 2010.
2   Recall that current UK guidance prefers to talk of (not) *attempting* resuscitation and hence DNAR (and sometimes DNACPR) orders: see British Medical Association, the Resuscitation Council (UK) and the Royal College of Nursing 2007.
3   *Schindler v Schiavo*, 792 So 2d 551, 557 (Fla Dist Ct App 2001).
4   *In re Schiavo*, 90-2908GD-003 (Fla Cir Ct, Pinellas Co, 11 February 2000).
5   *Schindler v Schiavo*, 800 So 2d 640, 647 (Fla Dist Ct App 2001).
6   *In re Browning*, 568 So 2d 4 (Fla 1990).

The Schindlers continued to resist the position taken by their son-in-law and the courts. They unsuccessfully petitioned to have oral feeding instated,[7] and also failed to have Michael removed as guardian,[8] when they argued that his decision to move Terri to a different hospital was a waste of funds.[9]

On 24 April 2001 Terri's feeding tube was withdrawn, only to be reinstated on 26 April, amidst a flurry of legal activity (known as *Schiavo II*) in which new arguments were heard about Terri's apparent wishes and her medical condition.[10] The latter issue then became the focus of *Schiavo III*, when the appellate court granted the Schindlers' wish that their daughter's situation be re-examined. Five medical experts were to be appointed: two nominated by Terri's parents, two chosen by her husband, and one independently assigned by the court.[11]

After conducting new tests plus a review of the evidence to date, three of these experts (all neurologists) confirmed that Terri was in a PVS; the remaining two (a neurologist and a radiologist), who were appointed by the Schindlers, concluded that she was in a minimally conscious state (MCS) and could benefit from alternative rehabilitation techniques. A disorder of consciousness distinct from PVS or the locked-in state, the patient in a MCS retains limited conscious awareness.[12] Six hours of videotape of Terri was provided to the judge, who ruled that she was indeed in a PVS and unlikely significantly to improve. Mindful that 'medicine is not a precise science', Judge Greer was nevertheless particularly critical of the Schindlers' experts.[13] In what became known as *Schiavo IV*, the Appeal Court upheld Judge Greer's decision to authorise the withdrawal of the feeding tube, finding that he had reached his conclusion according to 'a cautious legal standard designed to promote the value of life'.[14]

On 15 October 2003, the feeding tube was withdrawn for the second time. However, within a week, it was back in place, when Florida's Governor, Jeb Bush, passed 'Terri's Law', according to which he had authority to intervene.

7 *In re Guardianship of Theresa Marie Schiavo, Incapacitated*, File No 90-2908GD-003 Florida Sixth Judicial Circuit available at http://abstractappeal.com/schiavo/trialctorder0300.pdf (last accessed 25 April 2011).
8 By this time, Michael was in a relationship and had fathered a child.
9 *In re: the guardianship of Theresa Marie Schiavo, Incapacitated*, File No 90-2908GD-003 available at http://www.libertytothecaptives.net/petitiontoremoveguardian_amended.html (last accessed 25 April 2011).
10 *In re Guardianship of Theresa Marie Schiavo, Incapacitated. Robert Schindler and Mary Schindler, Appellants, v Michael Schiavo, as Guardian of the person of Theresa Marie Schiavo, Appellee*; and *Michael Schiavo, as Guardian of the person of Theresa Marie Schiavo, Appellant v Robert Schindler and Mary Schindler, Appellees* Case Nos 2D00-1269, 2D01-1836, and 2D01-1891 available at http://abstractappeal.com/schiavo/2dcaorder07-01.txt (last accessed 25 April 2011).
11 *Schindler v Schiavo*, 800 So 2d 640, 647 (Fla Dist Ct App 2001).
12 Giacino et al 2002.
13 *In re Schiavo*, 90-2908GB-003 (Fla Cir Ct, Pinellas Co, 22 November 2002).
14 *Schindler v Schiavo*, 851 So 2d 182, 187 (Fla Dist Ct App 2003).

Further litigation ensued, regarding the rights (or lack thereof) of Terri's family in relation to this new law and, moreover, its constitutional validity. Almost a year later, the Florida Supreme Court found the law to be unconstitutional.[15]

By the beginning of 2005, Terri Schiavo's case was known internationally. Her parents continued to petition the courts, in particular seeking a swallowing therapy and a functional magnetic resonance imaging (fMRI) test,[16] which Judge Greer declined to permit, since he doubted the appropriateness of the experimental therapy and the accuracy of the medical evidence provided.[17]

On 18 March 2005 Terri's feeding tube was withdrawn for the third and final time. At this point the legal picture became even more confusing, as the United States Congress intervened, with what became known as the 'Palm Sunday Compromise', according to which jurisdiction over the *Schiavo* case was passed from the state to the federal courts. President George W. Bush flew back from a vacation to sign the Bill into law in the small hours of 21 March. The legal saga effectively ended in the Supreme Court, with its ruling that the Schindlers had exhausted their legal options.

Terri Schiavo died on 31 March 2005, surrounded by police officers, who were present to ensure that no attempts were made to provide her with food or fluids. The autopsy ruled out bulimia and cardiac arrest as the causes of her death, which was certified as 'undetermined'.[18]

3.2 Best interests, incapacity and precedent autonomy

Terri Schiavo's case, and the substantial litigation it initiated, is undoubtedly remarkable, but the issues at stake are uncomfortably familiar across the (developed) world. Acute dilemmas like these respect no geographical boundaries: wherever life-sustaining techniques and technologies exist, legal and ethical anxieties attend questions concerning their initiation and continuation. Such questions were first considered by a court in the case of Karen Ann Quinlan, who (like Schiavo) was in a PVS.[19] The New Jersey Supreme Court authorised the removal of a ventilator at the request of Ms Quinlan's father, who was empowered to decide on the basis of his daughter's assumed wishes. Ms Quinlan unexpectedly survived the withdrawal of ventilation, and lived for another decade before succumbing to pneumonia. Throughout this period,

---

15 *Bush v Schiavo*, 885 So 2d 321, 324 (Fla 2004).

16 Research involving fMRI of a PVS patient has suggested that consciousness might be preserved in such patients: Owen et al 2006; Monti et al 2010. See further below, in the discussion of *B NHS Trust v J* [2006] EWHC 3152.

17 *In re Guardianship of Theresa Marie Schiavo, Incapacitated. Michael Schiavo, as Guardian of the person of Theresa Marie Schiavo, Petitioner v Robert Schindler and Mary Schindler, Respondents*, File No 90-2908-GD-003 available at http://abstractappeal.com/schiavo/trialctorder 030905.pdf (last accessed 25 April 2011).

18 http://www.abstractappeal.com/schiavo/autopsyreport.pdf (last accessed 25 April 2011).

19 *In re Quinlan*, NJ 355 A 2d 647 (1976). See Huxtable 2007: 116–117.

she continued to receive nutrition and hydration via a feeding tube. As we saw in Mrs Schiavo's case, it is usually the discontinuance of this life-sustaining measure which is at issue in these difficult cases. Thus, the parents of Nancy Cruzan took three years to convince the American courts that their daughter would not want this life-support to continue.[20] Two decades later, in Italy, Eluana Englaro's father saw a successful end to 17 years of attempting to persuade the judges, during which time – again, as in Schiavo's case – there was political intervention from the highest levels, including by the Italian prime minister Silvio Berlusconi.[21]

Despite the geographical spread, there are clear similarities in the ethical and legal principles at stake in these cases,[22] which (as the statement from Lord Goff quoted at the beginning of this chapter attests) English law also shares. As with children, a central consideration will be the best interests of the patient. But many of these cases introduce another concept, through which we might give substance to that assessment or which we might see as a stand-alone concept. This concept can be described as 'precedent autonomy', which here encompasses two types of decision: the 'advance directive' ('living will' or some other alleged synonym); and the appointment of a proxy decision-maker (surrogate or healthcare attorney). In either case, the autonomous person is seeking to make provision for a future in which his or her autonomy has been lost. Before we consider what it means to lose autonomy in English law and how one might attempt to provide for such a future, we will first trace those cases in which the decision to treat (or not) turns on the perceived best interests of the incapacitated adult. The jurisprudence begins, as will we, with patients in a PVS.

3.2.1 Best interests and the persistent vegetative state

In April 1989, aged 17, Anthony Bland was trapped in the crush of people at the Hillsborough football stadium disaster. He suffered a punctured lung, which resulted in his brain being deprived of oxygen. Like Terri Schiavo one year later, Anthony was ultimately diagnosed as being in a PVS, and as such – despite following sleep-wake cycles – he was judged to be unaware and insensate, and highly unlikely ever to recover. After three years, his doctors and his family decided to approach the courts for a declaration that it would be lawful to discontinue life-support, including nutrition and hydration, which was being provided to Anthony via a naso-gastric tube. The case, *Airedale NHS Trust v Bland* [1993] 2 WLR 316, reached the House of Lords, where permission was granted.

---

20 *Cruzan v Director, Missouri Department of Health*, 497 US 261 (1990).
21 Luchetti 2010.
22 See also Jox 2011.

Deprived of the power to decide on a patient's behalf,[23] the Law Lords focused on the legal duties of the doctors. According to the majority, artificial nutrition and hydration (ANH) – or, in today's terminology,[24] clinically assisted nutrition and hydration (CANH) – is a form of medical treatment. Medical treatment is intended to benefit the patient; it is directed at serving the patient's 'best interests'. The *Bolam* test,[25] according to which reference may be made to a responsible body of medical opinion, can guide this assessment. Here, a responsible body of doctors agreed that existence in a PVS did not benefit the patient and that further treatment or care could be considered 'futile'.[26] Anthony Bland was to be considered alive, both clinically and legally, and although English law recognised the sanctity of human life, the Lords held that this was not an absolute principle.[27] Neither could it be complained that the doctors would be murdering Anthony Bland: the *mens rea* (or 'mental' element) of the offence – the intention to end life – might be present, but the *actus reus* (or 'physical' element) was not. Stopping feeding amounted to an omission, which would only be culpable where there was a duty to feed. The necessity to feed (which arose from Anthony's inability to consent or refuse on his own behalf[28]) had gone and so, accordingly, had the justification for doing so. The duty – perhaps even the entitlement[29] – to treat was therefore absent, so there was no prospect of criminality, a point which was subsequently confirmed when a Reverend Morrow attempted (unsuccessfully) to obtain a summons charging Anthony's doctor with murder.[30]

Despite its familiarity and influence, the *Bland* ruling is not easy to pin down. The essential message seems to be: although doctors will owe a duty to treat their patients, the withdrawal of life-sustaining treatment in the form of CANH will not be unlawful where a body of responsible medical opinion finds continued treatment not to be in the patient's best interests, which means that they are released from the duty. The Law Lords certainly found the case challenging, calling on Parliament to consider the issues,[31] and instructing

---

23 *Airedale NHS Trust v Bland* [1993] 2 WLR 316. Lord Lowry, particularly, lamented the loss of the *parens patriae* jurisdiction (at 378).

24 General Medical Council 2010.

25 *Bolam v Friern Hospital Management Committee* [1957] 1 WLR 582. Lord Mustill's reservations on importing this test into a field dominated by criminal law are noteworthy (at 399G–H).

26 *Airedale NHS Trust v Bland* [1993] 2 WLR 316 at 372 (Lord Goff).

27 ibid at 367 (Lord Goff).

28 Necessity, understood in terms of the incompetent patient's best interests, was the basis for providing treatment, following *Re F (mental patient: sterilisation)* [1990] 2 AC 1.

29 *Airedale NHS Trust v Bland* [1993] 2 WLR 316 at 379 (Lord Browne-Wilkinson) and 386 (Lord Lowry).

30 *R v Bingley Magistrates' Court ex p Morrow* [1995] Med L Rev 86.

31 *Airedale NHS Trust v Bland* [1993] 2 WLR 316. Lords Browne-Wilkinson and Mustill called for Parliament to consider the wider moral, social and legal issues of the case (at 382 and 392, respectively). A review was subsequently undertaken: see House of Lords Select Committee 1994.

that future such cases should come before the courts, at least 'until a body of experience and practice has been built up'.[32]

Although there were varying estimates of between 170 and 1500 PVS patients in the UK,[33] it was a year before the Court of Appeal considered the next case, which concerned a dislodged gastrostomy tube. *Frenchay NHS Trust v S* [1994] 1 WLR 601 was unusual, given its urgency, the lack of independent medical opinion and the uncertain diagnosis. Upholding the decision not to reinstate the tube, Sir Thomas Bingham MR held that S was in a PVS and that the *Bland* guidelines had been followed as far as was practicable. He felt that the urgency of a case might sometimes preclude a thorough investigation or even time to come to court, although he noted that it remained the judge's task ultimately to determine the best interests of a patient like S.

Hinchliffe, from the Official Solicitor's office, doubted that *Frenchay* would recur, given the requirement – confirmed in a *Practice Note* [1994] 2 All ER 413 – for an independent medical report.[34] As this and subsequent Practice Notes stated,[35] the diagnosis had to be made according to the most up-to-date criteria.[36] The court had also to hear evidence (where available) of the views of the patient and the patient's next-of-kin. These latter views need not be determinative, as Ward J indicated in *Swindon and Marlborough NHS Trust v S* [1995] Med L Rev 84, in which he considered whether surgical reinsertion of a feeding tube was warranted for a patient being cared for at home. Sir Stephen Brown P also had cause to consider the issue in *Re G (persistent vegetative state)* [1995] 2 FCR 46, since G's wife supported the withdrawal of ANH, but his mother did not. He concluded that the treatment could be withdrawn: the mother's view was relevant but not decisive and this was certainly not 'equivalent to euthanasia' as she claimed. Brown P directed that these cases could be heard in open court, in view of the public interest questions at stake, but that anonymity should be preserved (including beyond the patient's death).[37]

1995 proved to be 'a busy year',[38] with the courts confirming that ANH could be withdrawn from two patients referred to as B and another dubbed C (whose case was widely publicised, since his condition resulted from an anaesthetic accident[39]), and that ventilation could be removed from Daniel Coe.

32 *Airedale NHS Trust v Bland* [1993] 2 WLR 316 at 363 (Lord Keith).
33 Andrews and Hinchliffe 1993: 138; Grubb 1995: 84.
34 Hinchliffe 1996: 1579.
35 *Practice Note* [1996] 4 All ER 766; *Practice Note (Official Solicitor: Declaratory Proceedings: Medical and Welfare Decisions for Adults who Lack Capacity)* [2001] 2 FLR 158; *Practice Note (Official Solicitor: Declaratory Proceedings: Medical and Welfare Decisions for Adults who Lack Capacity)* [2006] 2 FLR 373.
36 See the criteria described in Royal College of Physicians 2003.
37 *Re G (adult patient: publicity)* [1995] 2 FLR 528; *Re C (adult patient: restriction of publicity after death)* [1996] 1 FCR 605.
38 Hinchliffe 1996: 1580. The case of Mrs L did not come before a court in 1995 (as had been expected), because she died before proceedings commenced.
39 eg Dyer 1995: 8.

The following few years tended to see one or two cases a year coming before the courts (*W* and *D* in 1996; *L* in 1997; *MM* in 1998).[40] Although their task remained difficult, the judges' approach was by now relatively settled. However, the cases did sometimes introduce new features: for example, in one case from 1995, the court referred to the supportive opinion of the patient's flatmate, as well as her family's views.

Yet, while the law appeared increasingly clear, the clinical picture was – and is[41] – not always so. Reports of recovery from PVS and misdiagnosis featured in the medical[42] and the popular press.[43] After the 'near miss' of *Frenchay*, the courts again narrowly avoided these issues in 1995, when an independent expert found that a patient known as G had sufficient capacity to be able to indicate her desire to continue living. G's family had supported the withdrawal of treatment, recalling G's previously expressed wish that her life not continue in such a state.[44]

By 1997 the dilemmas could no longer be avoided. However, despite the patient in *Re D (medical treatment)* [1998] 1 FLR 411 failing to satisfy two of the diagnostic criteria for PVS, Brown P found her to be lacking any 'real possibility of meaningful life',[45] and he ruled that it would be lawful not to reinsert her feeding tube. He did not think that this extended the law.[46] The President then reached the same conclusion in *Re H (a patient)* [1998] 2 FLR 36: despite retaining some rudimentary awareness and thus failing to meet the PVS guidelines laid down by the Royal College of Physicians, it was in H's best interests that life support be withdrawn.

1998 also brought the Human Rights Act and a challenge to the reasoning developed in *Bland* and its progeny. In *NHS Trust A v M; NHS Trust B v H* [2001] 2 WLR 942, Butler-Sloss P ruled that the Act did nothing to affect the legality of withdrawing life-support from PVS patients. Article 2, the right to life, would not be violated by the withdrawal of life-support where treatment was futile or not in the patient's best interests, as determined by a responsible body of medical opinion.[47] Article 8, which was seen to protect 'the right to personal autonomy',[48] would only be violated where what was proposed was contrary to the incompetent patient's best interests;[49] the

---

40 Hinchliffe 1996: 1580, 1585; *The Times* 1997: 12; Glasson and Irwin 1997: 1390; *The Times* 1998: 7.
41 See further below in the discussion of *B NHS Trust v J* [2006] EWHC 3152.
42 Andrews 1993a, 1993b.
43 eg *The Guardian* 1997b: 1; *The Daily Telegraph* 1998: 3.
44 See Hinchliffe 1996: 1580.
45 *Re D (medical treatment)* [1998] 1 FLR 411 at 420G.
46 Some journalists disagreed, eg *The Guardian* 1997a.
47 *NHS Trust A v M; NHS Trust B v H* [2001] 2 WLR 942 at 953A–E. According to Butler-Sloss P, this standard 'approximates to the *Bolam* test', although the court did not necessarily have to accept medical opinion (see 952–53).
48 ibid a 954D–E.
49 ibid at 951C.

family's views might be relevant here,[50] but the patient took priority and, in any event, the family members and the doctors happened to agree that treatment should be stopped in the present case. There could also be no objection on the basis of Article 3: not only did responsible medical opinion support the proposed course,[51] but the patient in a PVS was not sensate and so could not be aware of suffering any inhuman and degrading treatment.[52]

Shortly after this ruling, Butler-Sloss P had cause to consider another apparently doubtful case, *NHS Trust A v H* [2001] 2 FLR 501, in which (as also occurred in Terri Schiavo's case) a neurologist had thought that minimally conscious state (MCS), rather than PVS, was the more appropriate diagnosis. However, other eminent experts found no evidence of awareness (and the neurologist's opinion appeared also to change), which led the judge to conclude that H was indeed in a PVS. Noting the support of H's carers and family (who also felt that H herself would not have authorised ongoing treatment), Butler-Sloss P ruled that the (perishing) PEG tube need not be replaced. She further opined that the trust might have considered attending court 'rather sooner' than it had.[53]

After H came G, who had been unresponsive in the nine months since she had sustained severe anoxic brain damage following surgery. Relying wholly on the evidence of one medical expert as to G's condition, the court in *Re G* (2002) 65 BMLR 6 decided that nutrition and hydration could be withdrawn. Like H, G had (reportedly) also declared that she would not wish to live in such a condition and her family supported the Trust's application to court. This was also the case in *NHS Trust v I* [2003] EWHC 2243, where Butler-Sloss P concluded that the patient should be permitted 'to die with dignity',[54] rather than continue to exist 'in a twilight world'.[55]

Trust A, Trust B, Dr V v Mr M [2005] EWHC 807 – in which the withdrawal of ANH from M was authorised at a time when Terri Schiavo's plight was before the American courts and assisted dying was before the English Parliament – is particularly notable for the clarity Hedley J sought to bring to the court's calculation of a patient's best interests:

> First, it must consider the medical evidence and the medical advice. It must consider whether it is satisfied [that the patient] is in a permanent vegetative state, and it must consider whether the continuation of

50 ibid at 954E–G.

51 ibid at 956C–D.

52 ibid at 956D–E. On this point, Baker J has since noted that 'medical understanding of VS has expanded significantly . . . and it may be that Butler-Sloss P's assertion would not now be applied without qualification' (*W v M and S and A NHS Primary Care Trust* [2011] EWHC 2443 para 92; the case is discussed below).

53 *NHS Trust A v H* [2001] 2 FLR 501 para 18.

54 ibid para 1.

55 ibid para 8.

treatment is, or is not, in his best interests. Secondly, it seems to me that the Court has to take close account of the views of the family and those who are closest to [the patient], not only because they are the family . . . and entitled to be heard in that regard, but because they may be able to be in the best position of conveying to the court what they think the views of [the patient] himself may have been . . . Thirdly, and in a sense over and above the other two, the court has a duty, in respect of its public policy, to scrutinise with the greatest of care any course whose inevitable result is the death of someone for whom the court is responsible because that person is not competent to make their own decisions.[56]

Considering this last dimension, Hedley J candidly admitted that the case before him 'stands close to concepts of euthanasia, and stands close to the fence which divides natural consequences from deliberately brought-about death'.[57] The judges, he argued, should 'stand sentry at the fence' and assume responsibility for these questions of life and death, since 'the court, as a publicly accountable body, is the proper repository of this responsibility rather than doctors and rather than the family'.[58]

The courts would soon acquire new responsibilities, since 2005 also saw the passing of the Mental Capacity Act, which was to come into force in 2007. The Act provided a new framework for the (non-)treatment of incompetent adult patients, including a revitalised Court of Protection. Central to the Act is the best interests test,[59] which is given statutory expression for the first time (for adults). The precise variables that should make up the calculation are not given, although the Act does instruct that, 'so far as is reasonably ascertainable', reference should be made to the person's 'past and present wishes and feelings', the 'beliefs and values' that would be likely to influence their decision, plus 'any other factors' they would be likely to consider if they were capable.[60] A decision to withdraw or withhold life-sustaining treatment in a patient's best interests would remain lawful, provided it was not 'motivated by a desire to bring about . . . death'.[61] As a Practice Note and the accompanying Code of Practice made clear, there remained the requirement to come to court (now the Court of Protection) when the removal of CANH from a patient in a PVS was contemplated.[62]

The 2005 Act evidently did not abandon the prevailing jurisprudence and,

---

56 *Trust A, Trust B, Dr V v Mr M* [2005] EWHC 807 para 16.
57 ibid para 11.
58 ibid para 12.
59 Mental Capacity Act 2005 s 1(5).
60 ibid s 4(6).
61 ibid s 4(5). See also s 62, which states that nothing in the Act affects the law of homicide.
62 *Practice Note (Official Solicitor: Declaratory Proceedings: Medical and Welfare Decisions for Adults who Lack Capacity)* [2006] 2 FLR 373; Mental Capacity Act 2005 Code of Practice 2007 paras 6.18, 8.18 and 8.19.

of course, there was still work for the judges to do before the Act came into force. In the next case, *An NHS Trust v D* [2005] EWHC 2439, numerous members of the patient's family disagreed with the doctors, who wished to withhold CPR, antibiotics or other 'invasive steps' from D, who they felt was likely to die within a year.[63] D's family detected some awareness and communicative ability in D, which the doctors interpreted as (only) reflexive. Siding with the doctors, Coleridge J ruled that D:

> . . . should be allowed as dignified a passing as is achievable. Some might say that her dignity has already been severely compromised by the progress and incidence of this awful disease. To subject her body to further grossly invasive procedure can only further detract from her dignity.[64]

While D's case differed from many of its predecessors in concerning interventions other than CANH, a more marked variation was to come with *B NHS Trust v J* [2006] EWHC 3152, in which the court authorised a short trial of a sleeping pill, Zolpidem, notwithstanding the objections of J's relatives, who felt that J herself would also have objected. Around the same time that a study using fMRI first suggested the retention of some consciousness in apparently vegetative patients,[65] another group had reportedly found significant, albeit temporary, improvements in consciousness in three patients who had taken the drug.[66] In court, leading expert Dr Keith Andrews suspected that none of the latter patients had been in a PVS, but he felt the potential benefits to J of a successful trial outweighed the (minimal) risks. Potter P concurred: the drug would take effect quickly if successful, and a limit of three days would be imposed. The judge dismissed the family's concern that, if she were to awaken, J might experience profound distress. In the event, the drug had no effect beyond putting J to sleep. Her case returned to court, where Potter P granted the order originally favoured by J's family, that ANH be withdrawn.[67]

Potter P reached the same result in *A Hospital v SW* [2007] EWHC 425, in which, like Butler-Sloss P before him, he found no conflict with the Human Rights Act 1998. However, another statute was on the horizon – although (to date) the enforcement of the Mental Capacity Act 2005 has effected no substantial change on the handling of these cases. So, in *Re C* [2010] EWHC 3448, Ryder J in the Court of Protection felt able to authorise the withdrawal of ANH. A balance sheet of benefits and disbenefits could guide the court in deciding where a patient's best interests lay but 'there is no balancing operation to be performed where a patient has a definite diagnosis of permanent

---

63 ibid para 2.
64 *An NHS Trust v D* [2005] EWHC 2439 para 44.
65 See Owen et al 2006; Monti et al 2010.
66 Clauss and Nel 2006.
67 *An NHS Trust v J* [2006] All ER (D) 73 (Dec).

vegetative state and where the futility of the treatment would justify its termination'.[68]

3.2.2 Best interests beyond the persistent vegetative state

A substantial – and, to some extent, predictable – body of jurisprudence has developed, founded (as Ryder J has it) on the perceived 'futility' of inflicting life-sustaining treatment on a patient in a PVS. PVS has been set apart from the many other conditions, howsoever caused, which undermine or eradicate a person's capacity to govern his or her life. The judges have also had occasion to consider whether or not life-sustaining treatment ought to be provided to some of these other incompetent patients, and the decisions rest on a familiar standard: the best interests of the patient.

The 23-year-old patient in *Re R (adult: medical treatment)* [1996] 2 FLR 99 was described as being 'in a low awareness state'. Seriously disabled R had been born with a severe malformation of the brain and cerebral palsy, and he had developed epilepsy, along with substantial and painful intestinal difficulties. The majority of his care was provided in a nursing home and a day centre, although he did spend periods with his family. After a year in which R had been hospitalised five times, his family and doctors agreed that resuscitation should not be attempted if he suffered a cardiac arrest, although staff at the day centre disagreed. Upholding the DNAR decision, Brown P felt that CPR was unlikely to succeed and might even inflict harm on R. Although R was an adult, Brown P cited *Re J (a minor)(wardship: medical treatment)* [1991] 1 FLR 366,[69] an authority pertaining to minors, because 'the overriding principle in my judgment is the same', that is, it was for the court to judge the quality of life R could expect to endure if treated and decide whether this would be 'intolerable' to him.[70]

The alleged futility of treatment took a rather different form in the case of *Re D (medical treatment: mentally disabled patient)* [1998] 2 FLR 22. There, dialysis could be withheld from a patient with a long-standing psychiatric illness and problems with alcohol and drug dependence, since the only way he would cooperate was if he was anaesthetised, which was considered dangerous and impracticable. Brown P felt that only such palliative care as the patient would accept was required.

Dialysis was also one of the treatments in issue in the case of *An NHS Trust v A and SA* [2005] EWCA Civ 1145, which concerned nonagenarian Mr A,[71] who was suffering from acute chronic renal failure, amongst other significant

---

68 *Re C* [2010] EWHC 3448 para 66.
69 See Chapter 2, section 2.2.2.
70 *Re R (adult: medical treatment)* [1996] 2 FLR 99 at 108B.
71 Although there was some uncertainty about his age, which may have been 86 years: *An NHS Trust v A and SA* [2005] EWCA Civ 1145 para 9 (Waller LJ).

difficulties. Mr A, who was being treated in the intensive treatment unit (ITU), was forcibly resisting attempts to insert a new line in his groin, which would continue his treatment. An interim declaration had been granted, authorising the administration of treatment, following the provision of a sedative or anaesthetic. At the full hearing, Kirkwood J decided that it was no longer in Mr A's best interests to continue receiving active treatment and that palliative care should commence. Mr A's son, Mr SA, challenged this decision on the basis that it was contrary to the principles of Islam and, accordingly, to his father's beliefs. He argued that neither these beliefs nor the views of the extended family had been accorded sufficient weight by the trial judge, who was also charged with inappropriately rejecting a contrary view expressed by a responsible medical expert.

The Court of Appeal dismissed the case. Ultimately, it was for the court to decide where the best interests of Mr A lay and in reaching its decision 'there is no reason in principle why the court should not assess the difference between medical experts'; indeed, this might even be required.[72] Where the patient's death is in issue, then (again relying on *Re J*) 'the judge is to be satisfied to a very high degree of probability that the medical evidence which he accepts or prefers is correct evidence'.[73] Here Kirkwood J had appropriately weighed the evidence germane to Mr A's quality of life and, having concluded that the 'discomfort' of treatment was not justified,

> . . . it was obviously going to be difficult for the religious views and the views of the family to overcome the obvious point that, since any decision to put Mr A through further suffering would produce no benefit to Mr A, it would be difficult to see that it could be in Mr A's best interests.[74]

Of course nowadays, cases like Mr A's will be determined by reference to the Mental Capacity Act 2005, coupled with the guidance periodically issued by professional bodies such as the General Medical Council (GMC)[75] and the British Medical Association (BMA).[76] There is still no general requirement that such cases be subject to any form of external oversight. However, the recent case of *W v M and S and A NHS Primary Care Trust* [2011] EWHC 2443 alerted clinicians and family members to another group of patients for whom judicial oversight is mandatory where the withdrawal of ANH is in prospect: patients in the minimally conscious state (MCS).[77]

---

72 ibid para 81 (Waller LJ).
73 ibid.
74 ibid para 84 (Waller LJ).
75 General Medical Council 2010.
76 eg British Medical Association 2007.
77 COP (Court of Protection) Practice Direction 9E, para 5; see also Huxtable 2012b.

After contracting viral encephalitis in 2003 and failing to regain full consciousness, M was initially diagnosed as being in a PVS, although further consultation led to the conclusion that she was in a MCS. However, the experts involved (who initially included Keith Andrews, before he retired) ultimately could not agree upon M's position on the MCS scale, or even whether such a scale existed. Having reluctantly concluded that M's condition was nonetheless irreversible, her partner and sister sought the removal of CANH. The family insisted that M would not wish to endure her current condition and that she had indicated as much both during the publicity attending Anthony Bland's case and when her father and grandmother had become incapable of caring for themselves.[78] However, the parties agreed that M had not issued any formal, valid or applicable expression of precedent autonomy and, in the Court of Protection, Baker J doubted that her prior indications carried 'substantial weight'.[79]

For Baker J, best interests once more provided the key: in a case like M's the decision 'would be made by weighing up relevant and competing considerations', as distinct from a case like Bland's, where such an approach was inappropriate as 'the treatment had no therapeutic purpose and was "futile" because he was unconscious and had no prospect of recovery'.[80] The evidence in favour of withdrawing treatment included M's previous opinions, her family's views, plus indications that she occasionally endured pain, discomfort and distress. But, for Baker J, more persuasive were the arguments in favour of continued treatment: M also responded positively to some stimuli, and she might be further enabled to do so, and, in any event, 'the importance of preserving life is the decisive factor in this case'.[81] Baker J accordingly declined to grant the declaration, although he allowed an order against attempting resuscitation to stand.[82] Amongst his closing observations, Baker J emphasised the need for MCS (as well as VS) cases to come to court.

Whilst some legal requirements are clear from these cases, others are less so. Certainly, the precise boundaries of (il)legality are open to question, particularly as the law of homicide apparently survives the 2005 Act intact.[83] In principle, then, failure to fulfil a duty to treat (or feed) might still result in criminal proceedings.[84] There is also the possibility of disciplinary action, as occurred in the case of Dr Taylor in 1999.[85] Dr Taylor had insisted on the withdrawal of a feeding supplement from an 85-year-old patient, who had suffered seven strokes, and had dementia and mild Parkinson's disease. Nurses

---

78 *W v M and S and A NHS Primary Care Trust* [2011] EWHC 2443 paras 107, 119.
79 ibid paras 230, 250.
80 ibid para 65.
81 ibid para 249.
82 ibid para 255.
83 Mental Capacity Act 2005 s 62.
84 See Chapter 2 section 2.2.1 and Chapter 4 section 4.2.
85 See Huxtable 1999.

defied the order until the supplement ran out; Mary Ormerod died 58 days later. The CPS declined to prosecute, apparently for want of evidence. The GMC, however, found Taylor guilty of serious professional misconduct and suspended him from practising for six months for failing adequately to respond to the nurses' opinions and to consult with colleagues.

3.2.3 Advance directives

Although Baker J felt that M failed adequately to do so, M's case indicates that (adult) patients can seek to make provision for their future, such that they retain some say – perhaps even complete authority – over whether or not life-sustaining treatment ought to be provided to them at a point at which they can no longer state their views. There are essentially two ways in which patients can make such provision for the future: by appointing someone to decide on their behalf or by articulating their views in an advance statement. We will address the former concept shortly. As for the latter, a plethora of terms have been used, including the 'advance directive' or the 'living will', which – classical antecedents like Odysseus aside[86] – was first proposed by Chicagoan lawyer Luis Kutner in the 1960s.[87] The central idea is that individuals indicate in advance which treatment(s) they would not tolerate should certain circumstances prevail.

Although sometimes viewed as controversial, one might be forgiven for thinking that the advance directive is self-evidently a part of English law and that it therefore requires no special consideration. This conclusion is powered by the weight accorded to an autonomous patient's consent to treatment and, by extension, his or her refusal of treatment. The same principle, respect for patient autonomy, underpins both decisions. Along with the respect accorded to consent comes the realisation that this is often furnished in advance of the relevant procedure being undertaken, rather than being provided continuously throughout its performance. A classic example is the patient who permits a surgical intervention to be performed whilst he or she is under general anaesthetic. This permission cannot be provided contemporaneously with the procedure: it must be issued in advance. Following from that example, it is seemingly but a short step to holding that an advance *refusal* of treatment – perhaps even life-sustaining treatment – is also legally acceptable.

No matter how self-evident it might appear, the advance directive has nevertheless attracted considerable attention in legal circles. The right of an autonomous patient to refuse treatment – here and now – 'for any reason, rational or irrational, or for no reason at all, even where that decision may lead to his or her own death' is trite law.[88] In such a case, the (adult) patient is to

---

86 See Morgan 1994.
87 Kutner 1969.
88 *In re MB (medical treatment)* [1997] 2 FLR 426 at 432.

be presumed autonomous but, where necessary, attention might focus on whether the patient is autonomous in the sense that he or she is competent, that is, he or she has the requisite mental capacity.

The test for competence was famously developed in the case of Mr C.[89] Mr C had paranoid schizophrenia and was detained in Broadmoor, where he was being treated under the Mental Health Act 1983. When Mr C developed gangrene in his foot, doctors recommended amputation, to which he objected, although he accepted antibiotics. The 1983 Act could only govern treatment directed at Mr C's mental disorder, so the question for the court was whether his refusal of amputation would continue to bind the doctors. Thorpe J found that it would, since Mr C could comprehend and retain information relating to the decision, believe that information, and weigh it in the balance to arrive at his choice.[90]

Mr C's case, in which a *functional* approach was taken to capacity, rather than one based upon the *outcome* of the patient's decision, effectively set the test for competence for over a decade.[91] Provided that the patient satisfied this test, his or her refusal of treatment had to be honoured, or else the intervening health care professional risked a suit in trespass to the person or even prosecution for battery. The former was indeed the finding in the case of Ms B, in 2002, when life-sustaining treatment (in that case, artificial ventilation) remained in place in the face of her (competent) refusal thereof.[92]

Health care professionals also needed to avoid committing trespass or battery when dealing with a refusal of treatment that was issued in advance of the patient's current incompetence. In short, an advance directive of this sort demanded compliance – subject, that is, to the satisfaction of 'two major ifs' identified by Lord Donaldson MR: if the choice is 'clearly established and applicable in the circumstances'.[93] The first of these 'ifs' essentially comprised the requirements associated with any consent that is contemporaneously issued, that is, the patient must have competently and voluntarily reached his or her decision, on the basis of sufficient information.[94] The second 'if – applicability in the circumstances – specifically applied to advance decisions and, as we will see, raises distinct difficulties.

The case before Lord Donaldson MR, *Re T (adult: refusal of medical treatment)* [1992] 4 All ER 649, concerned a pregnant 20-year-old woman who had been

---

89 *Re C (adult: refusal of treatment)* [1994] 1 WLR 290.

90 Cf *Re JT (adult: refusal of medical treatment)* [1998] 1 FLR 48. In the event, Mr C survived, with the 'dry' form of gangrene, which left him with a usable but 'mummified' leg. See Dickenson, Huxtable and Parker 2010: 107.

91 This has been framed as a two-stage test in *Re MB (medical treatment)* [1997] 2 FLR 426 at 436–37 (Butler-Sloss LJ).

92 *Re B (adult: refusal of medical treatment)* [2002] 2 All ER 449.

93 *Re T (adult: refusal of medical treatment)* [1992] 4 All ER 649 at 653.

94 *Re T (adult: refusal of medical treatment)* [1992] 4 All ER 649; the principle was also affirmed in *Airedale NHS Trust v Bland* [1993] 2 WLR 316.

involved in a road accident. She consented to a Caesarean section being performed the following day, but following a visit from her mother – who was a devout Jehovah's Witness – T declined to permit any blood transfusion. When T suffered life-threatening internal bleeding, her father and boyfriend sought the court's authorisation for transfusion. The court acceded because T was found to have lacked capacity at the time of the decision and sufficient information to reach that decision, with the judges further suspecting that T's mother had unduly influenced her.

Despite the result, Donaldson MR nevertheless affirmed the importance of respecting patient autonomy, including decisions issued in advance of incompetence. By the time of *Re AK (medical treatment: consent)* [2001] 1 FLR 129, as Hughes J put it, 'The law is so completely clear that in a sense a declaration is not really required'.[95] AK, whose motor neurone disease had advanced to the point that he was losing his only remaining means of communication (blinking), wanted his doctors to withdraw artificial ventilation two weeks after he had lost all such ability. The doctor responsible for AK's care had approached the court after receiving conflicting advice; the court confirmed that AK's wish should be honoured.

Mr AK therefore joins Mr C in the group of patients whose advance refusals of (apparently) life-saving treatment were upheld in court. It seems, however, that they are the only two members. The next significant case, *HE v A Hospital NHS Trust* [2003] 2 FLR 408, involving Ms AE, illustrates some of the problems that can arise, several of which will be familiar from Terri Schiavo's story. AE had been born with a congenital heart problem, which had required surgery when she was a child and which she knew would necessitate further treatment as an adult. Raised initially as a Muslim, she followed her mother in becoming a Jehovah's Witness after her parents separated. In 2001 she prepared an advance directive refusing consent to a blood transfusion 'in *any* circumstances'.[96]

In 2003 Ms AE became critically ill and her doctors believed that a blood transfusion was indicated. Her father supported this recommendation, arguing that AE had renounced her faith: she had not recently attended Jehovah's Witness' meetings, having become engaged to a Muslim, whose faith she was preparing to follow (as she had informed her family).[97] Munby J found these arguments persuasive and he concluded that the directive could not stand. He further noted that Ms AE had not mentioned its existence to the health care team in the two days she had been in hospital prior to the crisis escalating and that she had also stated to her family that she did not wish to die. He nevertheless felt that neither of these features necessarily undermined the directive as such;[98] it was, rather, the remainder of the evidence which 'raised

---

95 *Re AK (medical treatment: consent)* [2001] 1 FLR 129 at 136.
96 *HE v A Hospital NHS Trust* [2003] 2 FLR 408 para 4 (emphasis in original).
97 ibid paras 13, 14.
98 ibid para 47.

doubts – real doubts, not fanciful doubts or mere speculations – [which] must be resolved in favour of the preservation of life'.[99]

While Ms AE's directive had been executed relatively recently in 'pen and ink',[100] Munby J noted that a valid directive could take any form, provided (inter alia) 'that the patient's expressed views represented a firm and settled commitment and not merely an offhand remark or informally expressed reaction to other people's problems'.[101] In *W Healthcare NHS Trust v KH* [2005] 1 WLR 834, the Court of Appeal seemed to think that the latter was closer to the truth when it came to consider remarks made (verbally) by Ms KH to her daughter a decade earlier. Ms KH had apparently stated 'I don't want to be kept alive by machines' and had made similar remarks to a friend; in summary, said the trial judge, her loved ones believed that KH 'would only wish to remain alive so long as she enjoyed a reasonable quality of life'.[102] Now 59 years old and substantially afflicted by multiple sclerosis, Ms KH was minimally conscious and receiving 24 hour care. The court had to consider whether her earlier statements should have a bearing on the reinsertion (or not) of a percutaneous (PEG) feeding tube. The appellate judges felt that there might be a valid directive prohibiting the use of life-support machines and even artificial means of tackling infections,[103] but there was not a sufficiently clear direction that she 'be deprived of food and drink for a period of time which would lead to her death in all circumstances'.[104] The case therefore had to be determined by reference to KH's best interests and the Court of Appeal found no reason to interfere with the trial judge's decision to 'accede to the unanimous wish of those who are responsible for her treatment'.[105]

In the eyes of the appellate judges, Ms KH's directive failed because it seemed not to be applicable and because KH appeared insufficiently informed about the choice she was apparently making.[106] Around the same time, in *NHS Trust v T (adult patient: refusal of medical treatment)* [2005] 1 All ER 387, Ms T had her directive struck down (in an interim declaration) owing to her lacking capacity at the time of its execution. T, who had a borderline personality disorder, had a history of self-harm by cutting herself and bloodletting. On these occasions, she would often be admitted to hospital and transfused. She would typically refuse this treatment initially, but always came to accept it, following discussion with the health care team. In January 2004, with her

99 ibid para 50.
100 ibid para 41.
101 ibid para 34.
102 *W Healthcare NHS Trust v KH* [2005] 1 WLR 834 paras 6, 17.
103 ibid para 19.
104 ibid para 21.
105 ibid para 29.
106 ibid para 21.

solicitor, T drafted an advance directive declining blood transfusions. Despite this statement, in April of that year, she was again transfused, after the hospital received authorisation from a judge. Ms T subsequently consulted a solicitor again, who informed the Trust that T stood by her directive. The Trust sought advice from Charles J, who declared the directive invalid: Ms T's (persistent) beliefs in, for example, blood being 'evil' were evidence of 'a disorder of the mind and further or alternatively symptoms or evidence of incompetence'.[107] The court declared that future transfusions could be justified in T's best interests.

The next directive which came before the courts was markedly different, since it involved an attempt to stipulate that treatment *should* be provided in the future. Leslie Burke had cerebellar ataxia, a progressive neurodegenerative disorder, which would ultimately leave him entirely dependent on others for his care. Whilst his bodily control would gradually be lost, he could expect to retain his cognitive capacity, even beyond the point at which he had no ability to communicate. On his reading of guidance issued by the GMC,[108] Mr Burke feared that his doctors might seek to remove the CANH, on which he would come to rely, at a point when he was still conscious, albeit incapable of expressing his wishes. In *R (on the application of Burke) v General Medical Council* [2005] 2 WLR 431, Mr Burke sought judicial review, claiming that the guidance was incompatible with his rights at common law and under the Human Rights Act 1998, specifically Article 2 (the right to life), Article 3 (the right to be free from inhuman and degrading treatment) and Article 8 (the right to respect for private and family life).

At first instance, Munby J agreed that the guidance was amenable to judicial review. A central strand to his ruling was that the GMC accorded insufficient weight to the patient's autonomous wish. According to this judge, where competent patients opt for the provision of CANH (now or, in the event of incapacity, for the future), then they have determined the course that serves their best interests: a Trust may make provision for passing on that patient's care, but failure to provide the care would be a breach of the 1998 Act. Munby J therefore concluded that those provisions of the guidance which failed to reflect these principles were to be considered unlawful.

The Court of Appeal was unimpressed with the judge's reasoning and the result he reached, even cautioning 'strongly against selective use of Munby J's judgment in future cases'.[109] The case, said the appellate judges, concerned

---

107 *NHS Trust v T (adult patient: refusal of medical treatment)* [2005] 1 All ER 387 para 61.

108 General Medical Council 2002 paras 13, 16, 32, 38, 42, 81 and 82, which seemed to vest the ultimate responsibility for decisions with the treatment team rather than the patient. The latest guidance is General Medical Council 2010.

109 *R (on the application of Burke) v General Medical Council* [2005] 3 WLR 1132 para 24.

a hypothetical question, since Mr Burke was currently competent. In any event, no patient has a right to demand treatment, whether now or for the future:

> Autonomy and the right of self-determination do not entitle the patient to insist on receiving a particular medical treatment regardless of the nature of the treatment. Insofar as a doctor has a legal obligation to provide treatment this cannot be founded simply upon the fact that the patient demands it.[110]

This does not mean that there is no duty to provide CANH: once a patient is accepted into hospital, a positive duty 'to take such steps as are reasonable to keep the patient alive'[111] comes into being. But this duty is not absolute: it reaches its limits where the patient has made an advance refusal of treatment, is in a PVS, or is enduring 'an extreme degree of pain, discomfort or indignity'.[112] The duty nevertheless endures when the patient is competent and wants to receive CANH; withdrawal of treatment in those circumstances would violate the right to life and mean the commission of murder. Although there was no legal obligation to do so, in cases of doubt, the courts could be consulted to determine whether CANH should be provided. The European Court of Human Rights sided with the Court of Appeal, finding that English law generally favoured the protection of life.[113]

The next and (for now) final chapter in the advance directive saga came with the enforcement, in 2007, of the Mental Capacity Act 2005. Competence is now a statutory matter, with incapacity involving the inability to make or communicate a particular decision owing to 'an impairment of, or a disturbance in the functioning of, the mind or brain'.[114] As it was in the common law, capacity is to be presumed,[115] but this may be found lacking where the individual is unable '(a) to understand the information relevant to the decision, (b) to retain that information, (c) to use or weigh that information as part of the process of making the decision, or (d) to communicate his decision'.[116]

The incapable patient may still guide treatment, however, in three ways in particular. First, his or her wishes and values – and especially any contained within a prior written statement – will feature in the assessment of the incapable patient's best interests.[117] Here one might include those discussions (and associated notes) which form part of 'advance care planning', in which an

---

110 ibid para 31.
111 ibid para 32.
112 ibid para 33.
113 *Burke v United Kingdom* (Application No 19807/06 unreported).
114 Mental Capacity Act 2005 s 2(1).
115 ibid s 1(2).
116 ibid s 3(1).
117 ibid s 4(6)(a), (b).

individual patient communicates their wishes and values to their care providers.[118]

Secondly, the Act explicitly provides for a particular class of advance directives, now known as 'advance decisions to refuse treatment'. These decisions to decline 'specified treatments',[119] which can only be made by over-18s, are binding provided that they are valid and applicable. The decision will not be *valid* if it has been withdrawn (perhaps verbally[120] or through inconsistent subsequent behaviour) or directly conflicting authority has been conferred in a lasting power of attorney.[121] It will not be *applicable* if: it does not deal with the treatment in issue at the relevant time; circumstances specified in the decision are absent; or unanticipated circumstances have arisen, which would have affected the patient's decision.[122] Additional requirements attach to those advance decisions which purport to refuse life-sustaining treatment. The patient must explicitly acknowledge that the decision is to apply 'even if life is at risk',[123] it must be written and it must be signed by the patient (or a proxy) in the presence of a witness, who also signs.[124] No liability arises from honouring such a directive, although treatment may be provided while clarification of the validity and applicability of the decision is sought.[125]

3.2.4 Lasting powers of attorney

The third way in which a currently incompetent adult patient can seek to exercise their precedent autonomy involves a new phenomenon for English law, which also came with the 2005 Act: the lasting power of attorney (LPA). Although English law had previously made provision for the conferment of an *enduring* power of attorney in relation to property,[126] prior to the 2005 Act no one was entitled to make treatment decisions on behalf of incapacitated adults. Following an apparently inexplicable legal quirk, even the judges lacked the requisite authority, which had led to the development of the declaratory procedure.[127] With the 2005 Act came the new Court of Protection, plus such other personnel as the court-appointed deputy,[128] and the independent mental capacity advocate (IMCA), who (in the absence of suitable others) can

---

118   Henry and Seymour 2008.
119   Mental Capacity Act 2005 s 24(1).
120   ibid s 24(4).
121   ibid s 25(2) and see below.
122   ibid s 25(4).
123   ibid s 25(5).
124   ibid s 25(6).
125   ibid s 26.
126   Enduring Powers of Attorney Act 1985.
127   See *Re F (mental patient: sterilisation)* [1990] 2 AC 1; *Airedale NHS Trust v Bland* [1993] 2 WLR 316 at 378 (Lord Lowry). See further Bridgeman 1995.
128   Mental Capacity Act 2005 ss 16–20.

represent incompetent adults in discussions of their best interests, particularly when the removal of 'serious medical treatment' is proposed.[129] In terms of honouring precedent autonomy, however, it is the LPA that merits particular attention.

The Act provides that an adult with capacity may appoint one or more attorneys (who must also be adults) to make decisions on his or her behalf once capacity has been lost.[130] A specific form must be completed, in writing, which provides: information about the nature and extent of the LPA; a signed statement from the donor confirming that he or she understands the effect of the appointment; a signed statement from the donee (ie the attorney) confirming that he or she also understands the effect of the appointment, including the obligation to act in the donor's best interests; and confirmation by a third party that the donor is appropriately informed and that there has been no fraud or undue influence.[131] The LPA must then be registered with the Office of the Public Guardian before it is to have effect.[132] The scope of the LPA will depend, to some extent, on the donor's preferred wording; he or she may, for example, place specific restrictions on the donee's powers. Those powers that are granted are only acquired once the donor is incompetent. Moreover, the donee cannot consent to any treatment to which the donor has objected in a valid and applicable advance decision to refuse treatment, cannot refuse life-sustaining treatment unless expressly authorised to do so, and cannot demand that treatment be provided.[133] However, by far the most significant principle that simultaneously empowers and constrains attorneys is the best interests of the donor. In intractable cases of conflict over the patient's perceived best interests, the Court of Protection is available to decide what ought (not) to happen. That court has had occasion to consider the rights and roles of LPAs,[134] although, to date, there appears to have been no case directly engaging with the issue of non-treatment in circumstances where this would lead to death.[135]

3.3 Conclusion: autonomy or welfare?

Although the dispute will not always be quite as acute as in her unfortunate case, situations like Terri Schiavo's can give rise to complex conflicts of duty. Is there a duty to prolong the life of an irreversibly incapacitated adult, which

---

129 ibid ss 35–41.
130 ibid ss 9–10.
131 ibid sched 1.
132 ibid .
133 ibid s 11(7), (8).
134 See Judiciary of England and Wales 2011.
135 Although for discussion of some pertinent issues see *AVS v A NHS Foundation Trust and B PCT* [2011] EWCA Civ 7, appeal against *Re AVS v A NHS Foundation Trust* [2010] EWHC 2746.

should take priority over any perceived duty to honour that adult's prior wishes? When does an obligation to serve such a patient's best interests exist and what should that obligation entail? English law has sought to provide answers to questions like these. Both parliamentarians and judges recognise limits on the obligation to sustain life in two broad cases: where the patient's welfare seems so to require; and where the patient has insisted that such a limit has been reached.

The first set of cases in which the central concern is the patient's best interests are generally distinguished according to whether or not the patient has been diagnosed as being in a VS. The fate of patients so diagnosed must be considered by a court if the removal or denial of CANH is in prospect. In such cases, the judges will seek to ensure that the diagnosis (and, it would appear, prognosis[136]) is settled. They will also have due regard for the views of the patient's loved ones, although these will not be determinative. Such decisions – which will inevitably result in a patient's death – will be carefully scrutinised. However, as numerous cases indicate, the result is likely to be the withdrawal of treatment. Patients diagnosed in a MCS also require judicial oversight when the removal of ANH is contemplated, although in these cases – as in other cases involving incapacitated adults not in a VS – a different approach is taken, and a different outcome might well ensue. When considering the (non-)treatment of a patient who occupies this wide group, the judge must draw up a balance sheet of factors for and against treatment. Here, the best interests calculation comprises not only medical but also other interests, be they cultural, spiritual or familial. As the Mental Capacity Act 2005 makes clear, reference should be made to any past or present wishes of the incompetent patient when deciding on the best interests of the patient, and there should be due consultation, such as with an independent mental capacity advocate if the patient lacks someone to speak on their behalf.

The second set of cases involves efforts to ensure that the patient – and his or her autonomous wishes – is the clinician's guide. This set of cases also separates into two broad groups: situations where the patient has provided a prior instruction as to her wishes; and situations where she has appointed someone to speak for her. Prior statements can take various forms, but, if the patient is to refuse life-supporting treatment in advance, then the Mental Capacity Act 2005 insists on a valid and applicable advance decision to refuse treatment, which specifically acknowledges that life will be shortened through compliance with its terms. Equally, a lasting power of attorney must satisfy specific criteria before the donor can be confident that the appointed individual will be free to express that donor's wishes beyond the loss of capacity. The freedom is not unfettered, however: the donee is always bound by the obligation to serve the donor's best interests. As the court's caution over advance directives which purport to decline life-support further attest, efforts to safeguard a

---

136 *B NHS Trust v J* [2006] EWHC 3152.

patient's best interests are seldom far behind attempts to exercise precedent autonomy.

Whether the law as described in both this chapter and the last is ethically in the right place is a substantial question, to which we will return. No less significant is whether the law is achieving its central purpose, that is, guiding the behaviour of current and future patients, their loved ones and the professionals with whom they will come into contact. It is to this important question we turn in the next chapter.

4   The limits of law at the limits of life

To treat or not to treat?

... the answer which will be given in relation to a particular problem dealing with a particular set of circumstances, is a much better answer than an answer given in advance. The difficulty in this area is that there are conflicting principles involved. The principles of law are clearly established, but how you apply those principles to particular facts is often very difficult to anticipate.

R v Portsmouth Hospitals NHS Trust ex p Glass [1999] 2 FLR 905
at 911A–B (Lord Woolf MR)

4.1 Conflicts in the clinic: to treat or not to treat?

The fundamental question posed in the hearings pertaining to David Glass, Charlotte Wyatt and Terri Schiavo is essentially: to treat or not to treat? The cases do, of course, have their differences: Mrs Schiavo's previous status as an autonomous adult opens up the possibility of her having made provision for an incapacitated future, and the perceived interests of each of these patients might differ according to such factors as diagnosis, prognosis, and their family's perceptions and preferences. Chapters 2 and 3 reveal that not only might different legal frameworks be available for different incapacitated patients, but also the same legal principles might point in different directions for different patients.

Such differences might be entirely appropriate if we accept that each patient is different. But problems arise when the different frameworks and assessments fail to qualify as rational law, in the sense defended in Chapter 1. Central to this idea is law's action-guiding function: rules that contradict one another, or cannot be known, or cannot be performed will all fail to pass muster. Unfortunately, as we will see throughout this chapter, there are numerous such failings in the law pertaining to the provision and cessation of life-supporting treatment, which reveal what Annas has described as 'the limits of law at the limits of life'.[1] Remarkably, even the judges appreciate the problems, with those in *Airedale NHS Trust v Bland* [1993] 2 WLR 316

1   Annas 2001.

detecting problems with – but simultaneously affirming and applying – a set of rules they saw as 'misshapen', 'irrational' and 'illogical'.[2] In what follows we will look at these problems in detail, focusing particularly on the 'best interests' standard, since this underpins the legislation pertaining to both adults and minors and dominates the jurisprudence on withholding and withdrawing treatment.

4.2 Taking exception to exceptions: a duty to treat?

The first problem with the cases which hold that it can be permissible to withhold or withdraw life-supporting treatment – be they those pertaining to children or those pertaining to incompetent adults – is that it is difficult to see how these decisions can occupy the same terrain as rulings which insist that failure to care for people who are incapable of caring for themselves can amount to a homicide offence when such a person dies. The latter rulings are well known to criminal lawyers. In *Gibbins v Proctor* (1918) 12 Cr App Rep 134 the defendants were convicted of the murder of Gibbins's daughter, after 7-year-old Nelly starved to death. Darling J in the Court of Appeal upheld both convictions. Proctor 'had charge of the child', so it was her duty to ensure that Nelly was 'properly fed' and given 'medical attention if necessary'.[3] However, a murder conviction was appropriate because the jury found that 'she had deliberately withheld food'.[4] Gibbins may not actively have inflicted harm on his daughter but 'he knew that Proctor hated her, knew that she was ill and that no doctor had been called in'.[5] The jury accordingly found that he satisfied the *mens rea* (or 'mental' element) of the offence, that is, intention to cause death or grievous bodily harm. As this precedent demonstrates, parents and those *in loco parentis* evidently owe a duty to care to children in their charge; failure to fulfil such a duty, coupled with an intention to end life or cause grievous bodily harm, will amount to murder.

The duty to care need not be restricted to parents, nor the right to children who fall beneath the age of majority.[6] Where there is a failure to fulfil such a duty, whosoever it is who happens to come under the obligation, then the criminal law has an array of offences at its disposal, to deploy as circumstances dictate.[7] We might presume that cases like that of *Gibbins v Proctor*, in which there was a direct intention to cause harm, will be rare. Other charges might nevertheless result where the *mens rea* is different, such as where a defendant is

---

2 *Airedale NHS Trust v Bland* [1993] 2 WLR 316 at 387D–F (Lord Browne-Wilkinson) and at 389A (Lord Mustill).

3 *Gibbins v Proctor* (1918) 12 Cr App Rep 134 at 139.

4 ibid at 140.

5 ibid at 139.

6 eg *R v Smith* [1979] Crim LR 251. See also the analysis in Huxtable 2007: 68–77.

7 eg Children and Young Persons Act 1933 s 1; Infanticide Act 1938.

grossly negligent in failing to satisfy the duty. *R v Stone and Dobinson* [1977] QB 354 tends to be cited here. Stone and Dobinson were convicted of the manslaughter of Stone's (adult) sister, Fanny, who suffered from anorexia nervosa. As in the previous case, the couple's appeals against conviction were dismissed. Lane LJ talked in terms of 'a reckless disregard of danger to the health and welfare of the infirm person',[8] but nowadays the question is more likely to be whether the defendant was grossly negligent to such a degree that a criminal sanction is warranted.[9]

The message from the criminal courts seems clear: there is a duty to take care of those incapable of so doing. Failure to oblige, such as through a failure to feed, can lead to the dock – but not, it seems, if the defendant happens to be a doctor; at least, this looks like the message from cases like that of Anthony Bland. Anthony's judges did recognise that the law of murder presented a substantial obstacle to the removal of his feeding tube.[10] Controversially,[11] the judges suggested that his doctors would have the guilty intention.[12] This certainly seems to suggest that they would be guilty of the same crime as Gibbins and Proctor. Lord Mustill drew a direct parallel: 'Of course, the cases are miles apart from an ethical standpoint, but where is the difference on the essential facts?'[13]

The first step towards clearing the murder hurdle was to find that the withdrawal of clinically assisted nutrition and hydration (CANH) (via a naso-gastric tube) did not amount to a (positive) action but rather to a (negative) omission.[14] Like some philosophers,[15] the judges detected a degree of difficulty with this conclusion, with Lord Goff acknowledging that 'some positive step' was involved.[16] But Lord Lowry conveyed the mood of the majority when he suggested that to find otherwise, and thus distinguish between withholding and withdrawing treatment, would be 'illogical'.[17]

The next step was to find that Anthony's doctors would no longer be under a duty of the sort which bound Gibbins, Proctor, Stone and Dobinson. The duty question appeared to turn on the finding that CANH, by which nutrition and hydration are delivered by artificial means, amounted to 'medical treatment' (or, at least, part of Anthony's 'care').[18] This too is controversial.

---

8 *R v Stone & Dobinson* [1977] QB 354 at 363F.
9 *R v Adomako* [1995] AC 789; *R v Evans* [2009] EWCA Crim 650.
10 See *Airedale NHS Trust v Bland* [1993] 2 WLR 316 at 383D (Lord Browne-Wilkinson), discussing criticism of the Official Solicitor on this point.
11 eg Finnis 1993: 331–32.
12 *Airedale NHS Trust v Bland* [1993] 2 WLR 316 at 383D–E (Lord Browne-Wilkinson).
13 ibid at 395A.
14 Bingham MR in the Court of Appeal was particularly explicit about this (at 340E–F; see also Butler-Sloss LJ, at 344D, 349A–B). The House of Lords essentially followed suit.
15 See eg Rachels 1979; Singer 1995. For discussion, see Chapter 5 section 5.3.2.
16 at 369B–H.
17 ibid at 377H.
18 See Lord Goff at 372H; Lord Keith at 362C–D; Bingham MR at 335E–G; Butler-Sloss LJ at 343D–344A. See further Kennedy and Grubb 1993: 367.

John Keown, a vocal critic of the ruling, asks simply 'what is being treated?'[19] This manoeuvre nevertheless enabled the judges to invoke the *Bolam* test in determining what would be in the best interests of the patient.[20] This in turn allowed the doctor who sought to withdraw treatment to claim the backing of a responsible body of medical opinion. But this too is highly contestable. Sheila Maclean objects that the introduction of *Bolam* means that the decision rests on 'what some doctors actually do'[21] and Lord Mustill saw no reason why the doctors' viewpoint should be decisive.[22] More troubling was Lord Browne-Wilkinson's suggestion that doctors might justifiably differ about the prolongation of life.[23] As Kennedy and Grubb appreciated, if 'best interests' are determinative: 'Surely continuing *or* withdrawing is in the patient's best interests: not both!'[24]

Even leaving aside the deference shown to medical opinion,[25] the judicial attempts to grapple with the best interests assessment in the case were scarcely successful. Lord Goff, for example, saw fit to conclude that the nasogastric feeding could be withdrawn since it was no longer serving Anthony's best interests because its continuation was 'futile'.[26] Yet, if this truly had been the case, then the situation would never have come before a court.[27] In any event, the judges concluded that the doctors' duty to treat had dissolved, leaving them entitled – maybe even obliged[28] – to discontinue treatment, or else they would risk committing a different crime, this time of assault.[29]

Despite the Law Lords' misgivings about any precedent they might have been setting, the logic of *Bland* must apply beyond the relatively narrow confines of adults in a VS. The ruling certainly gives the most comprehensive coverage of the limits of the duty to treat and the boundaries of the criminal and civil law. Remarkably, one can trace the origins of the distinction being drawn back to *R v Arthur* (1981) 12 BMLR 1, in which the paediatrician was acquitted of attempting to murder John Pearson. There too one finds a judge apparently striving to carve out an exception for the doctor in the dock, as revealed in his eagerness to depict Arthur's conduct in the passive terms of a

---

19 Keown 1997b: 492.
20 *Bolam v Friern Hospital Management Committee* [1957] 1 WLR 582.
21 McLean 1994: 12.
22 *Airedale NHS Trust v Bland* [1993] 2 WLR 316 at 399H.
23 ibid at 386B–C.
24 Kennedy and Grubb 1993: 364.
25 However, the judges have somewhat departed from this deference, by adopting a wider approach to best interests in eg *Re A (male sterilisation)* [2000] 1 FLR 549 and the Mental Capacity Act 2005. How wide a departure this is will be considered further in section 4.5.
26 *Airedale NHS Trust v Bland* [1993] 2 WLR 316 at 372E (Lord Goff).
27 cf Keown 1997b: 492.
28 *Per Airedale NHS Trust v Bland* [1993] 2 WLR 316 at 384–85 (Lord Browne-Wilkinson) and at 379B–D (Lord Lowry).
29 ibid at 379B–D (Lord Lowry).

'holding operation' (a term otherwise unknown to the law) and his scant reference to the alleged attempt to suppress the child's appetite.[30] But, just as with *Bland*, it is possible to take exception to this exception, given the conflict with established precedent on the duty to preserve life.[31]

The summing-up in Arthur's case is also susceptible to challenge because it is clearly at odds with the decision in *Re B (a minor)(wardship: medical treatment)* [1981] 1 WLR 1421, which had been decided only months before but which did not appear to feature in the criminal trial. These cases certainly generate conflicting guidance about the duties owed by parents and doctors to infants with Down's syndrome: Alexandra, who was the subject of *Re B*, had been judged by her doctors to be in a worse condition than John Pearson, but her doctors were obliged to ensure that she would live, while Dr Arthur was apparently free to leave John Pearson to die, at the request of the boy's parents. Gunn and Smith have sought to argue that the two cases can be reconciled: each case acknowledges that a lower duty of care is owed to 'abnormal' infants,[32] and in both cases a decision taken jointly by parents and physicians to leave an infant to die is deemed acceptable (or, as it was put in *Re B*, 'entirely responsible'[33]). The different results might simply be explained by the fact that the judges in Alexandra's case, *in loco parentis*, chose 'responsibly' to exercise their discretion differently, that is, in favour of life.[34] This argument does not wholly convince, however. The quality of life thresholds are still drawn at different levels and, insofar as the law purports to protect all regardless of disability, there remains the conflict with hitherto unassailable principles about the duty to treat, feed and otherwise preserve and protect the lives of incompetent individuals.

This dispute might be best consigned to the history books, since *Re B* seems to emerge victorious and few believe that *Arthur* has any value nowadays as a precedent. But *Bland* undoubtedly remains, and so too does the difficulty with squaring that decision from the civil realm with prior precedent from the criminal courts. Perhaps, in contrast to the opening of this section, it is best to say that they do not occupy the same terrain at all, and so we should consider them – and their ensuing principles – separately. A perfectly clean separation eludes us, however, given the civil courts' willingness to settle criminal questions.[35] Furthermore, as Brownsword argued, the convenient creation of categories cannot convincingly cover up inconsistency.[36] Nevertheless, it is

30 See Brahams and Brahams 1983; Gunn and Smith 1985; Huxtable 2007: 111.
31 See eg Brahams and Brahams 1983: 1342.
32 Gunn and Smith 1985: 708.
33 *Re B (a minor)(wardship: medical treatment)* [1981] 1 WLR 1421 at 1424G (Dunn LJ).
34 Gunn and Smith 1985: 708, 715.
35 See eg *Airedale NHS Trust v Bland* [1993] 2 WLR 316; *R (on the application of Pretty) v DPP* [2002] 1 FLR 268; and *R (on the application of Purdy) v DPP* [2009] UKHL 45. Contrast *Re Z (local authority: duty)* [2005] 1 WLR 959. For discussion see Bridgeman 1995.
36 Chapter 1 section 1.2.2.

certainly apparent that decisions (not) to provide life-support are today most often viewed through a civil lens, and in particular one associated with medical law, in which the focus is upon the best interests of the patient.[37]

4.3 In the patient's best interests?

Even when we restrict our attention to civil cases including *Re B* and its successors, we find a body of jurisprudence that fails to measure up to the standards of rational law. Not only are fine lines drawn in an effort to avoid the appearance of conflicts in the case law, but also the objective rules with which the legal enterprise should be associated become increasingly difficult to detect. Too often one is left wondering precisely what the law in this area requires and how its edicts can be achieved.

4.3.1 Treating like cases alike?

Leaving the anomalies of *Arthur* aside, the legal framework governing contemporary decisions (not) to treat critically ill children can be traced back to *Re B*. It is here that the central (nowadays 'paramount') concern with the best interests of the child is emphasised and we find Templeman LJ's much-quoted statement that treatment might legitimately be abated where 'the life of this child is demonstrably going to be so awful that in effect the child must be condemned to die'.[38] From this line of thinking comes the idea, in *Re J (a minor)(wardship: medical treatment)* [1991] 1 FLR 366, that the child's quality of life is a key component of the balancing exercise that must be conducted, in which consideration should be given to whether the 'life would be so afflicted as to be intolerable to that child'.[39] Subsequent cases nevertheless confirm that any reference to 'intolerability' should not detract from the central concern, which is with the best interests of the child.[40] Whilst the presumption should be in favour of sustaining the child's life, this can be rebutted where to do so is not in the child's best interests.[41] That determination looks like a matter for the doctors and parents to decide together, but clinical opinion seems to carry particular weight,[42] notwithstanding the judges' reassurances that emotional and other features enter the equation.[43]

According to the Court of Appeal in its judgment in the case of Charlotte Wyatt, the cases may be difficult but the 'intellectual milestones' just outlined

---

37 For further consideration of the criminal law dimensions see Huxtable 2007.
38 *Re B (a minor)(wardship: medical treatment)* [1981] 1 WLR 1421 at 1424 (Templeman LJ).
39 *Re J (a minor)(wardship: medical treatment)* [1991] Fam 33 at 55 (Taylor LJ).
40 *Wyatt v Portsmouth Hospital NHS Trust* [2005] EWCA Civ 1181 para 91; *An NHS Trust v MB* [2006] EWHC 507 para 17.
41 *Re J (a minor)(wardship: medical treatment)* [1991] Fam 33.
42 *Re J (a minor)(wardship: medical treatment)* [1992] 2 FLR 165.
43 *Re A (male sterilisation)* [2000] 1 FLR 549.

are 'simple'.[44] A rational system of law – in the sense defended in Chapter 1 – should yield consistent answers to cases like these. The judges agree: 'They are always anxious decisions to make but they are invariably eventually made with the conviction that there is only one right answer and that the court has given it'.[45] Unfortunately, the decided cases do not wholly support this conviction.

The 1997 case of *Re T (a minor)(wardship: medical treatment)* [1997] 1 All ER 906, in which the court declined to authorise a life-saving liver transplant, is undoubtedly the most starkly aberrant decision, since it appears to be completely at odds with the decision in favour of life in *Re B*. Two-year-old T was residing abroad with his parents, who concluded that he should not be subjected to the transplant, which would require his mother to return to England with him for the treatment. At first instance Connell J found the mother's refusal unreasonable but the Court of Appeal rejected this approach and allowed the refusal to stand. As Lyons sees it, 'The court preferred that the child should have a short happy life rather than (most likely) a significantly longer life involving medical intervention where the level of happiness T might attain would be speculative'.[46]

He goes on to question whether the decision therefore necessitates a wholesale rethink of the permissibility of liver transplants for children: following the logic of *Re B*, the message from *Re T* appears to be that such procedures should cease as they condemn the recipients to 'demonstrably awful' lives. Of course, the vast majority of such patients are likely to experience the opposite, that is, a vast improvement in the quality of their lives. Butler-Sloss LJ nevertheless sought to distinguish the two decisions on the basis that T's surgery would be more severe than Alexandra's and would require considerable after-care.[47] Few find this attempt convincing, with Michalowski pointing out the considerable commitment required by the carers of children with Down's syndrome.[48] Indeed, this is certainly not the logic adopted by Holman J in the 2007 case of *A*, when he authorised a bone marrow transplant in the face of the parents' objections that A had endured enough.[49] Perhaps safer, then, to view *Re T* as an anomaly, dictated primarily by the trial judge's erroneous fixation on the 'reasonableness' (or otherwise) of the parents' position – and no doubt also influenced by the fact that they happened to be 'trained as health care professionals and are both experienced in the care of young sick children'.[50]

---

44 *Wyatt v Portsmouth Hospital NHS Trust* [2005] EWCA Civ 1181 para 87.
45 *Re A (Children) (conjoined twins: medical treatment)* [2000] 4 All ER 961 at 968J (Ward LJ).
46 Lyons 2010: 192.
47 *Re T (a minor)(wardship: medical treatment)* [1997] 1 All ER 906.
48 Michalowski 1997: 184.
49 *NHS Trust v A (a child)* [2007] EWHC 1696.
50 ibid at 908E–F (Butler-Sloss LJ). We should also note that, ultimately, the parents opted for treatment and, as Butler-Sloss reported in a lecture, 'the child recovered and appears well and thriving': Butler-Sloss 2006.

The apparent conflict between *Re C (medical treatment)* [1998] 1 FLR 384, in 1998, and *An NHS Trust v MB* [2006] EWHC 507, in 2006, might not be explained away in such terms. The children in question were suffering from the same condition, spinal muscular atrophy. In each case the parents wanted treatment to be provided, but only M's parents had the backing of the court. Holman J felt that distinctions could be drawn: C had only months left, whilst M's prognosis was far less certain and might have meant survival for a few years; M also enjoyed greater awareness than C, and was (again unlike C) wholly reliant on the breathing support. Perhaps, then, there is a case to be made for the different results issued in these cases. Yet, such a conclusion seems to require the drawing of some very fine lines, against which Brownsword advised. The difficulty here, in terms of law's capacity to guide action, should be apparent: had M's parents consulted the law books they might well have thought their case was destined to founder; and C's parents might also have believed they had legitimate grounds for complaint. The doctors, meanwhile, might have had cause to question the practical effect of the decisions here, as well as in cases such as *Re B*; notwithstanding the judges' insistence to the contrary, such rulings must amount to ordering the doctors to provide treatment.[51]

Similar difficulties arise in the jurisprudence as it pertains to incompetent adults. Once again, the best interests test is central and, as developing case law and the Mental Capacity Act 2005 make clear, this will usually (save in the case of the VS patient) involve a balancing exercise comprising not only medical factors but also any wider issues that should have a bearing on the patient's welfare.[52] Here too the judges think that the application of the 'best interests test ought, logically . . . give only one answer'.[53] But here too their optimism is misplaced.

Consider, first, the case which immediately succeeded *Bland*, *Frenchay NHS Trust v S* [1994] 1 WLR 601, involving the patient known as S. The Law Lords in *Bland* were acutely uneasy about the ruling they were making and its possible ramifications, hence their call for parliamentary input and insistence that future such cases be brought before the judges.[54] John Finnis wondered what would count as a 'similar' case.[55] Indications in *Bland* suggested that some of the Law Lords were resistant to extending their reasoning beyond patients who were irreversibly insensate, and specifically those in a PVS.[56]

---

51 James 2008: 73–74; Morris 2009: 369. See also eg *NHS Trust v A (a child)* [2007] EWHC 1696.
52 See eg *W v M and S and A NHS Primary Care Trust* [2011] EWHC 2443.
53 *Re SL (adult patient)(medical treatment)* [2000] 2 FCR 452 at 464 (Butler Sloss P).
54 *Airedale NHS Trust v Bland* [1993] 2 WLR 316 at 363 (Lord Keith), at 382 (Lord Browne-Wilkinson) and at 392 (Lord Mustill).
55 Finnis 1993.
56 *Airedale NHS Trust v Bland* [1993] 2 WLR 316 at 387C–D (Lord Browne-Wilkinson) and at 391B–C (Lord Mustill).

Yet, whilst Anthony Bland's brain had apparently liquefied, S seemed more like the patient with 'glimmerings of awareness' to whom Lord Mustill had referred.[57] This did not encourage Bingham MR to authorise the reinsertion of the feeding tube, even though, as he openly admitted, 'the evidence in this case is not as emphatic and not as unanimous as that in *Bland*'s case'.[58] Nor was the judge too perturbed by the lack of an independent investigation by the Official Solicitor on S's behalf, despite the ambiguity in the case and therefore the arguable need for such scrutiny.

Bingham MR seemed to think the court would not need to be involved in every PVS case but the requirement does remain, even following the 2005 Act.[59] Subsequent decisions, accompanied by Practice Notes issued by the Official Solicitor, helped to redirect the judges to the original parameters of *Bland*, so the case of *S* is probably (like *Re T*) something of an aberration. Indeed, the judges have since acknowledged that some early cases of alleged VS might actually have involved MCS.[60] However, this is not to deny that other unclear and somewhat contradictory cases have slipped through in the wake of *Bland*, such as *Re D (medical treatment)* [1998] 1 FLR 411, in which the doctors could not agree on D's diagnosis.[61] Brown P felt that he was not extending the law in authorising the removal of treatment but, as Caroline Sawyer spotted,[62] *The Guardian*'s typographical error inadvertently conveyed the confusion, when it described D as 'not not in a permanent vegetative state'.[63]

There are, of course, many adult patients that the law would consider incompetent whose condition is emphatically not one of PVS. The difficulty with this undeniably large class of patients is that it is not always apparent how decisions should be made in their cases or, indeed, why apparently fine lines should be drawn according to their age (minor or major?) or condition (PVS or not?). A case such as *Re R (adult: medical treatment)* [1996] 2 FLR 99, from 1996 (thus some considerable time before the Mental Capacity Act 2005), illustrates the potential difficulties. In that case one finds the judge – Brown P again – seeking to apply the jurisprudence pertaining to critically ill infants to a 23-year-old patient 'in a low awareness state'.[64] Now, of course, recourse can be made to the Mental Capacity Act 2005 but this leads one to wonder why the determination of best interests required by that Act should differ from that required by the Children Act 1989? There might well be

---

57 ibid at 400D.
58 *Frenchay NHS Trust v S* [1994] 1 WLR 601 at 608F.
59 COP (Court of Protection) Practice Direction 9E: Applications relating to serious medical treatment.
60 *W v M and S and A NHS Primary Care Trust* [2011] EWHC 2443 para 256.
61 See also *Re H (a patient)* [1998] 2 FLR 36.
62 Sawyer 1997.
63 *The Guardian* 1997a.
64 *Re R (adult: medical treatment)* [1996] 2 FLR 99; see similarly *An NHS Trust v A and SA* [2005] EWCA Civ 1145.

good reasons for making such a distinction. Nevertheless what should be apparent from the cases so far cited is that the judges (and perhaps also the legislators) have not always successfully defended the distinctions they seek to make. And perhaps these difficulties of application stem from the principle they must apply. It is to the best interests standard, as a legal rule, we should therefore turn.

4.3.2 Objective rule(s)?

So far we have considered some problems of formal rationality and in particular the inconsistencies inherent in treating arguably comparable cases differently and departing from seemingly established principles. The source of these problems might not be the judges; it might be the principle – or principles – with which they must work. Fuller argued that law must be general, in the basic sense that to qualify as law there must be rules. As Miers and Twining put it, a 'rule' can be understood as 'a general norm mandating or guiding conduct or action in a given type of situation'.[65] Does the best interests standard qualify?

Returning to the jurisprudence concerning children, the judges might insist that they reach their decisions 'by the application of an objective approach or test'[66] but there is a palpable lack of sufficiently general rules and, in their place, a strong emphasis on the particularities of the case at hand. There is certainly no attempt at providing a definition of the best interests or welfare of any child, let alone one who is seriously unwell. The merits of the law in this area have been commented upon in a lively exchange between Bridgeman, Baines and Lyons, who notably come from different disciplinary perspectives (law for Bridgeman, paediatric intensive care for Baines and Lyons, who at the time of writing were both working in academic bioethics).[67] Although the standard initially looks objective and (as Choudhry says) 'sensible',[68] Bridgeman accepts Baines's point 'that there is no one objective, best interests' but she insists that the courts have 'established the principles and approach to be adopted, establishing a very clear framework for assessment'.[69] She proceeds to list the main messages one can glean from the judges' aforementioned 'intellectual milestones'.[70] To these milestones we might usefully add Morris's detection of certain influential factors, such as the judges' suggestions (in cases like *Re C (a minor)(wardship: medical treatment)* [1990] Fam 26) 'that intellectual impairments are seen as especially burdensome'.[71]

65 Twining and Miers 1991: 131.
66 *An NHS Trust v MB* [2006] EWHC 507 para 16(iv).
67 Baines 2008, 2010; Bridgeman 2009, 2010; Lyons 2010.
68 Choudhry 2008: 240.
69 Bridgeman 2009: 16.
70 See section 4.3.1 above.
71 Morris 2009: 359.

None of this will persuade Baines, however. For him, no matter how purportedly clear the framework, this is not the same thing as identifying an objective standard; it involves *describing* what will be treated as objective, rather than defining what is actually so. According to Baines, the judges are merely drawing pictures of unicorns, but there will be no way of saying whether their depictions are accurate, because unicorns do not exist. Put more directly: there 'is no clear calculus' and nor can there be, given the plurality of ethical world views that can and do exist.[72]

Baines is scarcely the first person to detect these difficulties; others, like Herring, even invoke the same terminology of the missing 'calculus'.[73] The clearest insight undoubtedly comes from Gillian Douglas, who believes that 'uncertainty and inconsistency may be both the greatest strength and greatest weakness of the "welfare principle" '.[74] Herring picks up on the positive: he concludes that the opposition often levelled at the principle is more likely to be directed at its application in particular cases and contexts.[75] The strength surely resides in the flexibility the principle allows, and thus its capacity to respond to a vast array of situations that might arise in the life of a child.[76] Of course, the problem with this is that it can allow too much or even too little, and it becomes increasingly difficult to label this standard a 'rule' in the sense Fuller would have envisaged.

Similar things can undoubtedly be said in the context of incapacitated adults, not least because the same terminology is invoked. Once more, there is no definition and no definitive or exhaustive list of factors to which reference must be made in determining the patient's best interests. Coggon finds no single test – neither in the cases succeeding *Re F (mental patient: sterilisation)* [1990] 2 AC 1 nor in the 2005 Act – but instead 'a bundle of guiding factors rather than an expression of one concept'.[77] The courts appear openly to admit this.[78] And so, again, the cases are seen as fact-specific, in which conflicting accounts of what is 'best' for the patient can be accommodated, and so a multitude of results can be supported; here too, then, the inherent flexibility carries both promise and peril.

4.3.3 Know-ability and perform-ability?

Given the elasticity of the best interests standard, one is left pondering whether it has the potential to achieve its task as a legal principle, that is, to guide people's behaviour. Coggon seems to think so: 'As a construct, it is a

---

72 Baines 2010: 197.
73 Herring 2005: 160.
74 Douglas 2004: 173.
75 Herring 2005: 169.
76 cf Elliston 2007.
77 Coggon 2008: 225.
78 eg *R (on the application of Burke) v General Medical Council* [2005] 3 WLR 1132 para 63.

system of action guiding principles'.[79] However, I can detect numerous ways in which the principle and its progeny fail Radin's requirements of 'know-ability' and 'perform-ability'.

The problems essentially boil down to a lack of clarity and predictability. If we start with 'know-ability', then this requirement encompasses Fuller's call for constancy, clarity and consistency, as well as due publicity and congruence between the law-on-the-books and the law-in-action. To some extent these requirements are being satisfied: it is, after all, relatively easy for the law-in-action to comply with an inherently nebulous standard. More substantially, however, the degree of obfuscation should give cause for concern.

The problems begin with the differences in jurisdiction dictated by the age and condition of the patient and (it has sometimes seemed) the skills (or whim?) of counsel. Even after the introduction of the Children Act 1989, and with it the welfare principle, some cases continued to come before the High Court under its inherent jurisdiction, according to which the child would be made a ward of court and the decision based on the child's best interests.[80] The point need not be laboured since the distinction between the two jurisdictions and especially the respective criteria could be considered superficial. In *Re A (children) (conjoined twins: medical treatment)* [2000] 4 All ER 961, Ward LJ quoted Lord Hailsham LC:

> There is no doubt that, in the exercise of its wardship jurisdiction the first and paramount consideration is the well being, welfare or interests (each expression occasionally used, but each, for this purpose, synonymous) of the human being concerned.[81]

Nevertheless, there will be important differences between the two, such as the potentially longstanding ramifications of making a child a ward of court.[82] To this jurisdictional distinction might be added the purported differences, noted earlier, between the handling of those adult patients in a PVS and those not, despite the apparently uniform use of the best interests test as nowadays interpreted in light of the 2005 Act.

More troubling is the lack of clarity about what this test is and what it requires in any given case. It is not insignificant that Charlotte Wyatt's plight came before the courts on at least 11 occasions.[83] Proceedings like these bear out Wilkinson's suggestion that 'The best interests of the child is a laudable standard to appeal to; however, it may provide little practical guidance to

---

79 Coggon 2008: 220.
80 eg *Re C (a baby)* [1996] 2 FLR 43.
81 *Re A (children) (conjoined twins: medical treatment)* [2000] 4 All ER 961 at 993H (Ward LJ), quoting *Re B (a minor)(wardship: jurisdiction)* [1988] AC 199 at 202.
82 For a brief history of the best interests standard see Lyons 2010: 188–89.
83 Bridgeman 2010: 187.

decision-making'.[84] Beyond this general deficiency, four specific areas of difficulty arise, in relation to 'intolerability', 'substituted judgment', the patient's wishes and the standard's potential to go beyond the patient.

Judicial appeals to 'intolerability' are problematic because they are neither consistent nor clear. Dunn LJ first utters the idea that some lives might be considered 'intolerable' in *Re B*, with Taylor LJ adopting the nomenclature in *Re J*. The majority of his brethren nevertheless seem to resist the idea that this might amount to a test – although they notably said the same of Templeman LJ's much-cited reference to 'demonstrably awful' lives. Like that concept, 'intolerability' thereafter acquires some prominence, in cases such as those of Charlotte Wyatt and Luke Winston-Jones,[85] before the Court of Appeal – also in the Wyatt litigation – instructed that it 'should not be seen either as a gloss on or a supplementary guide to best interests'.[86] But it then resurfaces in *MB*'s hearing, in which Holman J may complain 'that use of that word really expresses a conclusion rather than provides a test'[87] but, as Morris implies, he does not entirely eschew the concept.[88]

Also unclear is the status of the 'substituted judgment' approach to best interests in English law. A substituted judgment involves donning the 'mental mantle of the incompetent'[89] and thus striving to make a decision that equates to or closely resembles that which the patient herself would make, if competent. The test has been used in the US, in cases such as *In re Quinlan* (1976) NJ 355 A 2d 647.[90] The judges in *Bland* felt that this formed no part of the English law pertaining to adults, but there was some confusion about this in the case of *Re R*, in which principles, which had been developed in relation to minors and that seemed to include a trace of substituted judgment, were applied to an adult.[91] The Mental Capacity Act 2005 does now allow for the appointment of a lasting power of attorney (LPA), as well as including reference to any past and current wishes expressed by the patient in the best interests assessment.[92] According to Samanta: 'The focus on wishes, feelings, beliefs, and values serves to emphasise the underlying and important subjective component of the standard to be applied by the decision-maker, and arguably inculcates characteristics of the "substituted judgment" approach'.[93]

---

84 Wilkinson 2006: 459.
85 *Re L (a child) (medical treatment: benefit)* [2004] EWHC 2713.
86 *Wyatt v Portsmouth Hospital NHS Trust* [2005] EWCA Civ 1181 para 91; see also *Re R (adult: medical treatment)* [1996] 2 FLR 99.
87 *An NHS Trust v MB* [2006] EWHC 507, para 17.
88 Morris 2009: 369.
89 *Superintendent of Belchertown State School v Saikewicz*, 373 Mass. 728, 370 NE 2d 417 (1977).
90 See Chapter 3 section 3.2.
91 *Re R (adult: medical treatment)* [1996] 2 FLR 99.
92 Mental Capacity Act 2005 s 4(6).
93 Samanta 2009: 386; but see also Foster 2009: 158.

Yet, Samanta continues, what remains unclear is the relative weight to be attached to such wishes and thus the extent to which the test can be tailored to the individual patient. What we might also question is the appropriateness of the law adopting such an approach in the first place. The substituted judgment seems to be the embodiment of a legal fiction, which Fuller defined as 'either (1) a statement propounded with a complete or partial consciousness of its falsity, or (2) a false statement recognized as having utility'.[94] This seems particularly apparent in cases, such as those involving critically ill infants, where the incompetent individual will never have been capable of indicating his or her views and values. Despite this and the 'doubt' expressed by some judges,[95] the concept can still occasionally be glimpsed in the paediatric cases.[96]

Following on from this problem, there is also uncertainty about the weight that is to be attached to an incompetent adult patient's wishes when assessing his or her welfare. An advance decision to refuse treatment, which has a specific legal form, is another matter, to which we will return. Of interest here is section 4(6) of the 2005 Act, which requires reference to the person's 'past and present wishes and feelings', the 'beliefs and values' that would be likely to influence their decision, plus 'any other factors' they would be likely to consider if competent. Noting the link with the substituted judgment test, Donnelly points out that the Act 'does not indicate how conflicts between past and present preferences or between past preferences and current interests are to be dealt with'.[97]

A fourth area of difficulty is the extent to which the welfare test can – and should – encompass the interests of those *other* than the patient. The orthodox position defended by the courts is that these cases involve only the patient: 'The judge must decide what is in the child's best interests'.[98] So much for the theory; the practice can seem rather different. *Re T* is again the most extreme example, as Butler-Sloss LJ explicitly conflated the interests of the child who was denied the liver transplant with those of his parents:

> This mother and child are one for the purpose of this unusual case and the decision of the court to consent to the operation jointly affects the mother and son and it also affects the father. The welfare of the child depends upon his mother.[99]

Checks might be needed to ensure the interests of such a patient are not inappropriately swamped or 'hijacked' by those of his or her family, or even society

---

94 Fuller 1967: 9; cf Harmon 1990.

95 *Re A (children) (conjoined twins: medical treatment)* [2000] 4 All ER 961 at 999 (Ward LJ).

96 eg *Wyatt v Portsmouth Hospital NHS Trust* [2005] EWCA Civ 1181 para 87.

97 Donnelly 2009: 27. See also section 4.4 below for further discussion of s 4(6).

98 *Wyatt v Portsmouth Hospital NHS Trust* [2005] EWCA Civ 1181 para 91; see also *An NHS Trust v MB* [2006] EWHC 507 para 107.

99 *Re T (a minor)(wardship: medical treatment)* [1997] 1 All ER 906 at 914J–915A.

as a whole.[100] But equally there might be a case for widening the scope of the assessment, so as more accurately and appropriately to account for the web of relations in which patients are often located and the full range of interests at stake.[101] What ought to happen is arguable; what is happening should be more settled, yet the law remains unclear as to whether and when the interests of people other than the patient will be encompassed in the (purported) assessment of their interests.[102]

It is, therefore, difficult to 'know' the best interests standard, and this in turn impacts negatively on its potential for performance. 'Perform-ability' encompasses Fuller's requirements that law be prospective, possible of performance and, again, neither contradictory nor incongruent. Some judges are alert to the need to provide detailed guidance.[103] However, the family and doctors of David Glass know all too well how unpredictable the law can be when posed with the question: to treat or not to treat? Whilst understandable, it cannot be entirely satisfactory for the judges to cite the unpredictability of the clinical situation as the reason for not issuing an answer – or, as also happened on the first occasion on which David Glass's case was contemplated, for providing an answer in which the applicable principles listed are those which even the judge admits are 'conflicting'.[104] Herring has some sympathy with the judges here, since their task seems to require clairvoyance and omniscience, in being able to identify 'what the good things in life are' and then predict the path to their satisfaction.[105]

But it might equally be retorted that the law will often generate predictable answers to the question: to treat or not to treat? Rightly or wrongly, there will be no problem in cases (which are undoubtedly the norm) where parents and doctors agree on a course: that line can be taken, apparently without the need for any additional oversight.[106] Of course, as the circumstances leading to the prosecution of Dr Arthur exemplified, it might still be a good idea to allow for some scrutiny of even agreed decisions.[107] But even leaving this aside, we might venture to say that there is also a high degree of predictability to those cases that do come before a court because the parties have failed to agree: the medical opinion will tend to win out.[108] Admittedly,

---

100 Choudhry 2008: 243, 248; Lyons 2010: 189; cf *Re A (children) (conjoined twins: medical treatment)* [2000] 4 All ER 961; Huxtable 2001.
101 Herring 2005: 166–67; Choudhry 2008: 243.
102 See Lewis 2002.
103 See eg *Re B (a child) (medical treatment)* [2008] EWHC 1996, in which Coleridge J appended to his judgment a report, prepared jointly by the experts, in the hope this would offer support to anyone caring for the patient in the future.
104 *R v Portsmouth Hospitals NHS Trust ex p Glass* [1999] 2 FLR 905 at 911B (Woolf MR).
105 Herring 2005: 160.
106 Butler-Sloss 2006: 'The courts are only involved in exceptional cases where the family and the hospital trust are in dispute over treatment'; cf *An NHS Trust v MB* [2006] EWHC 507 para 16.
107 cf Choudhry 2008.
108 cf Huxtable 2007: 84–114.

this is at odds with decisions like those of the Strasbourg court in relation to David Glass, and the more recent decision in relation to MB.[109] More apt and predictable are those pockets of case law where the results are routinely uniform, such as those pertaining to the removal of treatment from patients in a PVS and those concerning Jehovah's Witness parents who are opposed to their children receiving blood transfusions. In the first case, treatment is very likely to be withdrawn; in the second, it is very likely to be given.[110] According to Coggon, these latter cases demonstrate the judges' willingness occasionally to impose on the parties a 'stringent ("objective"?) code of values'.[111] Yet, piecemeal consistency is some distance from wholesale consistency, and so the case for coherence, and thus for rationality in the law, yet again founders.

4.4 Respecting autonomy?

Although it permits of pockets of uniformity and consistency, the nebulous best interests standard is neither easily pinned down nor evenly applied. Similar problems attend efforts to articulate and substantiate the idea of precedent autonomy, although we need not spend as much time in this particular territory, partly because the best interests standard still tends to dominate. We see this in the appointment of an LPA: although this undeniably involves an exercise of autonomy, the donee is bound to serve the patient's best interests and may be challenged on that basis.[112] Yet, provided they are deemed competent, patients themselves cannot be challenged in this way, and neither, apparently, can any advance directives they set down. Munby J considers such a directive to involve 'nothing more or less than the embodiment of the patient's autonomy and right of self-determination'.[113] Best interests therefore reach their limits where a valid and applicable advance directive exists; from there, respect for autonomy apparently has dominion. But how far does this authority really extend?

Respect for autonomy has been described as a central organising principle in English medical law.[114] The concept has spurred considerable developments in the jurisprudence of consent, including some remarkable pro-autonomy strides in recent rulings.[115] However, the idea is not given entirely free rein; seldom does the law straightforwardly concern itself with 'whatever you want', since it is just as often (if not more) likely to be concerned

---

109 *An NHS Trust v MB* [2006] EWHC 507.
110 For an example of the latter type of case see *Re E (a minor)(wardship: medical treatment)* [1993] 1 FLR 386.
111 Coggon 2008: 225.
112 Mental Capacity Act 2005 s 9(4).
113 *HE v A Hospital NHS Trust* [2003] 2 FLR 408 para 37.
114 Gunn 1994: 8.
115 eg *Chester v Afshar* [2004] 3 WLR 927.

with 'whatever you need'.[116] The right to consent is therefore bounded by the public interest, such that – no matter how autonomous the individual – certain behaviours will be judged to be beyond the pale. Resistance (thus far) to assisted dying is a classic example,[117] which attracts criticism when 'pretty fine lines' are drawn between cases involving the refusal of life-support (lawful) and those where positive assistance in dying is sought (unlawful).[118] Some think the asymmetry extends beyond requests to demands – that is, that it is wrong to deny a patient like Leslie Burke the right to issue a binding advance directive seeking specified treatment (there, clinically assisted nutrition and hydration (CANH)) in the event of future incapacity.[119]

Even the right to refuse, which looks like the strongest expression of autonomy, is not all that it appears. For one thing, the right is not extended to minors, no matter how autonomous.[120] Moreover, the right as expressed in the Mental Capacity Act 2005 is severely constrained, as we see from the provisions governing advance decisions to refuse treatment. Once again, lines are drawn according to age: the Act generally applies to those of 16 years and over but, in keeping with the common law, these particular provisions are restricted to those of 18 years and up.[121] A distinction is also apparently drawn between that which can be refused now and that which can be refused for the future. While the principle might imply that the position should be the same regardless of timing,[122] it seems an advance directive can only decline CANH: if the incompetent patient is capable naturally of ingesting food and fluids, then they must be given, no matter what any advance directive might say.[123]

The broader complaint, however, is that the rhetoric of autonomy obscures the reality of welfare. Built into the scheme surrounding advance decisions to refuse treatment are features that enable (perhaps encourage) their defeat, and which thereby preserve the sheen of consistent commitment to precedent

---

116 Huxtable 2008.
117 English law (overtly, at least) remains opposed to assisted dying, although the operation of the law – whilst variable – is not necessarily punitive: see Huxtable 2007. It may be too early to tell whether practice might differ in the wake of guidance that was issued by the Director of Public Prosecutions following a legal challenge by Debbie Purdy (*R (on the application of Purdy) v DPP* [2009] UKHL 45; Crown Prosecution Service 2010; Coggon 2010b), or, indeed, whether the legal position might change following a report which recommends legalisation (Commission on Assisted Dying 2011).
118 Biggs 2003.
119 *R (on the application of Burke) v General Medical Council* [2005] 3 WLR 1132. See also Biggs 2006; Brazier and Cave 2007: 504.
120 Huxtable 2000a; but see Butler-Sloss 2006.
121 Mental Capacity Act 2005 s 24(1).
122 Although the media reports were somewhat confused, a case like that of Kerrie Wooltorton, who refused life-saving treatment following a suicide attempt, demonstrates that doctors can appreciate the competent patient's right to decline treatment, whether now or for the future: McLean 2009b.
123 This appears to be the position in the Code of Practice: Department for Constitutional Affairs 2007: para 9:28.

autonomy. Maclean points to four such levers.[124] First, the directive may be found not to satisfy statutory formalities, with any such doubts resolved in favour of preserving life.[125] The statements uttered – but not written – by M prior to entering a minimally conscious state are a case in point.[126] Any uncertainty surrounding the patient's competence, their level of information or their freedom to decide at the time that the directive was executed will point towards the directive's defeat. Secondly, the directive may be found insufficiently specific. Thirdly, doubts might be expressed as to the endurance of the directive – especially, finally, where arguably inconsistent behaviours or statements are taken to indicate its revocation.

Although they are not formally acknowledged, one or more of various forces can push these legal levers into operation. Notwithstanding judicial rhetoric to the contrary, the judges do appear to be alert to the rationality of some patients' decisions. This rationality will sometimes be judged by reference to the consequences associated with a particular decision: a paralysed patient like Ms B might be considered to have a good case for seeking to escape an unwanted life of dependence and inability;[127] but a patient like pregnant Ms T might appear to have every reason for living, and will effectively be required to do so, despite her apparent refusal of a life-saving blood transfusion.[128] Much seems to rest on the ability of the directive's drafter to engage the judge's sympathy.[129] Account might also be taken of the motivation behind the decision: notice how notorious Moors-murderer Ian Brady was viewed as manipulative in his refusal of sustenance, which was accordingly imposed upon him.[130]

A great deal therefore depends on the perceived merits of the decision desired by the directive drafter and, in turn, on the person judging those merits. Doctors will tend, day-to-day, to have the casting vote, in judging whether the patient is competent,[131] and deciding whether or not any advance decision is up to standard.[132] There may be a great deal of symbolic support for precedent autonomy but no attempt to self-rule in advance will succeed if the doctors – or, ultimately, the judges – are unconvinced. Some argue that these gatekeepers are too quick to bar entry, and that prior statements deserve to carry more presumptive weight than they are currently accorded.[133] The

---

124 Maclean 2008.
125 cf Coggon 2007b: 239.
126 *W v M and S and A NHS Primary Care Trust* [2011] EWHC 2443; see Huxtable 2012b.
127 *Re B (adult: refusal of medical treatment)* [2002] 2 All ER 449; Huxtable 2002b.
128 *Re T (adult: refusal of medical treatment)* [1992] 4 All ER 649; Coggon 2007b: 246.
129 Coggon 2007b: 247; for a parallel argument in relation to euthanasia see Huxtable and Möller 2007.
130 *R v Collins and Ashworth Hospital Authority ex p Brady* [2000] Lloyd's Rep Med 355; Coggon 2007b: 250.
131 Harrington 1996.
132 Maclean 2008: 22.
133 Michalowski 2005; Maclean 2008.

ease with which an apparent advance decision to refuse treatment can be defeated in practice, borne out by empirical research,[134] suggests a lack of congruence between the avowed intention of the law and its practical ramifications. 'We see an application of the law that does not adhere perfectly to its precepts', as Coggon puts it.[135]

This is not the only point at which perform-ability is in doubt. The (literal) costs associated with exercising precedent autonomy might prove too much for some: there is, for example, a £130 fee for creating an LPA pertaining to health and welfare, although remissions and exemptions are available.[136] Even more inhibitive of effective action are those court decisions which appear to issue incompatible injunctions regarding advance decisions. AK's insistence that ventilation be stopped, which he communicated through blinking, involved matters of law 'so completely clear that in a sense a declaration is not really required';[137] but the law is simultaneously sufficiently unclear that a directive written by Miss AE, which was apparently to apply in 'in *any* circumstances', could be overridden.[138] Leslie Burke could not insist that treatment be provided – although, apparently, failure to follow his wishes could amount to murder.[139] Mr C, who erroneously believed he was a renowned surgeon, is found to have set down a binding refusal of amputation;[140] Ms T, who believes that blood is 'evil', is found to have 'a disorder of the mind and further or alternatively symptoms or evidence of incompetence' such that she cannot veto transfusion.[141] And, in declaring 'I don't want to be kept alive by machines', Miss KH may have refused the use of life-support machines; she may even (somehow) have refused antibiotics; but she apparently did not refuse PEG-feeding.[142]

The injustice inherent in failures to issue performable rules is perhaps most pronounced in the case of M, who was ultimately found to be in a minimally conscious state (MCS), having become incompetent in 2003 after contracting viral encephalitis.[143] According to her family, M would not wish to live an incapacitated life of dependence, having indicated as much on at least three occasions.[144] The parties agreed that there was no formal advance decision, as

---

134 Thompson, Barbour and Schwartz 2003; cf Fagerlin and Schneider 2004.
135 Coggon 2007b: 251.
136 See http://www.justice.gov.uk/downloads/global/forms/opg/lpa120-fee-guide.pdf (accessed 19 January 2012).
137 *Re AK (medical treatment: consent)* [2001] 1 FLR 129 at 136 (Hughes J).
138 *HE v A Hospital NHS Trust* [2003] 2 FLR 408 at para 4 (Munby J), emphasis in original.
139 *R (on the application of Burke) v General Medical Council* [2005] 3 WLR 1132 at para 34 (Lord Phillips MR).
140 *Re C (adult: refusal of treatment)* [1994] 1 WLR 290.
141 *NHS Trust v T (adult patient: refusal of medical treatment)* [2005] 1 All ER 387 at para 61 (Charles J).
142 *W Healthcare NHS Trust v KH* [2005] 1 WLR 834.
143 *W v M and S and A NHS Primary Care Trust* [2011] EWHC 2443; see Huxtable 2012b.
144 *W v M and S and A NHS Primary Care Trust* [2011] EWHC 2443 paras 107, 119.

did Baker J, who, guided by the Mental Capacity Act 2005 and cases such as *Bland*, decided that it was in M's best interests for treatment to continue. According to Baker J, 'the various statements made by M prior to her illness in 2003 were informal, and not specifically addressed to the question I have to decide',[145] and neither were they 'documented'.[146] These are pretty high standards for M to attain. As the MCS was only written-up in 2002, she presumably needed to be scouring the medical journals prior to her illness.[147] She seems also to have required either a time machine or else clairvoyant powers of prediction, by which she could observe how the law would develop and then ensure her compliance therewith.[148]

The lack of clarity is amplified by the plethora of concepts and distinctions surrounding precedent autonomy. An advance decision to refuse treatment has a narrower meaning than an advance directive or 'living will', which are themselves narrower than (but may form part of) an 'advance care plan', such as is favoured in contemporary end-of-life care policy.[149] Confusion is likely to ensue, not only for professionals,[150] but also for patients and their loved ones. The confusion – and mixed messages – carries over into the legislative realm. Foster thinks that the Mental Capacity Act 2005 even defeats itself.[151] He points out that, notwithstanding the requirements pertaining to advance decisions set down in sections 24–26, the determination of best interests described in section 4(6)(a) plays the trump card, insofar as it only requires that advance directives be 'considered'. As he adds, the issue was also considered in *R (on the application of Burke) v General Medical Council* [2005] 3 WLR 1132:

> The position of a patient in a PVS was addressed at length by the House of Lords in *Bland* and we do not consider it appropriate in this case to add to what was said by their Lordships, other than to make the following observation. While a number of their Lordships indicated that an advance directive that the patient should not be kept alive in a PVS should be respected, we do not read that decision as requiring such a patient to be kept alive simply because he has made an advance directive to that effect. Such a proposition would not be compatible with the provisions of the

---

145 ibid para 6.
146 ibid para 33.
147 Giacino et al 2002.
148 The requirements of the 2005 Act were eased in by way of a transitional order, which first introduced the written requirement: the Mental Capacity Act 2005 (Transitional and Consequential Provisions) Order 2007 s 5.
149 See generally the End of Life Care Strategy, launched by the Department of Health in 2008: Department of Health 2008. There is even one more layer of complexity, since beyond the advance care plan there is the 'values history': see Fagerlin and Schneider 2004: 35; Chapter 5, section 5.3.3.
150 cf Coggon 2007b: 253.
151 Foster 2009: 152–55.

Mental Capacity Act 2005, which we consider accords with the position at common law. While section 26 of that Act requires compliance with a valid advance directive to refuse treatment, section 4 does no more than require this to be taken into consideration when considering what is in the best interests of a patient.[152]

Foster's analysis seems to take the final sentence too far. The better view is surely that the court, in keeping with the facts of the case, was merely confirming that advance *refusals* which meet the terms of section 26 will be binding, whereas *other* advance decisions (including demands for treatment) will only form part of the best interests assessment. This reading also seems more in keeping with the preceding common law, to which the court referred.

Foster seems to overstate his argument but there is nevertheless a case to be made for declaring the position on advance directives ambiguous. Had he been subject to English law, Odysseus's crew might not have left him bound to the mast when he begged to be cut free.[153] Enough has been said of the lack of clarity and confusion inherent in this area of the law, problems that seem to stem from the strong welfarist counter-currents that flow against the tide of autonomy, which thereby hinder attempts at navigating a future course.

4.5 Subjective judgments? From law to ethics at the limits of life

When addressing the incompetent patient, English law therefore appears to lack a straightforward answer to our fundamental question: to treat or not to treat? Parliament and the courts claim to have at their disposal a variety of rules designed to provide the necessary answers, which are essentially concerned with the best interests of the patient and any efforts they have made to articulate their autonomous wishes concerning (non-)treatment. The problem, as we have seen throughout this chapter, is that the answers given do not always meet the standards associated with rational law, such as clarity, consistency and predictability. Far from the purported objectivity to which the judges and law-makers cling, the impression that inevitably emerges is one of radical subjectivity in the law, albeit in the guise of objectivity, which is tailored to the 'individual' situation presented by the patient's plight. Coggon sees no problem with this attempted meld:

> When, for example, a judge seeks knowledge of the best interests of a patient in a case, what he is looking for (or should be looking for) is (reasonably)

---

152 *R (on the application of Burke) v General Medical Council* [2005] 3 WLR 1132 at para 57 (Lord Phillips MR).
153 See Morgan 1994.

objective knowledge of factors relevant to the assessment. Subjective perspectives will necessarily and appropriately form part of this. For example, a previously competent patient's subjective values can be taken to have existed objectively, and are appropriately brought into consideration.[154]

But there is more subjectivity lurking in these assessments – and, we might add, in consideration of advance directives and the like – than the subjectivity associated with the specific patient: there is also the subjectivity of the person empowered to give effect to the final decision. Perhaps, in truth, it might be that person who counts as the ultimate decision-maker.

So whose subjective account counts? Writing about the trial of Dr Arthur, Ian Kennedy commented:

> It is said that the case lends support to the proposition that rules, principles, or guidelines – call them what you will – cannot be worked out except in the vaguest, most general way. The situation is too complicated, the argument goes. The doctor and parent must be allowed to judge what to do in the light of the situation . . . [This] is sometimes called 'situation ethics'; the situation dictates the response. But situations do not dictate responses; people do. The reality is that the person making the decision is bringing certain values and principles to bear, but is either unwilling or unable to articulate them. If he does so, he will have to deal with tiresome problems of resolving conflicts between clashing principles and dealing rationally with argument and counter-argument.[155]

Kennedy here throws down the gauntlet to those intimately involved in making these decisions: they should be prepared to scrutinise the values and principles embodied in their decisions. Before we side with Kennedy in this duel, we should first consider who these decision-makers happen to be.

As Kennedy suggests, doctors – and, to some extent, their colleagues on the wards – will be central to the decision-making process. This will be especially true in those many daily cases that do not come near to a court, but in which assessments of a patient's best interests or capacity are nevertheless required.[156] Of course, legislation also makes clear the need to involve those close to the incapacitated patient, whether they are a child or an adult. With parental responsibility comes not only a duty but also a right,[157] and studies reveal that parents do tend to play an influential role in neonatal decision-making across Europe.[158] The level of involvement seems to be higher in Britain than

---

154 Coggon 2008: 221; cf Donnelly 2009.
155 Kennedy 1991: 158.
156 cf Harrington 1996.
157 Thus reversing Spiderman's mantra: 'With great power comes great responsibility'.
158 Cuttini, Rebgliato, Bortilo and Hansen 1999.

elsewhere, with one study finding that parents frequently participate in 78 per cent of units.[159] However, the same study reveals that parents take full responsibility for the ultimate choice in only 11 per cent of units,[160] while another suggests that responses to parental preferences can vary according to the experience and age of the paediatrician.[161] Some health professionals reportedly feel that the final responsibility is 'too great a burden for parents to bear'.[162] McHaffie and colleagues found that only 3 per cent of doctors and 6 per cent of nurses believe that parents should take the final decision.[163] The professionals nevertheless agreed that many such parents, particularly those whose child had spent a considerable time in an intensive care unit, displayed 'an impressive ability to understand the issues and weigh up the consequences for their own child'.[164] Time will tell how the professionals will judge similar decisions to withhold or withdraw life-sustaining treatment from incompetent adults who have made explicit provision for the input of an LPA.

Of course, the judges are the ultimate decision-makers in any and all of these cases. This will be directly true in any case that comes before the court; as Holman J puts it, in disputed cases 'it is the role and duty of the court . . . to exercise its own independent and objective judgment'.[165] But it will also be indirectly true in every other case, in the sense that Parliament's injunctions to serve the welfare or best interests of the patient, or to honour the patient's prior autonomous choice, must all be interpreted in the shadow of the courts. The judges do take care to emphasise the significance they attach to any input provided by those close to the patient. One unusual example involved receiving evidence from the flatmate of a patient in a PVS;[166] more typical will be the opinions provided by the parents of a critically ill infant – or even infants, as in the case of the conjoined Attard twins, in which Ward LJ sought 'to emphasise to the parents, strangers in our midst, how we sympathise with their predicament, with the agony of their decision – for now it has become ours'.[167] He later stated 'that their wishes should command very great respect';[168] yet, as is well known, the Court of Appeal saw fit to reach a decision completely at odds with that of the parents, since it authorised the surgical separation of the twins.

Elsewhere too one can question the extent to which parental autonomy generally triumphs, even in the 1997 case of *Re T* (T's parents were, lest we forget, trained health care professionals). When disagreements reach the

159 ibid 87.
160 ibid.
161 Duffy and Reynolds 2011.
162 Boyle, Salter and Arnander 2004: 403.
163 McHaffie, Laing, Parker and McMillan 2001: 105.
164 ibid 106.
165 *An NHS Trust v MB* [2006] EWHC 507 para 16(i).
166 See Hinchliffe 1996.
167 *Re A (children) (conjoined twins: medical treatment)* [2000] 4 All ER 961 at 987B–C (Ward LJ).
168 ibid at 1006G (Ward LJ).

courtroom it seems all too easy for the judiciary to cast the parents as biased and relatively ignorant, in contrast to the more objective and technically knowledgeable doctors (and, we might add, judges themselves). As Morris points out, there is a temptation to view the parents of children such as Charlotte Wyatt and Luke Winston-Jones as susceptible to 'wishful thinking'.[169] But the expertise available to these different parties may be qualitatively different, and borne of quite distinct values. And, just like Charlotte Wyatt, David Glass teaches us that dire predictions are not always borne out: as the European judges appreciated, there will be occasions when 'maternal instinct has . . . more weight than medical opinion'.[170]

Although some caution is warranted, it is usually clear that professional opinion tends to compel the judges' conclusions. A host of 'welfare experts' are on hand to help the court, especially in proceedings pertaining to children. Choudhry notes how social workers, functioning as court reporters, can play a useful role and she laments the absence of a similar figure in the scheme of the Mental Capacity Act 2005.[171] She accepts, however, that fresh knowledge in the disciplines associated with such welfare expertise – like psychiatry and psychology – can take considerable time to filter down to the courts, so she advises the judges to tread carefully, despite their apparent enthusiasm for such input.[172]

More generally, in the cases with which we are concerned, it is the doctors to whom the judges are in thrall. *Bolam* is written through medical law as if it were a stick of seaside rock. The stranglehold of 'responsible medical opinion' on the determination of the best interests of an incompetent adult may have loosened with successive cases and Parliament's intervention,[173] but doctors' evidence continues to carry great weight. Morris cites cases including *A National Health Service Trust v D* [2000] 2 FLR 677, *Wyatt v Portsmouth Hospital NHS Trust* [2005] EWCA Civ 1181 and *Re L (a child) (medical treatment: benefit)* [2004] EWHC 2713 as examples where the judges adopted a clear 'preference for the clinicians' view', despite – in D's case at least – the possibility that a persuasive alternative account was available, albeit from people (including professionals) other than the doctors.[174] Medical experts undoubtedly bring essential specialist knowledge.[175] Their viewpoints might also encompass much more than the 'purely' scientific and they will also be

169 Morris 2009: 366.
170 *Glass v UK* [2004] 1 FLR 1019, Separate Opinion, para 2.
171 Choudhry 2008: 241–42, 247. Note, however, the role of the independent mental capacity advocate: Mental Capacity Act 2005 ss 35–41.
172 Choudhry 2008: 244; see also Holm 2008: 253.
173 See eg *Re F (mental patient: sterilisation)* [1990] 2 AC 1; *Airedale NHS Trust v Bland* [1993] 2 WLR 316; *Re A (male sterilisation)* [2000] 1 FLR 549; Mental Capacity Act 2005 s 4.
174 Morris 2009: 367.
175 ibid 363.

informed by more than one (if any) encounter with the patient – unlike the judge, who may only have met the patient once, if at all.[176] Nevertheless, neither we nor the judges should be tempted to assume that scientific input means objectivity.[177]

Many of these concerns touch on a theme familiar to medical law: fear of a perceived excess in the power granted, and deference displayed, to doctors.[178] According to Foster:

> In the context of end of life decision-making the woolly 'best interests' test is too subjective to be safe. It is impossible to police its use. Remember that the vast majority of 'best interests' determinations take place not in the Royal Courts of Justice but on the ward. They are made not by detached judges but by harassed clinicians and distraught parents.[179]

Morris thinks the former party will outweigh the latter; even those rulings (like the early *Re J* cases[180]) which appear to promote a partnership between the two parties ultimately grant the doctor the power of veto. She notes the judges' reluctance to challenge medical opinion, evident in their determination to protect clinicians' 'consciences' and respect 'clinical autonomy'.[181] Clinical judgment is often presented as monolithic, with disagreements between professionals typically hidden from the parents' view. Left unchallenged, experience gleaned from the wards inevitably becomes a self-fulfilling prophecy.[182] Doctors seem to think that they should carry the burden of the final decision, and the judges appear disinclined to disagree. This, of course, means letting decisions rest on the values of doctors, as the judges explicitly acknowledge:

> I myself am not concerned with any ethical issues which may surround this case . . . The ethical decision whether actually to withdraw or withhold it must be made by the doctors concerned. Judges are neither qualified to make, nor required, nor entitled to make ethical judgments or decisions.[183]

But what qualifies the doctors to make such decisions? Often their values will, as a matter of professional expectation (and, sometimes, requirement), be

---

176 See Baines 2010.
177 Herring 2005: 162.
178 Kennedy 1981; Montgomery 2000, 2006.
179 Foster 2005: 1241.
180 *Re J (a minor)(wardship: medical treatment)* [1991] Fam 33; *Re J (a minor)(wardship: medical treatment)* [1992] 2 FLR 165.
181 See Morris 2009: 353–55, 370.
182 ibid 365.
183 *An NHS Trust v MB* [2006] EWHC 507 para 24.

those enshrined in professional guidance, such as that issued by the General Medical Council,[184] British Medical Association[185] and Royal Colleges.[186] Yet, they might also be much more subjective in origin and outlook: studies show that religious convictions do influence the opinions that doctors form.[187]

Given all this, one could conclude that doctors dominate the decision-making process. But that would be too hasty since, in truth, the power must still reside with the judges. Expert testimony is not passively received and regurgitated. Notice again the true import of the ruling in MB's case: Holman J was effectively ordering the doctors to provide treatment to which they were opposed.[188] Such results are not strictly reached through deductive reasoning. No single answer will necessarily emerge from the mechanical application of precedents and principles like *Bolam* and the best interests standard, since they lack 'a fixed, univocal meaning'.[189] They are, says Harrington, 'guiding standards', which only indicate those factors worthy of consideration in the individual case, rather than compelling any particular result.[190]

According to Harrington, the operation of a guiding standard depends, to a large degree, on the facts of the case and 'the intuitive sense of reasonableness of the deciding judge. The meaning of the standard is yielded only in the moment of its application'.[191] Guiding standards have a normative function, in that they:

> . . . open the system up by allowing judges, under the influence of changing social mores and scientific developments, to fashion and refashion new criteria of best interests etc. This is never simply a question of receiving direct inputs from society. The courts respond to what they see as change by working and re-working a distinctively judicial common sense. Values and principles, but also stock images and stereotypes are the stuff of this common sense.[192]

Viewed in this way, a concept like the best interests of the patient might look like an end-point but it is actually where the real work begins. To do this work well, the decision-maker seems to need shamanic skills of prediction,[193] as well as ethically-attuned senses. A great deal will turn on the values of

---

184 General Medical Council 2010.
185 British Medical Association 2007; British Medical Association, the Resuscitation Council (UK) and the Royal College of Nursing 2007.
186 eg Royal College of Paediatrics and Child Health 2004.
187 Seale 2010; cf Morris 2009: 364.
188 *An NHS Trust v MB* [2006] EWHC 507; see also eg *Re B (a minor)(wardship: medical treatment)* [1981] 1 WLR 1421; *NHS Trust v A (a child)* [2007] EWHC 1696.
189 Harrington 2003.
190 ibid.
191 ibid.
192 ibid.
193 Breen 2002: 17, cited in Lyons 2010: 189.

individual judges, no doubt informed by the values which they see in their peers' decisions. Even their account of the 'facts' will be filtered through such values.[194]

One of the problems, of course, is that the judiciary is scarcely renowned for its diversity.[195] The values exhibited by its members may nevertheless be judged good or bad, depending on the observer's own ethical commitments. Some believe the judges have a 'bad track record',[196] and Quigley worries that a 'judge knows best' model will rise from the ashes of the old 'doctor knows best' paradigm.[197] Whether or not this comes – or has come – to pass, the judges who are likely to 'know best' will be those who appreciate that their task has an inherently value-laden dimension. As Lee and Morgan put it, the judges adjudicating on matters of medical law will have occasion to contemplate 'stigmata cases', which 'require courts to develop a social, even a moral vision with which to respond to the dilemmas created by the social and cultural revolution of contemporary medicine'.[198] So what is this moral vision? And does it view the dilemmas of treatment and non-treatment in the right light?

4.6 Conclusion: problems painting unicorns with Odysseus

The central problems revealed in this chapter can be summarised by reference to two of the more striking mythical similes we have encountered. First, we cannot be sure when we should leave Odysseus tied to the mast, as opposed to when we should release him, presumably to the mercy of the Sirens. Secondly, and of wider concern, recalling Baines's comparison, we cannot be confident about how best to paint a unicorn or, indeed, who can best depict this creature. Put more straightforwardly, exercises of precedent autonomy will not always succeed but we cannot decisively say in advance which will pass muster. Meanwhile, a patient's best interests might sometimes direct clinicians towards treatment, other times not, again without there being a clear way of predicting the direction. Amidst the voluminous jurisprudence on best interests at the margins of life is intolerable inconsistency, and, indeed, inconsistent appeals to intolerability; fine lines and apparent arbitrariness; and subjective judgments on purportedly objective matters. Much appears to hinge on the decision-maker and, crucially, the ethical values underpinning the vital decision. It is to these values we now turn.

194　Lyons 2010: 193.
195　eg Baines 2010: 197. See further Chapter 7 section 7.2.2.
196　Herring 2008: 164. Here we should note the concern expressed by Coggon (2008: 226–28) about the scope afforded to the inherent jurisdiction in relation to incompetent adults in *In the Matter of SA* [2005] EWHC 2942.
197　Quigley 2008: 238.
198　Lee and Morgan 2001: 298.

5 Calculating the value of life at the limits of life

> Is the court to assume the role of God and decide who should live and who should die? . . . This is not an area in which any difference can be allowed to exist between what is legal and what is morally right. The decision of the court should be able to carry conviction with the ordinary person as being based not merely on legal precedent but also upon acceptable ethical values.
>
> *Airedale NHS Trust v Bland* [1993] 2 WLR 316 at 350F–G (Hoffmann LJ)

5.1 Looking for values in English law

Legal rules may require objectivity but a central feature of the complaints canvassed in the previous chapter was the contamination of what (apparently) should be decisions based on the subjective wishes or interests of the individual patient with more 'objective' considerations, as judged by someone other than the patient, or his or her intimates. This does not mean that the patient is forced to adopt a 'view from nowhere',[1] since that view is inevitably clouded by the subjective lens through which the ultimate decision-maker – typically a judge or a doctor – experiences the world. This additional layer of subjectivity undoubtedly contributes to the inconsistency and confusion written through the law pertaining to the removal of treatment from incompetent patients.

The subjectivity in the law – and the irrationality it appears inevitably to spawn – is scarcely unexpected given the close resemblance of modern judgments to the proposals and predictions made in the wake of the landmark US ruling in *In re Quinlan* (1976) NJ 355 A 2d 647.[2] As we saw in Chapter 2,[3] in 1976, the New Jersey Supreme Court authorised the withdrawal of ventilation from Karen Ann Quinlan, at the request of her father, who was his daughter's surrogate. Like Ms Quinlan herself, who survived for another decade after the treatment was stopped, the ruling has endured, since it laid

---

1 Nagel 1986.
2 For an expanded version of the following argument see Huxtable 2007: 117–23.
3 Section 2.2.

the foundations for much of our current thinking about the withdrawal of life support, particularly in relation to clinically assisted nutrition and hydration (CANH).

In the wake of the decision, a host of scholars contemplated how English law would respond to a similar dilemma. They overwhelmingly concluded that permission to cease treatment would be granted, such that there would be no violation of the prohibition on homicide. *How* they arrived at this conclusion will be familiar: their first substantial manoeuvre involved viewing this as an omission in law, such that its lawfulness would turn on the duty of the doctor,[4] which might encompass a duty to honour a patient's refusal of treatment.[5] *Why* this was seen to be the result is also revealing: implicit in each of the accounts given is the moral judgment that this is the ethically appropriate outcome. In other words, the theorists sought an answer to a perceived legal dilemma by reference to the ethical intuitions or arguments with which they themselves were aligned or which they otherwise felt the judges would endorse. The meld of proposal and prediction is apparent in the terminology employed, as we see the writers moving between accounts of what the law purportedly 'will' or 'could' say,[6] and what it 'should' endorse.[7] This becomes particularly apparent when different accounts of the legal position are offered in response to the 'intruder' – a person who behaves exactly as the doctor does in removing treatment, albeit from seemingly malevolent motives: in contrast to the doctor, this person 'acts' and is guilty of a crime.[8]

Some of these early attempts to spell out the (likely) legal position were mentioned in one of the leading judgments in this area, *Airedale NHS Trust v Bland* [1993] 2 WLR 316, so it is unsurprising that one can detect a distinct ethical undercurrent to the decisions that have followed Quinlan's case. In which directions, then, do these currents pull the law, and from which wells do they spring? An immanent critique, along the lines described in Chapter 1, will allow us to surf the currents. We start, then, by looking for the waves they create, that is, for indications of the main ethical values which shape the law governing non-treatment decisions.

5.2 The value of life in English law

Embedded in the law pertaining to the best interests standard, alongside that governing attempts to give effect to advance decision-making (whether via

---

4 eg Kennedy 1977; Williams 1977; Leng 1982; Beynon 1982; Skegg 1988; see also Fletcher 1969.
5 Williams 1973: 27–31; Skegg 1974: 523–28; Kennedy 1977: 449–52.
6 eg Skegg 1988.
7 eg Fletcher 1969: 74, 78, 79, 81.
8 eg Williams 1977: 635; Skegg 1988: 177–79.

advance directives or through the appointment of surrogate decision-makers), appear to be three (relatively[9]) distinct sets of ethical claims. These claims map onto three accounts of the value of human life, which latch onto its intrinsic, instrumental or self-determined value.[10] The first two of these lurk within discussions of patients' best interests, as does the third, although this often comes much further out into the open.

John Keown would have us start with the *intrinsic* value of life, since this has 'consistently been stated by the courts to be a governing principle of English law'.[11] 'We all believe in and assert the sanctity of human life', as Lord Donaldson MR put it in the case of *Re J (a minor)(wardship: medical treatment)* [1990] 3 All ER 930,[12] with Anthony Bland's judges adding that the principle 'is the concern of the state, and the judiciary as one of the arms of the state, to maintain'.[13] Keown's view, to which others have subscribed,[14] finds support beyond the cases with which we are concerned, in the simple fact that English law prohibits homicide, with murder ranked as the most heinous crime, and in the Human Rights Act 1998, which contains (indeed, opens with) the 'right to life'.

For Keown, the basic idea to which the law clings is that there is a prohibition on the intentional ending of life. This prohibition might owe something to broadly Judeo-Christian (and often distinctively Roman Catholic) thinking, but it need not be so tethered, as more secular human rights accounts indicate. In the words of one Law Lord, when contemplating arguments against voluntary euthanasia, 'the arguments in support are transcendental, and I agree. Believer or atheist, the observer grants to the maintenance of human life an overriding imperative, so strong as to outweigh any consent to its termination'.[15]

Yet, the judges will sometimes invoke distinctively theological terminology and even invite religious opinion into the courtroom.[16] We see both in

---

9 'Relatively' because autonomy and quality of life arguments are sometimes advanced in tandem.

10 For expansion of some of the arguments in this section see Huxtable 2007: 131–40. Although the arguments I offered in my evidence were not endorsed, my typology was adopted by the Commission on Assisted Dying (2011: 73–75, 89).

11 Keown 1997b: 481.

12 At 938G–H.

13 *Airedale NHS Trust v Bland* [1993] 2 WLR 316 at 362F–G. Indeed, in keeping with the emphasis on protecting life, it is worth noting that the approach taken by Anthony Bland's judges was first developed in *Re F (a mental patient: sterilisation)* [1990] 2 AC, in which the appeal to the best interests of an incapacitated patient was tethered to the necessity to save life or limb.

14 eg Blom-Cooper and Drewry 1976: 187; see also Kuhse 1987: 5.

15 *R v Brown et al* [1993] 2 WLR 556 at 588G.

16 *Re A (children)(conjoined twins: surgical separation)* [2000] 4 All ER 961; see Skene and Parker 2002.

the Court of Appeal decision on the fate of the conjoined Attard twins: distinctions between intending and (merely) foreseeing death, as well as between acts and omissions, and also between 'proportionate' as opposed to 'disproportionate' treatment, all feature in the judgments, as do references to the submissions made by the Archbishop of Westminster and the Pro-Life Alliance. Keown himself is also cited, with approval.[17]

The problem – for Keown at least – is that English law does not restrict itself to the view that life has intrinsic value; the ensuing problem – which is potentially one for everybody – is that contradictory law seems to result. A statement such as the following from Cazalet J in the case of baby D conveys the essential message: 'The court's clear respect for the sanctity of human life must impose a strong obligation in favour of taking all steps capable of preserving life, save in exceptional circumstances'.[18]

The 'exceptional circumstances' are not always ones which Keown would accept,[19] since they sometimes pull in the opposite direction to where he wants law to be. One even sees this in the case in which Keown was favourably cited, since the court ruled in favour of separation and, in so doing, it appeared to adopt an ethic more concerned with the quality – rather than the sanctity – of the twins' lives (both together and apart).[20] According to this ethic, life has only an *instrumental* value: it is valuable only insofar as it enables the achievement of other goods. So, the argument goes, where the life is of sufficiently poor quality, it need not be preserved.

The emphasis on the instrumental value of life implicit in the twins' case can be traced back to *Re B (a minor)(wardship: medical treatment)* [1981] 1 WLR 1421, although it becomes most apparent in *Re J (a minor)(wardship: medical treatment)* [1991] 1 FLR 366. In the latter case, Munby QC (as he then was) made two submissions: one 'absolute'; the other 'qualified'. The absolute submission was that it would offend against the sanctity of life if artificial ventilation were to be withheld from seriously disabled J. The court felt that there were 'few, if any, absolutes';[21] in 'exceptional circumstances', like those in the present case, the strong presumption in favour of life would be outweighed.[22]

---

17 *Re A (children)(conjoined twins: surgical separation)* [2000] 4 All ER 961, especially at 999–1001.

18 *National Health Service Trust v D* [2000] 2 FLR 677.

19 As we will see below, according to Keown, life-supporting measures may be withheld or withdrawn where these are 'disproportionate', eg because the treatment is judged to be 'futile'. One might detect this sort of thinking in cases such as *Re L (A child) (medical treatment: benefit)* [2004] EWHC 2713 and *Re K (a child) (withdrawal of treatment)* [2006] EWHC 1007.

20 Huxtable 2000b.

21 *Re J (a minor)(wardship: medical treatment)* [1991] 1 FLR 366 at 937A (Lord Donaldson MR).

22 ibid at 938E–F (Lord Donaldson MR) and at 943C (Taylor LJ).

Munby's qualified submission, which he developed on the basis of *Re B*, also failed to find favour. Munby had argued that the balancing exercise encouraged by the judgments in *Re B* fell in favour of prolonging J's life. The Court of Appeal resisted the idea that the references to 'intolerable' and 'demonstrably awful' lives could be used as a 'quasi-statutory yardstick' for determining when a child could be allowed to die.[23] The test, as we saw throughout Chapter 2, was (and is) the best interests of the child. This would involve assessing 'the pain and suffering and quality of life which the child will experience if life is prolonged'.[24] It would not necessarily involve rigid adherence to the sanctity of life, which could prove 'inconsistent at its extreme with the best interests of the child'.[25]

Similar evaluations can be detected elsewhere in the jurisprudence,[26] including that pertaining to incompetent adults. Critics and defenders of the *Bland* ruling tend to agree that the decision rests more on the instrumental than on the intrinsic value of life.[27] Peter Singer puts this with characteristic clarity and zeal: he detects a 'revolution in British law regarding the sanctity of human life'.[28] As in *Re J*, the judges regarded the principle as 'not an absolute'.[29] Controversially, they accepted that the ending of Bland's life was not merely foreseen but also intended, although – in stark opposition to the prohibition promoted by the principle – this was viewed as justifiable.[30] The unified view of personhood inherent to the intrinsic value of life was supplanted by a Cartesian separation of mind from body:[31] with his mind apparently gone, Anthony Bland's value as a person diminished. He now seemed to lack 'best interests of any kind',[32] and merely endured an existence offering 'no affirmative benefit'.[33] The message seems to be

---

23 ibid at 938F–G (Lord Donaldson MR); see also 942G (Balcombe LJ).

24 ibid at 938E–F (Lord Donaldson MR), emphasis added; see also 942C–F (Balcombe LJ) and at 945G–H (Taylor LJ).

25 At 944D–E.

26 Amongst numerous examples (some of which are discussed by Lyons 2010: 191–92), see eg the judgments of 'normality' and 'abnormality' reflected in *NHS Trust v A (a child)* [2007] EWHC 1696 and the judge's reference to 'meaningful life' in *Re D (medical treatment)* [1998] 1 FLR 411. For a socio-legal perspective on the attitudes to disability revealed by some of these cases, see Read and Clements 2004.

27 *Airedale NHS Trust v Bland* [1993] 2 WLR 316.

28 Singer 1995: 337; see also Finnis 1993; McLean 1996.

29 *Airedale NHS Trust v Bland* [1993] 2 WLR 316 at 362F–G (Lord Keith) and at 367D–E (Lord Goff).

30 ibid at 379C–D (Lord Lowry), at 383D–E (Lord Browne-Wilkinson) and at 388G–H (Lord Mustill).

31 ibid. See in particular at 355F–G (Hoffmann LJ) and at 400B–C (Lord Mustill). Keown 1997b: 493; Finnis 1993: 334.

32 ibid at 398E.

33 ibid at 386H (Lord Browne-Wilkinson).

that inhabitants of such a 'twilight world' need not have their occupancy extended.[34]

Keown continues to resist the advance of instrumental accounts of the value of human life, which he fears are gaining ground in the professional guidance succeeding *Bland* (from the British Medical Association, for example) and in developments including the Mental Capacity Act 2005.[35] The latter presents an additional threat to the intrinsic value of life since it unites with case law to provide a third account of the value of life, which is *self-determined*, by the autonomous individual. Whether the decriminalisation of suicide amounted to a victory for autonomy at the expense of the sanctity of life is a moot point,[36] but we can certainly see its dominance in the proclaimed priority of an autonomous refusal of treatment, even if this means death will follow and even if that is precisely what the patient wants.[37] Case law has confirmed that such a refusal may be issued here and now, or in advance of anticipated future incompetence: either way, provided that the refusal comes from a competent patient, it must be honoured, or else an action in trespass or prosecution for battery might ensue.[38] Advance decisions of the sort with which we are concerned (that is, those in which life is at stake) now fall within the ambit of the 2005 Act and they come subject to particular conditions, but, where these are satisfied, the end result should be the same: the patient's refusal should be respected.[39]

Keown and like-minded scholars are troubled by these inroads into the idea that life is inviolable. For them, English law misconceives autonomy, which should be tethered to – and given meaning by – the sanctity of life.[40] The law certainly goes too far, they think, when it respects even suicidal decisions to decline life support.[41]

---

34 *NHS Trust v I* [2003] EWHC 2243 at para 8 (Butler-Sloss P). These sorts of arguments are sometimes couched in terms of 'dignity', which is a contested concept (eg Ashcroft 2005). Adherents to the sanctity of life position essentially see dignity in terms of the intrinsic value of life (Huxtable 2007: 11). However, when the judges make explicit reference to the concept (as Butler-Sloss P did in this case), then their reasoning often seems more inclined towards the idea that life has only an instrumental value: see eg *A National Health Service Trust v D* [2000] 2 FLR 677, *Re A (children) (conjoined twins: medical treatment)* [2000] 4 All ER 961, *NHS Trust A v M; NHS Trust B v H* [2001] 2 WLR 942, *An NHS Trust v D* [2005] EWHC 2439, *R (on the application of Burke) v General Medical Council* [2005] 3 WLR 1132 and *Re OT* [2009] EWHC 633. It remains to be seen how the concept might best be understood, particularly in the law governing the end(ing) of life (cf Coggon 2006; Foster 2011).

35 eg Keown 2000; Gormally and Keown 1999.

36 See Huxtable 2007: 68–77, 137.

37 eg *Airedale NHS Trust v Bland* [1993] 2 WLR 316 at 393B–C (Lord Mustill).

38 *Re B (adult: refusal of medical treatment)* [2002] 2 All ER 449; *Re AK* [2000] 1 FLR 129.

39 See Chapter 3 section 3.2.3.

40 Linacre Centre 1993: 129, 132.

41 Keown 2002b: 238.

5.3 Calculating the value of life

We see in English law three prominent accounts of the value of human life vying for a primary (perhaps even an exclusive) position. But which, if any, should be law's guide to making decisions about (not) treating incompetent patients? An answer to this question should come into view as we extend the immanent critique, by exploring the logic of each set of claims, and comparing that which they appear to endorse and require with that which actually obtains in English law at present. The criteria developed in Chapter 1 will help us to judge the adequacy of each of these moral contenders, examining (inter alia) their clarity, consistency and empirical 'fit'. We begin, again, with the intrinsic value of life.

5.3.1 *The intrinsic value of life: the disutility of futility?*

Central to the principle of the sanctity or inviolability of human life is the idea that death should not intentionally be sought, either by action or omission. This idea owes much to Judeo-Christian thinking and specifically to Roman Catholic doctrine. This is certainly true of the version visible in English law, notwithstanding its more recent secular expression in human rights discourse.[42] The harm of intentional killing may be inflicted on God, in its rejection of his gift of life,[43] or it may be conceived as an affront to human dignity.[44] Everybody has worth – and, indeed, every *body* has worth, such that the mind cannot reject a failing body, as the two exist in partnership.[45] This does not mean that life is accorded an *absolute* value, requiring its defence in all circumstances.[46] Insistence on the absolute value of life amounts to *vitalism*; the intrinsic value of life is different, because it recognises that there are limits on the obligation to protect and preserve life. Two such limits are particularly pertinent in the cases with which we are concerned.

The first limit arises from the doctrine of double effect, which distinguishes between intending to end life (which is prohibited) and merely foreseeing that death will ensue (which may be permitted). Striving to secure a positive outcome can be permitted, even if this incidentally involves inflicting harm, provided that on balance it was better to proceed than not. Different defenders describe the idea differently, but usually four conditions must be met: the action (or omission) must not be morally wrong; the agent must intend to secure the good result; the good result must not be brought about by the bad result; and the harm in the bad result must be outweighed by the benefit

---

42 Keown 2002a: 40–41.
43 Gormally 1978a: 22–24.
44 Keown 2002a: 40.
45 Finnis 1993: 334; Linacre Centre 1993: 188–89.
46 Keown 2002a: 39.

brought by the good result.[47] The terms 'good' and 'bad' are undoubtedly given content by the overarching philosophy, which strives to safeguard life against its intentional ending. Although (too often) the doctrine is associated with the use of powerful pain relieving drugs,[48] it can apply to the removal of life-support, where the aim may be to remove burdensome treatment but not with the direct purpose of ending life.

The second limit comes with the distinction that is drawn between *acting* and *omitting*. Both will be prohibited where the intention is to end life, but where there is no such intention, a degree of flexibility is allowed in relation to omissions. AH Clough famously satirised the basic idea: 'Thou shalt not kill; but need'st not strive/Officiously to keep alive'.[49] Proponents of the sanctity of life replace Clough's reference to taking 'officious' steps with terms like 'extraordinary' or, more often nowadays, 'disproportionate'. Such efforts are not morally required. These labels can be applied when a treatment is judged 'futile' or when its burdens outweigh its benefits; if the reverse holds, then intervention looks 'proportionate' (or 'ordinary') and is therefore morally obligatory.[50] The requisite judgments do not hinge on the 'heroic' or 'hi-tech' nature of the intervention in question and nor do they involve judging the instrumental value of the patient's life. Keown seeks to make the latter point by distinguishing between 'quality of life' judgments and 'Quality of life' judgments.[51] The former attach to the *treatment* ('Given this patient's quality of life and condition, does this treatment offer a reasonable prospect of improving it?'); the latter concern the patient's *life* ('Given the patient's Quality of life, is it a life worth living?').[52]

There is much to commend the intrinsic value of life and its associated precepts. The long history of the principle, plus its occupation of various theological and secular domains, mean that ample attention has been given to its coherence and robustness as a source of moral guidance. The idea that life should be protected certainly has a strong intuitive appeal, but it also appears capable of withstanding critical scrutiny. As Keown argues, the inviolability of life offers something of 'a middle way' between the opposite extremes of vitalism and an approach in which the instrumental value of life is all that counts.[53] Even leaving aside any historical religious affiliations, it is not surprising that the concept continues to echo throughout contemporary law and professional guidance.

47 Gormally 1978a: 9–13; Keown 2002a: 19–30.
48 See Huxtable 2007: 89–92.
49 Quoted in Singer 1994: 194.
50 Gormally 1978b; Keown 2002a: 42–43.
51 Keown 2000: 71.
52 ibid .
53 ibid.

At the same time, there are numerous ways in which this approach fails to meet the standards we can expect from moral guidance. The clarity, applicability and consistency of the principle warrant particular scrutiny. First, the judgments and injunctions associated with the intrinsic value of life are seldom sufficiently clear. The key terms on which the principle and its associates rely – like 'intention', 'omission', 'futility' and 'burden' – are all contestable. James Rachels complains that adherents to the doctrine allow agents to 'purify the intention' by using such words to describe their behaviour in ways that demonstrate compliance.[54] Notice, indeed, how Johnson J in his initial ruling authorising the separation of the conjoined twins Jodie and Mary felt obliged to characterise this as the 'omission' of life support from Jodie to Mary, since he apparently felt unable to embrace the (inevitable) bringing about of Mary's death by positive means.[55]

Confusion and obfuscation like this means, secondly, that the idea is not simple to apply in the real world. Agents are required to draw sometimes extremely fine lines between (for example) the intended and the foreseen, and between an action and an omission. Even Keown has not indicated precisely what he would decide in a case like Anthony Bland's. One would presume, given the force of his objections to that ruling and its progeny, that he would require the continuing provision of life-support in such a situation. But that is not quite what he concludes: instead, he says, the 'traditional ethic does not, as yet, unequivocally rule out the withdrawal of tube-feeding on the ground that it is futile medical treatment'; indeed, 'the ethic may currently allow for a legitimate range of answers on tube-feeding those in pvs'.[56] If Keown cannot bring himself to issue a clear instruction in such a case, then what hope have clinicians and families of finding the moral steer which the sanctity of life purports to provide? Although the respective parties may have varied in their personal accounts of the principle, it is telling that different parents who claim to be guided by the same beliefs have arrived at conflicting decisions for their offspring, even in strikingly similar cases, such as those pertaining to the care of conjoined twins.[57]

Both of these groups of problems have a bearing on the third, major area of difficulty, which concerns the traditional ethic's claim to consistency. Keown's approach initially looks internally consistent but appearances deceive. This becomes particularly apparent when we reflect on the moral load being borne by terms like 'futile' and 'burdensome' treatment. It emerges that the moral load can only be laid down in one of two locations, neither of which Keown wishes to visit.

---

54 Rachels 1986: 92.
55 Burnet 2001.
56 Keown 2002a: 233.
57 See Huxtable 2002a.

Let us start with the words Keown actually uses, when he discusses the possible use of cardiopulmonary resuscitation (CPR) in the hypothetical case of Mary:

> Given that Mary is dying, CPR would offer no prospect of improving her quality of life. It would therefore be medically futile. Moreover, the treatment could well impose grave burdens on her. Not only could it prove very distressing to her, but it could easily, in view of her age and frail condition, result in painful fractures.[58]

Every significant term in this passage requires further ethical evaluation, before Keown's chosen ethic can be said to work. 'Futility', as Halliday summarises, permits of *quantitative* and *qualitative* readings.[59] Qualitatively, a 'futile' treatment will produce an effect but will fail to 'benefit' the patient; quantitatively, the label might be applied when experience suggests that the probability of producing the desired effect is low. But how low is 'low'? And what is the source of the evidence informing this conclusion? Indeed, who counts as 'dying' and who is to make that judgment? Presently this is a matter for doctors,[60] but we should not forget that such judgments, however conscientiously reached, can prove wrong.[61] More fundamentally, both readings shunt us from what *is* to what *ought* to be: they signal that the treatment *is* unlikely to have an effect and therefore it *should* be labelled 'futile' and *should not* be offered.

There are several problematic assumptions here. Why should we view medicine as concerned with the body as a machine, rather than the patient as a whole? What about the effects that offering allegedly futile treatment might have beyond those on the body, such as offering hope to the family? The term evidently 'requires a context of value-laden decisions and positions, a normative social context'.[62] In other words, judgments of futility and burden only acquire meaning when they are informed by prior ethical judgments about the goal of medicine and the nature of the relationship between patient and health professional.[63] And these judgments will, in turn, point us in two very different directions.

The first option is to embrace the instrumental value of life, that is, to have open regard for the 'Quality' of life, as Keown puts it. He denies that this can play any part in the calculations associated with the intrinsic value of life; yet, although David Price sympathises with Keown's concern, he remarks:

---

58 Keown 2002a: 48.
59 Halliday 1997: 149.
60 See *Re A* [1992] 3 Med LR 303.
61 See Huxtable and Forbes 2004; Price 2007: 552–54.
62 Halliday 1997: 151.
63 eg Singer 1993: 211; Brock 1993: 167–69, 198–99.

Quite rightly, it *is* an evaluation of the *treatment* not the patient with which one is concerned here, but the condition of the patient, which would include underlying impairments and handicaps, is an essential pre-requisite of assessing the former.[64]

Their shared concern is that such thinking could lead to judgments of social worth.[65] Raanan Gillon has similarly observed that the word 'futile'

> . . . carries with it a strongly negative connotation – 'uselessness' in the face of life-threatening disease is not generally appreciated, especially in doctors, and the natural anger of a dying person and his or her relatives is often directed not only at the interventions that fail to preserve life but also at the medical and nursing staff who carry them out.[66]

Such judgments appear unavoidably tethered to judgments about the worth of the patient's life. Consequentialist critics of the traditional ethic detect the same evaluation elsewhere in the theoretical framework, such as in the doctrine of double effect, which appears also to signal that death might sometimes be preferable to continued life.[67]

The only way to save the principle seems to involve a radically different line, according to which a vitalistic approach should be taken. Keown, of course, resists this. Indeed, Keown lays some of the blame for the current dismantling of the sanctity of life ethic with Munby QC, whose submissions to the courts in the cases of baby J and Anthony Bland are accused of inaccurately conflating sanctity with something stronger.[68] Of course, the judges are capable of creating this caricature without input from Munby (who is now also a judge).[69] The problem for Keown is that he probably needs the caricature if he is going to escape Quality's embrace. So, argues Kuhse, the only way of avoiding the consequentialist critique is to define the relevant terms so narrowly that life must ultimately be defended at all costs.[70] Price puts this more gently, when he opines that the sanctity of life *'tends strongly towards vitalism* rather than being vitalistic per se'.[71] On both accounts, logic appears to require rather more than Keown wants to admit.

---

64 Price 2001: 643 (I would prefer not to use the term 'handicap').
65 ibid 640.
66 Gillon 1997: 340.
67 Singer 1993: 210.
68 Keown 2002a: 231.
69 *Airedale NHS Trust v Bland* [1993] 2 WLR 316 at 367D–E. For example in *Re C (medical treatment)* [1998] 1 FLR 384 the court apparently believed that Jewish parents were adhering to the sanctity of life ethic, when it looks more likely that they were supporting a stricter (vitalistic?) ethic.
70 Kuhse 1987.
71 Price 2007: 549, emphasis in original.

5.3.2 *The instrumental value of life: worthless lives?*

Either the intrinsic value of life is more stringent that its defenders insist or it is more accommodating of judgments about the relative worth of lives than it claims. The latter theme has also been detected in English law. So how does this approach fare when judged as a moral guide?

The central idea here is that some lives are not worth continuing, given the poverty of the quality (or, according to Keown, Quality) of life endured or anticipated. The judgment – effectively that the patient will be better off dead – is essentially relative, either to the patient's previous quality of life or to the quality of life enjoyed by others. The ensuing argument tends to have a consequentialist tone, with death seen as the best outcome for the patient and perhaps even for others in society. For Mill's brand of utilitarianism, this is expressed in terms of maximising 'happiness';[72] more recently, thinkers like Rachels and Singer prefer to talk of 'welfare'.[73]

These ideas have been applied to incompetent adults and children alike. Harris, for example, does not recognise Anthony Bland as a 'person' – defined, by Harris, as someone capable of valuing of their own existence.[74] A young infant will also fail to qualify, so, Singer continues, neither is owed the full respect due to 'persons' and 'non-voluntary euthanasia' (that is, where the subject cannot consent) can sometimes be in their interests. So, he says:

> When the life of an infant will be so miserable as not to be worth living [and] there are no 'extrinsic' reasons for keeping the infant alive – like the feelings of the parents – it is better that the child should be helped to die without further suffering.[75]

Doyal has developed a parallel argument for incompetent adults like Anthony Bland, which involves recourse to the patient's loved ones, including (but not limited to) the patient's parents.[76]

Beauchamp and Childress agree that it can sometimes be better not to treat the incompetent patient but they do not embrace non-voluntary euthanasia.[77] They also resist any judgment founded entirely on the patient's medical condition; instead, they want the decision-maker, such as the attorney, to be bound by the patient's best interests, 'as judged by the best obtainable estimate of what reasonable persons would consider the highest net benefit among the available options'.[78]

---

72 Mill 1962: 257.
73 Rachels 1993: 46–48; Singer 1993, 1994.
74 Harris 1997: 41–42.
75 Singer 1993: 182–83; see also Hare 1973; Harris 1985.
76 Doyal 2006.
77 Beauchamp and Childress 2001: 138–39.
78 ibid 139. Of course, this raises the question: who is the 'reasonable' person? See eg Coggon 2010a: 551.

These sorts of arguments possess some intuitive appeal.[79] At a glance, Anthony Bland's life scarcely resembles life as many of us understand it. They also have critical bite: Rachels, for example, has famously used a thought experiment to demolish the distinction between acts and omissions on which the intrinsic value of life substantially relies.[80] Smith and Jones are each determined to end the life of their young cousin, in order to receive an inheritance. Smith enters the bathroom in which his cousin is bathing and holds his head under the water until he drowns; Jones enters the bathroom with the same intention and motivation but, noticing the child slip, hit his head and fall unconscious into the water, Jones (merely?) refrains from rescuing him. Rachels finds these situations ethically and logically indistinguishable and he goes on to argue that quality of life arguments can ground a decision to allow the patient to die, so they should equally justify some instances of active killing. If this logic succeeds, then surely the sanctity of life should be swept away by considerations of its quality (or, rather, Quality)?

Clinicians tend to doubt that this demolition succeeds, given how far removed the experiment is from clinical reality.[81] Indeed, quite apart from encouraging the embrace of more active means of causing death, perhaps the experiment instead teaches us to reflect more critically on what we already allow.[82] The tenacity of the distinction between acts and omissions should certainly give us reason to pause before attempting any dismantling. We might similarly hesitate before embracing active non-voluntary euthanasia of patients like Anthony Bland, despite the increase in such proposals both in the academy and in the world's clinics.[83]

Among the main difficulties with the wholesale adoption of the instrumental value of life are that it is not clear what types of judgments and injunctions are required (which also makes the account difficult to apply in practice) and that consistent commitment to the core idea serves to promote some wholly undesirable results. Fundamentally, the quality of life threshold needs to be set: when is a life sufficiently 'miserable' for a scholar like Singer to endorse its ending?[84] And who is to make the call?[85] One might start with a seemingly straightforward case (severe spina bifida is one of Singer's examples) but a hard line will be difficult to discern or defend, when 'suffering' is such a malleable concept.[86] Moreover, once one judgment is made about the poverty

---

79 cf Crane 1977.
80 Rachels 1979.
81 Forbes 1998.
82 cf Burt 2005.
83 Amarasekara and Mirko 2004; Manninen 2006.
84 Singer 1993: 182–83.
85 Recall Taylor LJ's determination in *Re J (a minor)(wardship: medical treatment)* [1991] 1 FLR 366 at 383H–384A that a child's life should be judged intolerable 'to that child', rather than 'to the decider' (see Chapter 2 section 2.2.2).
86 cf Huxtable and Möller 2007.

of existence with condition 'X', say with the support of the patient's relatives, the next might be easier, and the next easier still, until it potentially matters not what the relatives say; life with condition 'X' is not worth living and so effort should not be expended on its continuance. Once the need for 'extrinsic' support begins to fall away, how long before the involuntary ending of life is justified, that is, without the consent of the competent patient? This might seem entirely contrary to the self-determined value of life, but the instrumental value of life – and this alone – cannot tell us that such judgments are 'wrong'. Equally, how long might it be before permission becomes obligation, that is, before a 'duty to die' comes into being?[87]

Singer argues, from consistency, that quality of life judgments underpin much that society already allows, from termination of pregnancy to euthanasia of animals. Thus, he says, we should openly adopt the same judgments in (not) treating incompetent patients.[88] He would be advised, however, to explore further the extent to which such reasoning can be taken. Roger Scruton puts his opposition to Singer's thinking forcefully:

> Anybody who has had to choose between saving a child or a cat from drowning, between feeding his small surplus to his starving neighbour or his starving rabbits, between nursing a dying friend or leaving him out for the vultures, will know that Singer's view is nonsense.[89]

Indeed, it should tell us something that Singer devoted funds to his mother's care when she succumbed to Alzheimer's disease and so, on his account, no longer counted as a 'person'.[90] Sometimes, it seems, the apparently logical appeal of a concept must be bathed in the light of experience.

5.3.3   *The self-determined value of life: autonomy unbound?*

Respect for autonomy, from the Greek *auto* (self) and *nomos* (governance), underpins the idea that life has a self-determined value. The concept dominates healthcare ethics in the developed world; Gillon, for example, sees it as 'first among equals' in Beauchamp and Childress's list of four principles (the others being beneficence, non-maleficence and justice).[91] Philosophers with very different core commitments have signed up: for example, the deontologists, following Kant, emphasise the right to self-determine,[92] while consequentialists, following Mill and Bentham, promote liberty because the

---

87 See eg Hardwig 1997; Battin 2005: 280–99.
88 Singer 1993: 212–213.
89 Scruton 2001.
90 Bailey 2000.
91 Gillon 2003; Beauchamp and Childress 2001. See further Chapter 8 section 8.4.
92 Kant 1991: 90–91; Beyleveld and Brownsword 2001.

preservation of autonomy will lead to the best outcomes in terms of human coexistence.[93] The terminology may vary – it is not uncommon to encounter dignity, freedom and privacy in these discussions[94] – but the basic idea seldom wavers: an autonomous individual should be free to decide what can and cannot happen to his or her body. This decision might be expressed contemporaneously with treatment or specified in advance, such as through an advance statement or through the appointment of a proxy, who would take the decision at the relevant time, purportedly guided by what the patient would want.

Respect for autonomy has immense intuitive appeal and can withstand a great deal of critical probing. There are, however, some problems with the concept and, in the bioethics literature, signs of a backlash.[95] O'Neill neatly summarises the core concern, when she observes how modern theories have tended to 'reduce autonomy to some form of individual independence, and show little about its ethical importance'.[96] She argues that Kant and Mill kept a critical edge to their accounts: Kant's autonomous agent ensured that duties to others were met, while Mill's subject was not guided by the whims of the moment but rather took charge of her desires.[97] Of course, these two thinkers did differ in their arguments and modern thinkers might differ again. The problem here, which Coggon picks up, is that there are competing accounts of respect for autonomy at work in many bioethical discussions (and in law). Coggon detects three categories: current desire autonomy, best desire autonomy and ideal desire autonomy.[98]

Current desire autonomy promotes action which is based upon the agent's unreflective inclinations; these may be the whims of the moment or more durable desires to which the agent has nonetheless directed little or no attention. This concept of autonomy rests on what Frankfurt and Dworkin dub 'first-order desires'.[99] It finds legal expression, says Coggon, in the famous dictum from *Re T (adult: refusal of medical treatment)* [1992] 4 All ER 649 that treatment may be refused by a competent patient 'whether the reasons for making that choice are rational, irrational, unknown or even non-existent'.[100]

Best desire autonomy demands something more of the agent. This version of autonomy leads to an action that reflects the patient's overall wishes, informed by his or her values, even where this is contrary to the patient's immediate

---

93 Mill 1962; Singer 1993.
94 Hill 1991: 44.
95 eg Donchin 2000.
96 O'Neill 2003: 5.
97 O'Neill 2002: 31, 83.
98 Coggon 2007b.
99 Frankfurt 1971; Dworkin 1988.
100 *Re T (adult: refusal of medical treatment)* [1992] 4 All ER 649 at 653 (Lord Donaldson MR). See also *Re B (adult: refusal of medical treatment)* [2002] 2 All ER 449 at paras 81–83, 94, in which Butler-Sloss P cites Atkins (2000).

desire. One might see this, in law, when needle phobic patients are subjected to treatment of which they approve but to which they cannot currently consent.[101] For Frankfurt and Dworkin this better represents respect for autonomy since it reflects an agent's 'second-order desires'.[102]

Ideal desire autonomy asks for something more again: here, the agent's behaviour should reflect what that agent *should* want, as judged against some allegedly objective or universal set of values. This captures the Kantian conception and its successors, like O'Neill's own 'principled autonomy'.[103] Here the agent must acknowledge her place in a community of agents, and be able to universalise the precept associated with her action. We might detect something similar to this account in decisions that overrule a patient's choice because this should not be what he or she wants, in view of other values.[104]

With these fuller accounts of autonomy we can see more clearly why there was such disarray in the cases which sought to give expression to the concept. Unfortunately, the opacity and inconsistency carries over into the ethical domain. It is not apparent which of these accounts should be our guide, nor is it always clear how the given account should play out in practice.

Often, as Coggon appreciates, the three accounts will tend in the same direction. When they do not, however, a choice must be made. Current desire autonomy looks least able to meet the demands of moral theory, and it is telling that Coggon cites no support for this principle. The other contenders appear more robust but, as he concedes, 'the bounds of the legitimate use of the conceptions are unclear'.[105] Best desire autonomy seems to require some way of discerning what the person 'truly' desires. This looks like a sound limitation until we see its potential to limit choice, on the basis that a particular decision does not genuinely reflect the patient's values. It also says nothing about the values in question, which might be questionable indeed. Ideal desire autonomy does purport to say something here, but any objective list of values it seeks to serve will itself need strong defence. In developing the logic of autonomy, we appear to be left with two choices: either we tend towards a wholly-individualistic stance in which 'I want' translates into 'I should get' or we arrive at a more objective position, where I will only get what I want if it features on a pre-approved list of what I should get. Neither extreme seems wholly satisfactory.

Even attempts to give the concept concrete practical expression can fail to work in the real world. Consider Fagerlin and Schneider's demolition of

---

101 cf Coggon 2007b: 249–50, discussing *Re W (adult: refusal of medical treatment)* [2002] EWHC 901.

102 Frankfurt 1971; Dworkin 1988.

103 O'Neill 2002.

104 cf *R v Collins and Another ex parte Brady* (2000) 58 BMLR 173; *R (on the application of Pretty) v DPP* [2002] 1 FLR 268.

105 Coggon 2007b: 246.

advance directives.[106] Although their central concern is with health policy (and expenditure) in the USA, many of their shots also hit targets closer to home. Fagerlin and Schneider identify five problems with advance directives. First, people simply do not execute such statements, and efforts to educate and persuade tend to fail. Secondly, people do not know what they want. Contemporary decisions are challenging enough; harder still are attempts 'to conjure up preferences for an unspecifiable future confronted with unidentifiable maladies with unpredictable treatments'.[107] Thirdly, people cannot articulate what they want: indeed, 'you cannot state clearly on paper what was muddled in your mind'.[108] Drafting such statements is difficult, which is reflected in the evolution from general to specific formulations and, more recently, to the advent of the 'values history' (as if this contributes any clarity). Fourthly, even if these hurdles are cleared, the advance directive will not necessarily be available when it is needed. Finally, the decision-maker might not interpret the directive 'accurately' – assuming, that is, such a reading can be said to exist. As research from the UK suggests, plausible conflicting interpretations might be available.[109] Fagerlin and Schneider conclude that unavoidable facets of human psychology and coexistence conspire to condemn advance directives not only to fall short of the aspirations of self-determination but positively to undermine them.

These are cogent criticisms, which cast considerable doubt on the 'fit' of the theory of precedent autonomy to healthcare practice. It is not even apparent whether such a theory has any business in the affairs of patients who lack autonomy. Arguments abound to the effect that the subject of the advance directive is not the same individual who originally executed the statement.[110] So should the current, competent Odysseus bind the future, incompetent Odysseus? The same might be said (and asked) of the individual entrusted to the attorney or surrogate. These appointments also claim support from respect for autonomy, but once more the reality does not bear out the theory.[111] Evidence suggests that family members of the patient tend to decide according to their own values or through a desire to prolong their loved one's life.[112] Despite its considerable appeal, precedent autonomy, premised on the self-determined value of life, seems to prompt as many questions as those approaches concerned with either the inviolability or the quality of life.

---

106 Fagerlin and Schneider 2004.
107 ibid 33.
108 ibid 34.
109 Thompson, Barbour and Schwartz 2003.
110 See eg Maclean 2006.
111 See eg Samanta 2009.
112 Fagerlin and Schneider 2004: 37.

5.4 Subjective judgments or objective judgments?

In 1995 David DeGrazia detected 'the following hierarchy of medical decision-making standards: (1) informed consent; (2) substituted judgment; and (3) best interests'.[113] Respect for autonomy seems still to dominate both philosophical bioethics and medical law. However, it is not entirely clear that autonomy should trump the application of the best interests standard (or, if so, when), but neither is it evident when the reverse should hold, at least in relation to the provision of life-support. What we have seen on excavating the values buried in the law is that moral theory encounters the same deficiencies and difficulties as the law itself. Whether subjective or objective accounts of the 'right' course should dominate appears to be the main area of tension.

The question 'to treat or not to treat?' thus attracts a variety of answers along a spectrum, from a highly subjective patient-centred pole, all the way to a more detached and impersonal, objective extreme. At the subjective end are claims that what should happen should depend on what the individual patient decides she wants or needs. What the patient wants might be understood (and judged) as an expression of her *current desire autonomy* or in terms of her *best desire autonomy*. What the patient needs might be characterised (and assessed) in terms of what I will label *mental state welfare* or *preference welfare*. Let us take a moment to consider these latter concepts.

DeGrazia's paper attempted to inject the philosophical insights gleaned from value theory into bioethical discussions of best interests. *Mental state welfare* maps onto what DeGrazia describes as the mental state account of prudential value, or 'mental statism'.[114] On this account, the good consists in the possession of certain mental states, such as, for Bentham and Mill, pleasure and the avoidance of pain, or, for some later thinkers, satisfaction, as opposed to suffering or distress. This sort of account of welfare is not without difficulty. What if the mental state experienced is a sham, as depicted in films like *The Matrix*?[115] And where is the harm in painlessly killing someone, even if her or she wishes to continue living?

Worries like these prompt a different account, here dubbed *preference welfare*, in which the good consists in satisfying the individual's desires or preferences.[116] Advocates of this account have insisted on the desire first passing muster as appropriately informed or rational. However, disagreement lingers over whether the individual should (consciously) experience the satisfaction of their preference for it to count as good.[117]

---

113 DeGrazia 1995: 50.
114 DeGrazia 1995: 52–53.
115 ibid: 53.
116 ibid: 53–55.
117 I may desire that you see the film *Star Wars: A New Hope*; this you subsequently do, without me knowing that my desire has been satisfied. Has there been any positive contribution to my welfare?

As DeGrazia acknowledges, both of these versions of welfare 'may be understood as subjective accounts of prudential value';[118] and Coggon's first two categories of autonomy were similarly concerned with the individual, and her subjective desires. But at the opposite extreme are claims that what should happen should depend on what someone other than the individual patient decides they should want or should need. What the patient should want is reflected in *ideal desire autonomy*, in which the ideal desire is formulated in terms of some objective standard. This standard is likely to reflect *objective welfare*, which seeks to determine what the patient should need. DeGrazia notes that objective lists tend to feature concepts such as health and life, although subjectivity can creep in, given the appearance, in some lists, of autonomy.[119]

As DeGrazia implied, there will be a middle ground between subjectivity and objectivity, featuring intermediate accounts like the substituted judgment or even, I would suggest, the appointment of a surrogate decision-maker. Standards like these seem designed to promote decisions, taken by someone other than the patient, which reflect what that person thinks the patient would (rather than should) want if they were currently capable of deciding.

The three accounts of the value of life we have surveyed span the entire spectrum from the subjective to the objective. Thus, the self-determined value of life is capable of encompassing subjective accounts of autonomy (current desire and best desire) and objective accounts (ideal desire). The instrumental value of life also looks amenable to description in either of these terms; quality of life might be judged good or bad by the patient herself, or by some other, on the basis of objective criteria like health. Of course, the intrinsic value of life more obviously occupies objective territory.

The problem remains that there is no simple formula for choosing between these different accounts. As DeGrazia notes, there will be radically different lists of objective goods, such as those promoting life and those promoting quality (or, according to Keown, Quality) of life, 'without any of them being clearly unreasonable'.[120] The critical reflection encouraged by an immanent critique and the critical framework provided by Regan and company can help us to identify the weaker candidates, which are those that fail adequately to satisfy such criteria as clarity, consistency and empirical plausibility.[121] Each extreme has its weakest representative: for the objectivists, this looked like vitalism, which seemed to require an unrealisable commitment to protecting life, while for the subjectivists, current desire autonomy seemed to take too

---

118   DeGrazia 1995: 55.
119   ibid.
120   ibid 60.
121   See Chapter 1 section 1.3.2. Regan's talk of the 'best' (as opposed to the 'right') moral
        theory arguably leaves open the possibility that there will be more than one contender.

permissive a line, in which anything goes. Beyond these likely exclusions, however, the framework has not really helped us to settle on a victor.

5.5 Conclusion: beyond conflict?

It is striking to note that English medical law seems to reflect all of the themes we have encountered in this chapter. Of course, as a result, it looks irrational, as scrutiny reveals 'a plethora of arbitrary definitions and dividing lines which do little to enhance the law's reputation for consistency and rationality'.[122] The fundamental ethical conflict does not entirely bypass the judges. As Butler-Sloss P noted in a widely-reported case of treatment refusal: 'the principles of autonomy and beneficence would appear to be in conflict in this case'.[123] On that occasion, autonomy won out, contrary to the wishes of those who would prefer the intrinsic value of life to hold sway;[124] elsewhere, however, we see autonomy ousted by other concerns, much to the chagrin of its many defenders.[125]

Throughout this chapter we have seen how finely balanced the arguments can be, both for and against treatment at the limits of life, on the basis of one or other account of the value of life. The idea that life has intrinsic value understandably commands great respect but – like the law – apparently depends upon some fine lines and distinctions, plus its own plethora of addi-tional – contestable – concepts, like 'futility'. The instrumental account of the value of life commendably brings suffering and quality of life into focus, but does so at the expense of signalling that some lives lack sufficient worth to merit protection against their premature ending. A currently popular rallying point, respect for autonomy, also does well in allowing each individual to determine the value of his or her life, but threatens to descend into a free-for-all of whimsical assertions and counter-assertions.

In the cases with which we are concerned we do not appear close to consensus, but neither do we appear to have established a conquering concept, capable of providing the answers in all contested contexts. The available answers tack between extremely objective and extremely subjective poles, without providing a wholly convincing case for their own merits or for their rivals' demerits. Yet, still the lawyers, clinicians, patients and their families will require conclusions to the conflicts arising in the clinics. Where and how should such answers be sought? In the next chapter I aim to show that appropriate answers can be found in the space between competing moral positions – at least where certain conditions are present and certain ground rules observed. I will therefore argue that we can move beyond conflict by contemplating not consensus or conquest but, instead, compromise.

---

122 Blom-Cooper and Drewry 1976: 188.
123 *Re B (adult: refusal of medical treatment)* [2002] 2 All ER 449 para 27.
124 Keown 2002b.
125 eg Michalowski 2005; Maclean 2008; Samanta 2009.

6 A case for compromise at the limits of life

In the past decade an increasing number of cases have come before the courts where the decision whether or not to permit or to refuse medical treatment can be a matter of life and death for the patient . . . They are always anxious decisions to make but they are invariably eventually made with the conviction that there is only one right answer and that the court has given it. In this case the right answer is not at all as easy to find. I freely confess to having found it exceptionally difficult to decide – difficult because of the scale of the tragedy for the parents and the twins, difficult for the seemingly irreconcilable conflicts of moral and ethical values and difficult because the search for settled legal principle has been especially arduous and conducted under real pressure of time.

Re A (children) (conjoined twins: medical treatment) [2000] 4 All ER 961 at
968J–969A (Ward LJ)

6.1 Beyond conflict in the clinic: towards compromise

The difficulty Ward LJ describes in reaching the 'right' decision on the fate of the Attard twins amidst 'seemingly irreconcilable conflicts of moral and ethical values' brings to mind the central themes encountered in the previous chapter. In that chapter we saw how the different accounts of the value of life which vie for primacy in English law each carry promise but also peril. This threatens to leave us at an impasse, at which we are unlikely to reach consensus about whether (or not) to treat the incapacitated patient and we are equally incapable of determining which (if any) of the principled positions available is best.

English law seems to reflect this dilemma, in sending different signals about the (legal) value of life. This looked like a problem, at least for rational law, but perhaps that is not the whole story. Maybe, at the substantive level, the law is right to ebb and flow as it does, seemingly sceptical of the merits of allowing any one account to dominate. Various commentators do seem to glimpse a compromise of values in the law, if only fleetingly on their journey towards a destination where one value is proclaimed to be the only 'true' guide. Thus, for Maclean, the formalities surrounding advance decisions to refuse treatment are 'perhaps a reasonable compromise between facilitating the uptake of advance directives and protecting vulnerable patients'.[1] Lyons, meanwhile, thinks the ruling in MB's case did a good job of steering a way through the competing opinions of the baby's parents and doctors, since Holman J seemed to 'identify a middle ground position. Because of this compromise settlement, perhaps *An NHS Trust v MB* is a paradigm case'.[2] To this list, we might add the ruling in the case of minimally conscious M. M's clinically assisted nutrition and hydration was to remain in place, thereby reflecting the intrinsic value of life: as Baker J put it, 'the importance of preserving life is the decisive factor in this case'.[3] Yet, cardiopulmonary resuscitation (CPR) was not to be attempted if M suffered a cardiac arrest, in view of the 'significant harm' that would be caused to M by such an attempt, and the judge left open the possibility of administering antibiotics in the event of an infection.[4] These limits on the obligation to preserve life might comply with the sanctity of life doctrine, in acknowledging the option to forego 'burdensome' interventions, but the judge might have had in mind a different ethic, premised on the instrumental value of life and its concern with avoiding suffering. Here too, then, we might view the courts as seeking to occupy the middle ground.

Not everyone welcomes efforts to find the space between apparently opposing moral positions. The Mental Capacity Act 2005 attempts to preserve the sanctity of life doctrine by insisting that the removal of treatment 'must not, in considering whether the treatment is in the best interests of the person concerned, be motivated by a desire to bring about his death'.[5] Coggon has great difficulty with this section, and understandably so, since it (deliberately?) employs terms with no particular legal relevance, seemingly so that it can preserve the veneer of sanctity, without retreating from the instrumental value of life adopted in *Airedale NHS Trust v Bland* [1993] 2 WLR 316.[6] This, says Coggon, is 'a sorry compromise'.[7]

But how 'sorry' is this? And should the effort to compromise necessarily prompt an apology? I think not – at least, not always. Rotten compromises might rightly be a source of sorrow,[8] but *principled compromises*, which seek to afford space to competing moral perspectives, could be another matter. In this chapter I will mount (and defend) the case for seeking to occupy the middle

---

1 Maclean 2008: 11.
2 Lyons 2010: 193. *An NHS Trust v MB* [2006] EWHC 507: see Chapter 2 section 2.2.2.
3 *W v M and S and A NHS Primary Care Trust* [2011] EWHC 2443 para 249. See Chapter 3 section 3.2.2.
4 *W v M and S and A NHS Primary Care Trust* [2011] EWHC 2443 para 255.
5 Mental Capacity Act 2005 s 4(5).
6 eg Ann Winterton's Medical Treatment (Prevention of Euthanasia) Bill: see Morris 2000.
7 Coggon 2007a: 125.
8 Margalit 2010.

ground, when certain specific circumstances obtain, and subject to particular constraints.[9]

6.2 Contemplating compromise

The cases with which we are concerned involve a particular type of conflict, which we may describe as a *principled conflict*, since it involves a clash of values. The source and nature of the clash might vary in and between particular interests, values, rights and principles;[10] indeed, it might exist in the space between theory and application, as when different advocates of a single principle find themselves in dispute over what it requires of them in practice.[11] One and the same person might sense and experience any of these sorts of conflicts, although, mindful of the cases in which we are interested, it is conflict between one person and another (or others) on which we should concentrate.

What we seek is termination of the conflict.[12] There are many routes by which we might arrive at this destination and no fewer methods by which we might travel. A party might accede, concede or supersede; agreement, appeasement or capitulation might ensue; and such outcomes might derive from direct discussion and dispute or, whether by desire or dictate, from the intervention of some third party.[13] However, not just any resolution will suffice: we need a *principled resolution*.[14] Moral principles will thus constrain the resolutions reached: for example, a brute exercise of power by one party, by which they secure their victory, will probably not measure up. Law too will provide some of the pertinent principles and will accordingly stake out some of the principled boundaries within which the resolution must be sought.[15] Yet, as we have seen throughout the analysis so far, there may be numerous moral principles within law's boundaries; as one judge has put it, there are 'few, if any, absolutes'.[16]

We therefore need some way of deciding which moral principle or principles should guide us out of an ethical conflict. Unfortunately, in the conflicts we have surveyed, success cannot be secured by proclaiming the primacy of

---

9 Earlier versions of the arguments in this chapter can be found in Huxtable 2007: 149ff, 2012a, 2012c and 2012d.

10 Nachi 2004.

11 Winslow and Winslow 1991. Recall that eg parents with purportedly identical moral (Roman Catholic) commitments have reached different decisions about whether or not their conjoined twin offspring should be separated: see Chapter 5 section 5.3.1; see Huxtable 2002a.

12 Golding 1979.

13 See Benditt 1979.

14 See also Dubler 2011, discussed in Chapter 8 section 8.1.

15 cf Golding 1979: 18.

16 *Re J (a minor)(wardship: medical treatment)* [1991] 1 FLR 366 at 937A (Lord Donaldson MR).

one set of moral judgments and principles. It is in such circumstances, I suggest, that compromise might be not merely permissible but also morally laudable. This involves seeking a particular type of resolution: a *principled compromise*, by which compromise is achieved in relation to conflicts of principle, in a manner which is itself also principled.

Understanding of compromise has been advanced by studies in economics, international relations and mathematical game theory but, as Golding appreciated in 1979, the question has been surprisingly neglected in ethical and legal discourse.[17] Pennock and Chapman's collection, in which Golding's essay appeared, helped shed much-needed light on the issues, but progress has otherwise been slow, save for substantial work by Benjamin,[18] and my own more modest contribution, in a previous book focusing upon the bioethical and legal dilemmas attending euthanasia.[19] In the remainder of this chapter I aim to expand considerably on this work and in so doing suggest why there is merit in contemplating compromise in relation to some of the other dilemmas arising at the limits of life.

Etymologically, compromise refers to an agreement which has been reached through mutual concessions;[20] it is, by definition, always suboptimal.[21] The term can refer to the *procedure* (process) by which the mutual concessions are secured, or alternatively to the resulting *product* (solution, end-state, outcome or substance). Kuflik thinks that both features will often be present (to some extent) for each party to a compromise, that is, 'give-and-take by each (process), resulting in some gain and some loss for all (end state)'.[22] The negotiation on which compromise, whether in form and substance, rests can be conducted directly (face-to-face) or through third-party intervention,[23] and it can be consensual or compulsory.[24]

Many have commented on the ambivalent attitude compromise commands: Kuflik, for example, associates compromise with both 'moral turpitude' and 'moral goodwill',[25] and he suggests that there can be both bad and good compromises.[26] Even more positively, Ricœur viewed compromise as 'a barrier between agreement and violence', which 'keeps society from falling apart'.[27] Indeed, many commentators describe compromise as a classic feature of

---

17 Golding 1979; cf Nachi 2004.
18 Benjamin 1990a.
19 Huxtable 2007.
20 Nachi 2004; Cohen-Almagor 2006.
21 Van Willigenburg 2000.
22 Kuflik 1979: 40.
23 Golding 1979.
24 Cohen-Almagor 2006; *contra* Benditt (1979), who doubts that compromise can be forced on a party.
25 Kuflik 1979: 38.
26 See also eg Golding 1979; van Willigenburg 2000.
27 Quoted in Nachi 2004: 297.

democratic societies, in which there is a plurality of people, interests and values.[28] As we shall see, there is much to commend this view. But still compromise attracts criticism, hence the common pejorative sense of the word, according to which one's scruples 'are compromised' or one is found 'in a compromising position'. As Pétrovici noted in 1937, compromise is 'perpetually condemned in theory and always used in practice'.[29] So, what are these theoretical challenges and do they withstand scrutiny?

6.3 Criticising compromise

The disdain with which compromise is often regarded is well captured by Santayana: 'Compromise is odious to passionate natures because it seems a surrender; and to intellectual natures because it seems a confusion'.[30] Here, then, we encounter two standard objections to the idea that compromise can be compatible with morality: that compromise signals a surrender of (moral) integrity; and that, on moral matters at least, to contemplate compromise is to be confused about the nature of morality.

Integrity can be a 'puzzling' term,[31] but the essence of the *surrender objection* is that the compromiser in some sense undoes himself. As Benditt puts it:

> We expect people to stand for something, and we think less of a person who is not willing to espouse any principles, and even worse of one who vacillates . . . So to compromise on matters of principle is to risk a loss of esteem, not only on the part of others, but even on one's own part.'[32]

Where principles are concerned, 'there is an investment of personality'.[33] Benjamin steps in here to argue that we each invest in our own personal world view:

> A *world view* is a complex, often unarticulated (and perhaps not fully articulable) set of deeply held and highly cherished beliefs about the nature and organization of the universe and one's place in it. Normative as well as descriptive – comprised of [sic] interlocking general beliefs about knowledge, reality, and value – a world view so pervades and conditions our everyday thinking that it is largely unnoticed.[34]

28 Kuflik 1979; Winslow and Winslow 1991; van Willigenburg 2000.
29 Quoted in Nachi 2004: 293.
30 Golding 1979: 4–5.
31 Cox, La Caze and Levine 2008.
32 Benditt 1979: 31.
33 ibid 32.
34 Benjamin 1994: 267–68, emphasis in original.

A world view, in turn, structures and grounds a way of life. Integrity, says van Willigenburg, conveys a state of relative *wholeness*, which requires sufficient consistency in one's principled commitments and sufficient coherence between one's principles and one's actions; or, following Benjamin, one's world view and one's way of life. There must also be *wholeheartedness*, that is, sincere self-direction towards particular commitments, rather than slavishly following one's peers or passions.[35]

Holm has criticised the argument, which he attributes to me, that we can compromise (or, in Holm's words, 'agree to disagree') on euthanasia. His attribution may be accurate but, as we shall see, his interpretation of that argument is flawed and there are good reasons to resist his charges. One of his claims is indeed the integrity complaint, since he fears the 'significant cognitive dissonance and unease' that compromise will bring.[36] Certainly, one can see why (on the preceding accounts) compromise seems such an affront to integrity. But we need not admit the offence.

Kuflik counters the surrender objection by reminding us that there is usually more at stake than the disputed issue itself. The promotion or preservation of peace, the avoidance of force, the importance of open dialogue, and the acknowledgement of reasonable moral diversity will all be important features on the landscape of compromise.[37] One's world view (and corresponding ways of being) will admit of such variety; indeed, as Benjamin says, 'our identity is constituted in part by a complex constellation of occasionally conflicting values and principles'.[38] Sometimes these values will change, as we saw in the case of AE, who at different times aligned herself with Muslim and with Jehovah's Witness doctrines.[39] The self might therefore be seen as a web of commitments, rather than an impermeable core set of values.[40] Sometimes consistency must give way to this plurality, in keeping with the complicated entirety of the integrated life. 'The resulting ambivalence is part of the price we must pay to avoid the dehumanization of simple consistency in an unavoidably complex situation', concludes Benjamin.[41]

In a similar vein, van Willigenburg suggests that compromising on some of our values in order to safeguard others might actually preserve (rather than undermine) the wholeness with which integrity is associated. But he does not think that 'anything goes': there must still be fidelity to one's core principles,

---

35 Van Willigenburg 2000: 388. Notice the link here with autonomy, at least in the 'best desire' sense explored in Chapter 5 section 5.3.3.
36 Holm 2010: 4.
37 Kuflik 1979: 51.
38 Benjamin 1990b: 385.
39 *HE v A Hospital NHS Trust* [2003] 2 FLR 408. See Chapter 3 section 3.2.3.
40 See Goodstein 2000: 809.
41 Benjamin 1994: 277; see further Goodstein (2000) on integrity and regret.

that is, to those that express one's specific identity.[42] And he also does not think that we can label someone a 'person of integrity' regardless of the particular principles to which they subscribe. Van Willigenburg refers here to integrity also involving *purity*: we should have no truck with principles that appear to be destructive of humanity, agency and personality as such. Van Willigenburg accordingly sees personal and moral integrity as part of the same continuum, according to which Hitler cannot be dubbed a man of integrity, and personal integrity necessarily involves a commitment to morality's cause. The person of moral integrity could not therefore reach a principled compromise with Hitler. But we are still presented with a problem, since, generally, that person should stand up for what he or she believes are morality's demands. On this account, morality is not a 'negotiable commodity' suitable for compromise.[43] It is here that the *confusion objection* arises: if we are considering compromise on moral matters then we must be confused about the nature of morality.

Numerous moral theories and theorists purport to tell us that they – and, apparently, they alone – can illuminate (or even dictate) the right way to act or the best way to be. To take but a few examples: deontologists point us towards the duties to be acted upon by moral agents, consequentialists steer us towards securing the best outcomes, while virtue ethicists describe the ideal character traits we should exhibit. What they all appear to share is an 'objective' outlook on good and bad, or right and wrong. We each occupy our own 'moral space', but if we encounter a 'transgressor', then morality should be able to distinguish which (if either of us) is right from which is wrong.[44] The 'objective' nature of morality, and hence the contended truth of a particular moral position, would appear to be immune from negotiation and barter.[45] And if we have reason to think that we are right (and therefore in the right) then, leaving aside extraneous considerations, why should we consider accommodating an opponent whom we judge to be morally mistaken?[46]

These considerations lead some commentators to doubt that compromise is either conceivable or possible on those disputed moral issues, like euthanasia, which expose fundamental differences in moral commitment and outlook. Cohen-Almagor, for example, is sceptical about the prospects for compromise where ideology and identity are as intricately engaged as in a case like this,[47] and Tännsjö concludes similarly.[48] Yet, as we have seen, it is Holm who has particular difficulty on those occasions when:

42 Van Willigenburg 2000: 389.
43 ibid 395.
44 Kuflik 1979: 48.
45 Van Willigenburg 2000: 387.
46 See Benditt 1979: 31, 34.
47 Cohen-Almagor 2006: 438.
48 Tännsjö 2007.

. . . it is sometimes claimed that what should happen in a liberal society is (merely?) that the two sides in the debate 'agree to disagree' or 'split the difference' (Huxtable 2007); and the Netherlands is taken as an example of this kind of accommodation.[49]

First, I should clarify that I nowhere defend the view that the Netherlands exemplifies a compromise position on euthanasia (for which reason Holm does well to include his citation of my work before the semi-colon). Although one can detect a social compromise in the policy of pragmatic tolerance adopted in the Netherlands,[50] I see that jurisdiction as adopting a distinctively *permissive* approach to euthanasia, premised on such values as respect for autonomy and the obligation to eradicate suffering.[51] I argue instead that a compromise approach would allow space for these values, whilst also affording room for competing (more *prohibitive*) arguments, premised on the intrinsic value of life and the alleged risks associated with allowing the practice.[52]

However, secondly, and more importantly for present purposes, we must consider Holm's resistance to compromise where one's identity appears to be at stake. Like Golding before him,[53] Holm is open to the possibility of compromise where interests are contested, but he sees values as different, since these are more intimately connected with the disputants' respective world views, and with all the metaphysical commitments these necessarily presuppose. Some ethical disputes will degenerate into irresolvable stand-offs, with the parties becoming more (rather than less) firmly entrenched and each pointing to the alleged absurdities entailed by the other's claims. Although Holm does not mention it, there is an excellent illustration of this in the euthanasia literature, in the exchange between Harris (pro) and Finnis (anti) in Keown's *Euthanasia Examined*.[54] Holm undoubtedly has disputants like these in mind when he mentions those to whom 'the mere suggestion that there is a possible compromise is seen as grotesque and improper'.[55] Holm does foresee other problems with compromise, not least the likely barriers to effective implementation posed by the fragility of the settlement and the dearth of incentives that might entice the more powerful party to compromise, but he is undoubtedly most critical of what he views as the moral incoherence and implausibility of attempts to locate the middle ground.

49   Holm 2010: 1. 'Huxtable 2007' refers to Huxtable 2007.
50   Gordijn 2001: 231.
51   eg De Haan 2002.
52   See further Huxtable 2007, in which I defend the adoption of an offence (and partial defence) of 'assisted dying' (or some other suitable label).
53   Golding 1979.
54   See Keown 1997a: 6–61.
55   Holm 2010: 2.

In order to answer these charges, it is instructive to return to Benditt. Unlike Golding, who wants to focus upon interests, Benditt sees no problem with contemplating compromise on questions of principle. Contemplation of the latter might pose greater conceptual and practical problems than will arise with the former but in both cases, 'strictly speaking, it is not interests or principles that are compromised but claims that have been put forward or policies that are favored'.[56] In short, the conflict is likely to be about some expression or implementation of the underlying principles, rather than the principles themselves. Alternative ways of expressing or implementing the principles are likely to be available, such that positions lying somewhere between those advanced by the opponents can be formulated, that is, 'when principles conflict, there may be *room* for compromise'.[57] And, Benditt continues, the principles might be given different weight in different circumstances without being cancelled out altogether.

Benditt's arguments become more secure when they are anchored in moral (or normative) pluralism. Moral philosophers do not necessarily agree about which moral claims are true; as we saw earlier, deontologists, consequentialists and virtue ethicists will reach different conclusions on this. Indeed, different exponents situated within the same school of thought will also disagree: for example, monist utilitarians who point to a single value (like welfare or pleasure) will not always come to agree on the morally right course in relation to a particular dilemma.[58] Pluralists appear better equipped to account for such moral conflicts: their fundamental point is that there are different values in play, which cannot be reduced to a single overarching value.[59]

Isaiah Berlin, for example, saw conflicts of values as 'an intrinsic, irremovable part of human life'; in the world we do (and even in the world we could conceivably) inhabit, 'we are faced with choices between ends equally ultimate, and claims equally absolute, the realisation of some of which must inevitably involve the sacrifice of others'.[60] According to Berlin, normative pluralism thus requires us: 'to look upon life as affording a plurality of values, equally genuine, equally ultimate, above all equally objective; incapable, therefore, of being ordered in a timeless hierarchy, or judged in terms of some absolute standard'.[61] Normative pluralism therefore holds that there is no one ultimate value from which other principles can be derived

---

56 Benditt 1979: 27.
57 ibid 34.
58 Contrast the different conclusions reached on euthanasia by utilitarians Singer (1993) and Velleman (2004).
59 eg Ross 1930.
60 Berlin 1968: 168.
61 Berlin 1991: 71. Hoffmann LJ also made reference to this passage in his judgment in *Airedale NHS Trust v Bland* [1993] 2 WLR 316 at 355C–D.

('simple-mindedness', says Benjamin[62]) and there is not always a single 'correct' solution to a moral dilemma.[63] W.F. May thus refers to:

> ... the wisdom of the ancient observation that moral principles/laws are true for the most part. 'For the most part' is not a loophole in and through which one escapes into the sea of the relative. They are true for the most part in the sense that they reach their territorial limit in those cases where they must yield to another principle or good ... Further, even in that yielding, the original principle does not simply vanish. It maintains pressure upon one, and how one pursues the supervening good, and it generates in some cases duties of reparation and gratitude for losses imposed and benefits received. Such is the rough landscape of policy-making in which one may need to compromise, not in the sense of defecting from duty but honoring duties which are multiple.[64]

Van Willigenburg picks up this line of argument: sometimes we can establish an order of priority between the various conflicting values or 'duties', but often there will be grounds for indeterminacy, such that we cannot agree upon the relevant criterion for according weight or the criterion tells us that the different values have the same priority.[65] When we find ourselves at such a crossroads, the moral pluralist would permit – perhaps even encourage – us to contemplate compromise.

6.4 Cause to compromise: six reasons to compromise

It seems, then, that rather than compromising on our causes, we will sometimes have cause to compromise. But in which circumstances might this appear permissible or even laudable? Here we should distinguish between those factors which *drive* compromise (ie the circumstances or preconditions which lead one to contemplate compromise) and those which *govern* compromise (ie the ground rules according to which a compromise solution might be brokered or a compromise procedure might be conducted). I will focus first on the former, which appears to comprise six features.

Simple *prudence* provides the initial reason for contemplating compromise, at least in situations where not to do so is to risk losing out entirely.[66] Diluting one's claims makes sound pragmatic sense when the likely alternative is the emptying of the whole draught. If defenders of the intrinsic value of life fail

---

62   Benjamin 1994: 272.
63   Van Willigenburg 2000: 395.
64   May 2003.
65   Van Willigenburg 2000: 396.
66   Benditt 1979: 34.

to press their claims in, say, evidence to (or even membership of) a committee tasked with making recommendations in relation to neonatal intensive care,[67] then disenfranchisement is likely to result. However, once they engage in the process, these same advocates should appreciate the possibility that ground will be lost, as well as gained.

Secondly, *scarcity* of resources can compel compromise. Such limitations will often have an unavoidable – albeit not often overt – bearing on the question: to treat or not to treat? According to Benjamin:

> We often lack the time, money, energy, and other human and natural resources to satisfy everyone's rights or interests, let alone their wants and desires. And when rights or interests conflict because of scarcity, compromise may seem to be both necessary and appropriate.[68]

Thirdly, compromise will undoubtedly look more attractive in situations where a decision is *needed*. Benjamin describes a case in which a nurse and a doctor clash over whether aggressive treatment should be given to a patient.

> To postpone the matter while maintaining present efforts is ipso facto to come down on the side of continued aggressive treatment, and this is exactly what is at issue. If there were a way to 'freeze' the situation to delay taking action until one side is able to persuade the other that it is correct, compromise will be less appealing. But in a hospital as well is in other practical contexts we cannot always suspend judgment and action. In such circumstances compromise may be better than settling the matter by rank or by force or by simply leaving it unresolved.[69]

This need to reach resolution recalls Kuflik's point that we should appreciate more than the issues directly at stake, such as the importance of achieving peace.[70]

Indeed, peaceful *coexistence* also permeates the fourth driver for compromise: the need to preserve the relationship between the disputants. Kuflik seeks to distinguish between the methods of compromise that might be required when the relationship in question is transitory as opposed to longer term but, in either case, I would suggest that the relationship must be safeguarded, even if only for as long as it takes to resolve the present dispute in an otherwise brief transaction.[71] In any case, the relationships with which we are concerned are likely to be more enduring and established, since they will involve

---

67 For example the Nuffield Council on Bioethics 2006; cf Huxtable 2007: 155–58.
68 Benjamin 1990a: 32; see also Kuflik 1979: 49.
69 Benjamin 1990a: 31.
70 Kuflik 1979: 51.
71 ibid 54.

professionals working together, as well as patients and their families coming into contact not only with those professionals but also with the health care system at large.[72] Compromise will be indicated in contexts like these where, as Winslow and Winslow put it, we cannot simply 'quit the game'.[73]

The fifth and sixth features can run together and, as will become apparent, they are also ubiquitous in the cases we have surveyed. Thus, the ethical disputants are likely to be mired in empirical and metaphysical *uncertainty*. Benjamin provides a pertinent illustration, when he refers to ongoing disputes about the nature and significance of 'personhood'. He refers to the philosophically contested status of the embryo but, as we have seen, similar controversies attend infancy and mental incapacity, which might afflict (and thus span) a wide range of individuals, from the demented older patient to one in a PVS. Such metaphysical difficulties are matched by empirical uncertainties, like the prospects 'for seriously ill, low-birthweight infants in newborn intensive care units' and the retention of capacity in individuals with disorders of consciousness.[74] What certainties there are should, of course, be established and conveyed to interested parties as appropriate: misconceptions over, for example, what CPR entails,[75] the properties of morphine[76] and the perceived thirst and hunger of dying patients should be dispelled.[77] Yet, although medical science will progress and knowledge can and will improve, the eradication of uncertainty seems a will-o'-the-wisp.

These problems, in turn, indicate the existence of a final reason to consider compromise: the presence of moral and conceptual *complexity*.[78] Even where the stronger party has the power to impose their will, Benditt believes that uncertainty about their own principled position and recognition of the force of the opponent's case should give them reason to pause: 'An attitude of humility together with a recognition of one's opponent as a sincere and intelligent, though mistaken, surveyor of the moral landscape, seems to me to give one good ground to compromise in a conflict of principles'.[79]

Here we see again the importance of the pluralistic underpinning, according to which we should recognise the indeterminacy of the contested values. Van Willigenburg neatly summarises the indeterminacy we face, which might be ontic or epistemic in origin: either 'there *is* no superior way of mixing values or *we* are unable to rationally trace that superior mix'.[80] In either case, then,

---

72 See eg the case of David Glass, described in Chapter 1 section 1.1.
73 Winslow and Winslow 1991: 311.
74 Benjamin 2003: 138–39; Monti et al 2010.
75 eg Huxtable and Forbes 2004: 349.
76 eg Huxtable 2007: 88–91.
77 eg Dunphy, Finlay, Rathbone, Gilbert and Hicks 1995.
78 See Benjamin 1990a: 29–30.
79 Benditt 1979: 35.
80 Van Willigenburg 2000: 400; see also Tännsjö 2007.

we have reason to countenance compromise. Indeed, coming together in this way might yield broader benefits: as Kuflik comments: 'controversy is sometimes more to be welcomed than lamented, for it can become the occasion for persons to broaden their perspectives and enlarge their understanding'.[81]

Prudence, scarcity, necessity, coexistence, uncertainty and complexity combine to provide the conditions under which compromise might (maybe must) be countenanced. They need not all be present, but the greater they are in number and scale, the more pressing the case for compromise.[82] As should be apparent, each of these features is readily discernible in the dilemmas attending the provision or cessation of life-support at the limits of life. The stage therefore appears to be set for compromise in this context. The next thing to consider is how such a compromise should be played out.

6.5 Constructing compromise: three virtues of compromising

At this juncture it is worth reminding ourselves of the object of our search: we want to resolve a principled dispute. If the resolution is to count as sufficiently principled, then the process by which peace is achieved will need careful attention. Ideally, the process will encourage and enable the parties to reach a principled consensus, such that a strict compromise may not be needed.[83] Through discussion the disputants may therefore come to agree that the arguments on one side of the dispute are most compelling. Winslow and Winslow see less room for splitting the difference as the parties become more certain about the facts, clearer about the concepts in issue, and more convinced about the morality of the case at hand.[84] Even if the parties have not (yet) dispelled their difference through discussion in this way, they will still need to negotiate about the outcomes that seek to split that difference.[85] As such, whether the final resolution occupies the borders of the dispute or some mid-point, the parties need to be able to find the path to that location.

Here, process comes to the fore and with it the factors which should *govern* compromise, that is, the ground rules according to which we might say a compromise can be found. We want the necessary and sufficient conditions of

---

81 Kuflik 1979: 50.

82 See Benjamin 1990a: 32.

83 Smith 1942: 8. Of course, interesting questions might linger about the appropriateness of the consensus, whether it is a true agreement or there has been capitulation, coalition etc. See for discussion of some of these issues eg Moreno 1995.

84 Winslow and Winslow 1991: 320. One is left wondering when it will be possible to say that there is sufficient certainty; these authors do admit that, in the types of moral conflicts in which we are interested, uncertainty will often dominate, such that compromise might frequently be indicated.

85 Sometimes a compromise position can be identified, but even this will require further discussion: see eg Huxtable 2007, discussed further in Chapter 7 section 7.2.3.

compromise, so far as these can be said to exist.[86] This is not necessarily a search for the conditions which govern any compromise; it is, instead, an investigation into the conditions which should underpin compromise on matters of (moral) principle. Where moral principles (or, as Benditt corrected us,[87] our expressions or attempted applications of moral principles) come into conflict and the conditions are favourable towards compromise, we need some ground rules for ensuring that we achieve 'integrity-preserving'[88] or 'principled' compromise.[89]

The relationship between morality and compromise is, of course, amenable to different characterisations. Golding distinguishes between morality *in* compromise and the morality *of* compromise. Recalling the analysis with which this book began, Golding explains how morality *in* compromise

> . . . refers to the question of whether the compromise process requires adherence to certain intellectual and moral constraints as conditions for reaching a compromise, analogously to Lon Fuller's notion of the 'internal morality of law' as a condition for lawmaking.[90]

As Nachi explains, this characterisation regards compromise 'as the profound expression of a "moral sense" '.[91] So, Kuflik continues, if we scrutinise compromise we are likely to find that we can illuminate the nature of morality itself, since at the heart of each will be notions like peace, mutual respect, tolerance and cooperation.[92]

The morality *of* compromise, meanwhile, considers whether and how it is moral to enter into compromise in the first place. Some consideration has already been given to this question, and a case for moral pluralism has been made. Undoubtedly more could be said here, particularly about the relationship between morality *in* and *of* compromise. I would venture that if we have due regard for the morality *of* compromise (and especially the pluralistic position advanced earlier), then we are likely to fix upon the conditions that entitle us to say that we have met the demands of morality *in* compromise. In any event, it is the latter with which I am primarily concerned at this point, that is, the set of conditions that should be met if we are to secure a principled compromise. I suggest there are three such conditions – or virtues of compromising – which require disputants seated at the compromise table to be reflective, reliable and respectful.

86 Golding 1979: 4.
87 Benditt 1979: 27.
88 Benjamin 1990a; Winslow and Winslow 1991.
89 Cohen-Almagor 2006: 440.
90 Golding 1979: 5–6.
91 Nachi 2004: 300.
92 Kuflik 1979: 62; see also Kuflik 1979: 55–62.

The first of what Kuflik would dub my 'constitutional constraints' insists that participants advance *reflective* moral positions.[93] Van Willigenburg comes closest to what I have in mind here, when he mentions affording room to 'plausible arguments endorsed by thoughtful and intelligent people', and remarks that 'only answers that we can reflectively endorse will be answers that we can trust'.[94] His comments also recall Benditt's earlier points about exhibiting 'appropriate humility' and recognising the other as a sincere 'surveyor of the moral landscape'.[95] What this should involve, in the present context at least, is a suitable fit between the purported moral position being advanced and the requirements to which Regan and Pollock referred in the opening chapter. We should not be willing to endorse – as 'moral' principles – any old bias or prejudice; and there should be little place for such non-reflective thinking when we are contemplating principled compromise. As such, the disputants must come to the negotiating table with considered moral positions, which strive to satisfy the criteria outlined at the end of the first chapter.

Secondly, principled compromise requires the participants to be *reliable*. Ideas like good faith and trustworthiness take centre stage here. Such reliability is undoubtedly also intrinsic to the reflective criterion (at least) but the likely importance of this criterion merits it being spelt out in its own right – if only so we can be alert to and seek to temper the strategic problem Benditt perceived, where parties might defend moral positions to which they do not genuinely hold, in an effort to secure a compromise that is closer to their true commitments.[96] As Golding insists, we need each party to 'be trusted to mean what he says and to mean it sincerely – one must tell the truth and sincerely intend to do what one says one intends to do'.[97] In her seminal treatment of autonomy and trust in bioethics, O'Neill reminds us that: 'Trust is not a response to certainty about others' future action. On the contrary, trust is needed precisely when and because we lack certainty about others' future action: it is redundant when action or outcomes are guaranteed'.[98] It does not seem fanciful to suggest that a position of moral conflict is highly likely to be one where certainty is lacking, so an insistence on veracity here should bolster the negotiations.[99]

Thirdly, the participants must deal with one another *respectfully*. This involves a variety of constraints on the negotiation process. Negotiation is the

---

93 Kuflik 1979: 43.
94 Van Willigenburg 2000: 400, 401.
95 Benditt 1979: 35; see also Smith 1942: 13.
96 ibid 36.
97 Golding 1979: 18.
98 O'Neill 2002: 13.
99 cf Cohen-Almagor 2006, who links trustworthiness to negotiation and communication skills.

art of compromise;[100] if it is to be successful, it requires effective communication with one's opponent. And communication, says Golding,

> . . . presupposes a common language. But it presupposes more than this: it presupposes a commonality or, more exactly, a community. The compromise process is a conscious process in which there is a degree *of moral acknowledgement* of the other party. The other party is accorded some degree of *moral legitimacy*, and so are some of his interests. This is the special quality that characterises the cooperative attitude in the compromise process.[101]

Although they note that MacIntyre has mourned the loss of a shared moral language, Winslow and Winslow urge us not to inflate the sometimes 'artificial' problems detected at the level of theory: in practice (and, I might add, probably in theory too[102]), 'disagreements usually exist within wide areas of agreement'.[103] The disputants' interests in peaceful resolution of the dispute are very likely to coincide.[104] What the respect criterion asks of each party is that, in striving for such resolution, they recognise their opposing number and the moral case that party is sincerely seeking to advance.

However, there is more to this criterion, which might variously be described in terms of tolerance, mutuality, cooperation, a 'democratic spirit' or reciprocity. On closer inspection, each of these successive elements seems to build upon the last. We start with tolerance. Although the parties might converge in some of their interests, there will also be some divergence – hence the dispute. As Benditt says:

> . . . if the opponent's interests are different in kind from one's own, compromise is possible only if one recognizes a plurality of interests or some principle of tolerance. A fanatic does not recognize a plurality of interests or a principle of toleration, and a fanatic will not compromise (though he may make deals). Clearly, then, compromise is related to recognizing a plurality of interests or a principle of toleration. It is worth noting that an idealist, though not necessarily rejecting the possibility of a plurality of interests, regards some claimed interests (or merely actual wants) as illegitimate, and is to that extent unable to compromise.[105]

---

100 ibid.
101 Golding 1979: 16, emphasis in original; see similarly Benditt 1979: 29.
102 See Huxtable 2007: 146–49 regarding the options and prospects for consensus in relation to assisted dying.
103 Winslow and Winslow 1991: 316.
104 Golding 1979: 14; Nachi 2004: 296–97.
105 Benditt 1979: 30–31.

Benditt's comments seem no less pertinent in the realm of principles. In that realm, according to Winslow and Winslow, we should seek to understand and acknowledge the different principles in play, by, first, frankly admitting the areas of factual uncertainty, conceptual ambiguity and moral perplexity.[106] Not only will doubt and complexity help to explain why we are at the point of contemplating compromise but they will also help to ground our discussions now that we are. Such openness should enable our opponents to see why compromise is preferable to continuing the dispute or to complete inaction.

Accompanying this understanding of and tolerance for world views other than one's own should be mutual respect.[107] 'Compromise without reciprocal respect is likely to be mere capitulation', say Winslow and Winslow.[108] Such mutual recognition will involve recognising one's opposing party as a morally autonomous agent,[109] which in turn entails a cooperative attitude, as Golding outlines:

> The fact that the parties accord one another a degree of legitimacy has an important implication: it enhances the roles of rational argument and moral considerations in the compromise process. The party will have to attempt to *persuade*, rather than intimidate, the other side to accept its offers. It must do this by appealing to norms accepted by the other side. So the bargaining is conducted under intellectual and moral constraints, and it begins to take on the characteristics of a debate.[110]

Bargaining in this manner should enable the disputants to approach Kuflik's ideal of mutual accommodation.[111] The democratic temperament to which Benjamin, Nachi and many others refer is evidently closely entwined with the cooperative attitude on which principled compromise depends.[112]

The cooperative attitude obviously affects the compromise process but, notably, the same attitude places constraints on the outcome which might be reached through such negotiation, that is, on that which can be described as a principled compromise in substance (as well as in form). For Golding, 'bargaining in "good faith"' means 'responding to a concession with a concession'.[113] Van Willigenburg takes up this argument. For him, mutuality 'will

---

106 Winslow and Winslow 1991.
107 cf Cohen-Almagor 2006.
108 Winslow and Winslow 1991: 317.
109 Cohen-Almagor 2006; van Willigenburg 2000. We will return to the question of autonomy in the next section.
110 Golding 1979: 17–18, emphasis in original.
111 Kuflik 1979: 43.
112 Benjamin 1990a; Nachi 2004.
113 Golding 1979: 17.

favour evenly balanced compromises (splitting the difference)';[114] a 'willing-ness to strive for some balance in the sort and amount of concessions by different parties'.[115] Balance need not mean absolute equality, however. Van Willigenburg also thinks that there should be due recognition of situations in which the stakes are considerably higher for one party than for the other. A degree of agent-relativity is therefore required, since there will be circum-stances which are not fully appreciable from a subject-neutral perspective; for example, where, from the perspective of one party, the position and person we are contemplating 'is the result of *my acts*, and this other person is *my* child or friend or fellow countryman'.[116] Mutual respect seems therefore to require appropriate recognition of those intimately implicated in the conflict (at least, where one party in particular appears to have more at stake) and attention to such issues as the balance of power around the negotiating table.

These three requirements – that the participants be reflective, reliable and respectful – are undoubtedly closely linked. Taken together they might be described as the virtues or 'internal morality' of principled compromising, that is, the conditions which must be satisfied if an integrity-preserving compromise, premised on ethical pluralism, is to be attained. Like some other attempts to resolve disputes over values, they emphasise *process* over product, such that a principled outcome is sought through compliance with a princi-pled process.[117]

6.6 Conclusion: compromise in theory and practice

Although the idea can be met with scepticism and hostility, principled compromise is not an oxymoron.[118] The concept could benefit from further critical inquiry but there is much that can already be said. Complexity and uncertainty, both in the realm of values and in the realm of facts (as far as these can be separated[119]), are at the centre of the case for compromise. But so too

---

114 Van Willigenburg 2000: 400.
115 ibid 401.
116 ibid 402.
117 For example Daniels and Sabin (1997) have developed procedural criteria for ensuring 'accountability for reasonableness' when people disagree about the principles that should determine priority-setting in situations of scarcity. Their process, which has been adopted in the development of guidance by the National Institute for Health and Clini-cal Excellence (NICE 2008), involves: transparency about the grounds for decisions; appeals to rationales which should be shared by fair-minded citizens who recognise their obligations to cooperate; and procedures for revising decisions in response to challenges. Like the virtues of compromising (and, indeed, the rule of law, discussed in Chapter 1) their process requires mutual respect and has, at its core, a democratic spirit, such that there may well be merit in combining the two. This is work that might be usefully taken up elsewhere.
118 Goodstein 2000: 805.
119 See eg Gouldner 1962; Smajdor, Ives, Baldock and Langlois 2008.

are inadequate resources and the inability to honour every competing value, coupled with a prudent desire to ensure that one's values are voiced, an ongoing relationship with one's moral opponents and the need to reach a decision on a contested issue. The circumstances are ripe for compromise when such features are present in sufficient number or scale. The achievement of a principled compromise presumes communication and negotiation between the positions available and their respective defenders. In order for them to arrive at a principled compromise, they must be appropriately reflective, reliable and respectful in their dealings around the compromise table.

There is good reason to apply these insights in the context of withdrawing and withholding life-supporting treatment from incompetent patients, both young and old. Each of the circumstances driving compromise is present here: personhood, capacity and even death are strongly contested concepts in morality and science; the morality of abating treatment continues to divide discussants; and, in any decision, policy or recommendation, there is the risk that opposing viewpoints can be overlooked too easily. Yet, still these diverse discussants will occupy the same territory (literally) and a decision cannot be ducked: when the conflict concerns whether or not to treat an incapacitated patient, even no decision is a decision in one direction or another.

English law therefore appears to have good reason for accommodating different moral outlooks, even sometimes apparently in a single ruling, like those in the cases of *MB* and *M*, as we saw at the outset of this chapter. But does English law do enough to satisfy the conditions associated with *principled* compromise? I will take up this question in the next chapter, in which I will consider how best to translate the theory of principled compromise into practice.

7 Crafting compromise

Courts or clinical ethics committees?

> We observe . . . that it would be far better if judges were not called to patients' bedsides and required to make quick decisions on issues of life and death. Because judgment in such a case involves complex medical and ethical issues as well as the application of legal principles, we would urge the establishment – through legislation or otherwise – of another tribunal to make these decisions, with limited opportunity for judicial review.
>
> *Re AC*, 573 A2d 1235 (DC 1990) at 1237 (Terry J)

7.1 Conflicts in the clinic revisited: to treat or not to treat?

To treat or not treat? This book began by asking this seemingly simple – albeit fundamental – question, in relation to a range of critically ill patients who are incapable currently of expressing their views on the matter. The question was premised on the existence of conflict, such as might be detected between the professionals caring for a patient and the members of his or her family. High-profile cases like those of David Glass, Charlotte Wyatt and Terri Schiavo exemplify the dilemmas that can arise. Less acute cases, like that of Mr W from the introduction to the book, will also be familiar in the health care setting, although these too will not be free from difficulty and anxiety for the parties involved.

The existence and persistence of such conflict should not be overstated, but neither can it be denied. Where conflict is present, an answer will be needed and, indeed, unavoidable, since even failure overtly to tackle the matter will lead to an outcome, such as continued treatment, or failure to treat. Law tends to reign supreme here since, by its very nature, law is concerned with guiding human behaviour through the imposition of rules. But the problem we have seen is that the law which seeks to govern these cases fails frequently to do so: the rules are absent, inconsistent or unclear, making it difficult to say how best to answer the fundamental question.

The reason why law appears to fare so badly in guiding behaviour is that it seeks to give expression, and afford respect, to competing ideas of what it means to value life in cases like these. The legislation and jurisprudence seek simultaneously to declare that the value of life is a matter for the individual, and that it has an intrinsic worth, thus meriting protection from premature ending, and that its value resides in the uses to which it can be put, such that failing 'machines' need not be repaired. In doing so, the law oscillates between the personal and subjective at one extreme, and the abstract and objective at the other.

On this view, conflict in the clinic and in law will often derive from conflict between ethical principles – *principled conflict*, as I described it earlier. Little wonder, then, that the emergent legal messages appear so confused. Yet, a case can be made for commending not only English law's capacity but also its willingness to accommodate a plurality of ethical viewpoints in these cases. On this view, law is trying to do the right thing by articulating a compromise at the level of principle, that is, affording space to plausible, competing values, through its dealings with precedent autonomy and the best interests of incompetent patients. The problem nevertheless remains that professionals, parents, proxies and even patients are left in confusion and uncertainty, since they do not know whether, for example, respect for autonomy or the sanctity of life will be the ultimate guide in any individual case; and nor can they necessarily conclude which *should* be their guide.

What we appear to need is a mechanism that is capable of providing an answer to the fundamental question, 'to treat or not to treat?', and thereby guiding the affected parties, and resolving the conflict. But we need more than this: we need the mechanism in question to be capable of drawing hidden – but undeniably influential – values out into the open, so that they can be scrutinised, with a view to securing not only resolution but *principled resolution*. In other words, what is needed is a place in which the values that obtain in any given case can be investigated, and practical proposals plotted.[1] Although there may be a myriad of contenders, in this chapter I will consider two prime candidates: the courtroom and the clinical ethics committee. We will see that neither forum is entirely up to the task, although each has its merits, such that – in Chapter 8 – our concluding discussion will concern how best to capitalise on the opportunities, whilst avoiding the major risks.

7.2 Viewing values in the court

I suggested, in the previous chapter, that the principled compromise table will be a place where values can be examined, with a view to resolving principled disputes, and thus guiding the parties who find themselves in conflict. The achievement of principled compromise presupposes that the parties are capable of articulating their positions and bargaining effectively. Such

---

1 This may require some engagement with matters more often associated with the political realm: see Coggon 2010a.

bargaining will be bound by three ground rules, which hold that the parties will: advance reflective moral positions; behave sincerely, such that their opponents can rely on their words and deeds; and negotiate in a reciprocal, mutually respectful fashion, in which they recognise the legitimacy of their opponent's interests. The peaceful coexistence of people with diverse moral perspectives is at the heart of the principled compromise process. The presence of a third party can help to ensure that the negotiation stays on these tracks. Is this a role suitable for members of the judiciary?

7.2.1 *For the courts as vehicles of values*

There are three particular features of the judicial enterprise which suggest that a compromise table can indeed be moved into the courtroom. First, the courts are already engaged, to some extent, in the sorts of *value enquiries* we seek. Some members of the judiciary openly acknowledge the ethical import of their endeavour: Lord Coleridge CJ famously opined that 'It would not be correct to say that every moral obligation involves a legal duty; but every legal duty is founded on a moral obligation',[2] a sentiment echoed by some of his successors in *Airedale NHS Trust v Bland* [1993] 2 WLR 316.[3] On occasion, the courts have also been willing to examine the particular ethical commitments professed by the health care professionals they encounter, which are enshrined in guidance issued by the General Medical Council (GMC) and the like.[4] There are also moral presumptions stitched into the very fabric of the law, such as the presumption that illegal contracts are unenforceable.[5] All of this suggests that the language of ethics can be translated into the language of law. Indeed, the legal lexicon in the cases we have considered appears sufficiently flexible (or malleable?) that it can convey the plurality of ethical positions and thus the main parameters of principled disputes. Precedent autonomy and best interests each find a place in English law and permit of sufficiently broad interpretation as to facilitate reflection on the values they might ensnare in the individual case. By such means communication, on which compromise relies, is fostered.

Secondly, the courts have *authority*, which will be useful in setting the legal parameters within which resolution may be sought and in settling ongoing disputes. Judges therefore tend to be the officials most obviously empowered to declare which behaviours or outcomes are il/legal. Jurisprudential disagreements about whether the judicial role really involves making, as opposed to

---

2 *R v Instan* (1893) 1 QB 450 at 453 (Lord Coleridge CJ).

3 *Airedale NHS Trust v Bland* [1993] 2 WLR 316 at 379H–380A (Lord Lowry) and at 380D (Lord Browne-Wilkinson).

4 eg *R (on the application of Burke) v General Medical Council* [2005] 3 WLR 1132. See Miola 2007.

5 eg Golding 1979: 18.

declaring, law might persist,[6] but either way the judges are able to declare when a purportedly principled compromise has crossed the line into illegality. The judges can also say when a particular result *must* obtain; in other words, they have the power to make a principled compromise attainable, since their decisions are backed by sanctions. Decisions will therefore be binding, with evidence given under oath, and there are rules and procedures governing contempt of court and the like. Such backing can promote the goal of action-guidance, whilst helping to ensure that ground rules such as reliability are observed.

Thirdly, the courts aspire to *procedural rigour*, with rules governing such matters as rights of audience, equality of arms (in the sense of evidence disclosure) and the role of expert witnesses. Rules like these can help to ensure that each of the parties has their case heard, thus promoting communication and negotiation, which is reflective, reliable and respectful.

7.2.2 *Against the courts as vehicles of values*

Although the courts therefore could be viable vehicles for values-based decision-making, there are at least three obstacles in their path. First, and central to the analysis in this book, there is the objection that the courts frequently fail to issue sufficient guidance. Secondly, underpinning these failures, there is the persistent ethics-resistance of the judges. More common than remarks like that from Lord Coleridge CJ (above) are comments to the effect that 'I myself am not concerned with any ethical issues which may surround this case',[7] and 'this is a court of law, not of morals'.[8] Even where the ethical dimensions of a case do come to the fore, as in *Bland*, many judges would prefer to look away or to push the problem in the direction of some other, purportedly more suitable, arbiter (like Parliament). But the ethics of the case at hand do not simply evaporate and, as such, they deserve more substantial scrutiny than they currently receive.

What scrutiny there is would scarcely satisfy the standards Regan and Pollock would set for moral discourse:[9] hasty reference to a single – contested – argument about the primacy of respect for autonomy does not count as a robust assessment of the merits of the ethical arguments.[10] Parodies of autonomy and welfare fail to convince.[11] Neither is the plurality of ethical

---

6 Dworkin 1975.
7 *An NHS Trust v MB* [2006] EWHC 507 at para 24 (Holman J).
8 *Re A (children) (conjoined twins: medical treatment)* [2000] 4 All ER 961 at 969 (Ward LJ). See also eg *R (on the application of Pretty) v DPP* [2002] 1 FLR 268 at para 2 (Lord Bingham).
9 See Chapter 1 section 1.3.2.
10 See *Re B (adult: refusal of medical treatment)* [2002] 2 All ER 449 at paras 81–83, 94 in which Butler-Sloss P cites Atkins (2000); see also Nagasawa (2004).
11 Dunn and Foster 2010.

perspectives available on a particular scenario necessarily represented. As we saw in the previous chapter,[12] unlawful outcomes fall outside principled compromise – but this does not mean that lawfulness entirely equates to ethicality. Significant ethical arguments may be left out of the legal account, such as resource considerations in cases concerning the provision of costly life-prolonging treatment.[13] Those ethical viewpoints that are explicitly allowed in – as provided by *amici curiae* – tend to offer a distinctive religious (Christian or Catholic) account.[14] We might therefore doubt whether all the (appropriate) voices are heard, especially in a system where appeals to law are seldom cheap. Little wonder, the critics might say, that conservatism reigns in the rulings, with doctors trumping families, and life trumping choice. On this account, the effective and sincere communication on which compromise relies is not best served by the courts.

The fact that one party can trump another discloses a third problem with the courts' capacity to craft compromises: courts are adversarial arenas, in which conflicts may be settled, but seemingly only by a loser submitting to a winner. This inclination towards 'winner-take-all outcomes'[15] seems to be not only ill-suited to the clinical encounter,[16] but also at odds with the compromising spirit.[17] Indeed, sometimes there appear only to be losers: Charlotte Wyatt's case, for example,

> ... ended in a lose-lose-lose situation: an embittered and fragmented family, a child in foster care and six-figure costs for the hospital trust. The medical staff were left feeling battered and bruised and there was no real closure to this tragic case.[18]

As Meller and Barclay comment:

> Using the courts to decide cases of ethical complexity inevitably leads to a position in which there are perceived to be winners and losers in situations which are not black and white, but are often composed of multiple shades of grey which would be better resolved by ethically acceptable compromise.[19]

12 Chapter 6 section 6.2.
13 cf Alldridge and Morgan 1992.
14 eg *Re A (children) (conjoined twins: medical treatment)* [2000] 4 All ER 961; *R (on the application of Pretty) v DPP* [2002] 1 FLR 268; see Skene and Parker 2002.
15 Shapiro 1979: 173; cf Dworkin 1996: 7, 165.
16 Ward Platt and Ward Platt 2005: 331.
17 Although Shapiro (1979) argues that compromise and the courts are not mutually exclusive.
18 Meller and Barclay 2011: 620.
19 ibid 619.

7.2.3 *Law and ethics in the courts and beyond*

We find ourselves at another crossroads: one fork points us towards the courts as the location for principled compromise; another fork points us away. In their favour, the courts have procedural rigour and the power to decide; they are equipped to guide. Legal officials are, as Annas notes, 'expert at procedure'.[20] Sheila McLean adds that law's capacity to direct action is also beyond doubt:

> ... irrespective of the ethical views of decision-makers – legal or medical – there are rules under which they must operate, like it or not. Whether or not they are based on moral obligations ... they nonetheless are superior (in practical terms) to the outcome predicted by adherents to one ethical school of thought or another.[21]

On this account, law triumphs over other alleged authorities – like moral philosophers – who purport to say how we should (not) live. As Birks puts it:

> Moral philosophers are not obliged day by day to solve the real problems of real people, nor are they called to daily account to justify to those same real people the substance of their tenets and the even handedness of their procedures. The law by contrast is under constant surveillance. Vigilant critics quite rightly pick over the substance of every judgment. And it is an unrelenting question whether, through time, but allowing for the changes of perception which come with the passage of time, the courts are or are not, can or cannot be, true to the aspiration impartially to treat like cases alike.[22]

James also recognises the burden of the judicial task,[23] recalling Thorpe LJ's extra-judicial opinion that

> ... what is consistent in principle may not be practical in application. It is, perhaps, easier for an appellate court to discern principle than it is for a trial court to apply it in the face of judicial instinct, training and emotion ... The responsibility and sense of duty of the judiciary are no less in the Family Division than in the other Divisions, but it is, perhaps above all for their humanity that they are appointed.[24]

---

20 Annas 1992, quoted by Jonsen 1998: 343.
21 McLean 2007a: 196.
22 Birks 2000: 2–3.
23 James 2008.
24 Thorpe 1997: 663–64.

These references to humanity and duty remind us that the judges do not wholly eschew the moral dimensions of their work. But, McLean insists, these latter dimensions come second to the law:

> Commitment to a particular ethical position may not be sufficient to guide practice, particularly when there are legal rules which differ from it or which require that other values are more important. Ethics and law are ultimately both interlinked and separate.[25]

The interlinked point is surely right, perhaps more than McLean would admit. It is, after all, frequently the case that health care law cannot do its job without recourse to the ethical framework on which it rests. In short, legal arguments will often appeal to ethical justifications. Disputes about the *necessity* of this relationship are, of course, long-standing, as ongoing debates between natural lawyers and legal positivists demonstrate.[26] Amongst the more famous exchanges was that between Hart and Devlin about the legal enforcement of morality.[27] An additional layer of complexity has been added by the advent of 'bioethics' in the 1970s, which Brownsword sees as occupying the midway point between the respective domains of law and morality.[28] Philosophical and theological arguments about moral concerns have made a significant impression in this new field, but so too have contributions from the law. Annas, for example, believes that:

> American bioethics has been driven by the law . . . The stress on autonomy and self determination comes from our Bill of Rights, our Declaration of Independence and the whole common law tradition. And law's primary contribution to bioethics is procedural. Lawyers are expert at procedure. The common law itself is based on deciding individual cases and using these cases as the basis of creating law. Bioethics has adopted this technique. In the United States, with its pluralism of beliefs and people, the law is what holds us together. There is no other ethos. Thus, the law – procedural, autonomy based and case focused – came into bioethics.[29]

However, the transfer of ideas that Annas describes does not flow equally in both directions, since bioethical discourse – at least that which is associated with its academic expression – cannot necessarily claim to shape the law, neither in America nor, indeed, in England and Wales. James remarks that 'English judges have only slowly, indirectly and tacitly absorbed academic

25 McLean 2007a: 196.
26 See Chapter 1 section 1.2.1.
27 Hart 1963; Devlin 1965.
28 Brownsword 2008.
29 Annas 1992, quoted by Jonsen 1998: 343.

critique into their decisions'.[30] Legal training retains a distinctive vocational character, with extra-judicial opinion seen as lacking the requisite authority. Formally, at least, the judges decline to cite living academic scholars. Naturally, there are exceptions: as we saw in Chapter 5, academic articles anticipating a case like *Bland* featured in the actual ruling,[31] while Keown's opinion on the sanctity of life appeared alongside Sheldon and Wilkinson's pioneering analysis of the surgical separation of conjoined twins in *Re A (children) (conjoined twins: medical treatment)* [2000] 4 All ER 961.[32] Yet, reference does not equate with influence, as indeed we see in *Re A*, in which the Court of Appeal managed to depart from the scholarship on which it purportedly relied.[33]

Having said all this, ethical considerations do, as an undeniable matter of fact, continue to exert influence on medical law; the two domains enjoy (or endure?) what Miola dubs 'a symbiotic relationship', each reliant on the other.[34] We have seen how different accounts of the value of life have their counterparts in law. Confronted with these rival ideas, law seeks a compromise of principles. Unfortunately, this prompts considerable confusion, since competing ethical principles are advanced, often discretely and covertly (perhaps even hidden from the judges themselves). This carries both the opportunity and the threat of indeterminacy;[35] a threat, since we are left with no clear way out of any conflict; an opportunity, because a plurality of answers appear to be available. The compromise that law has reached effectively signals that sometimes the intrinsic value of life will be our guide, sometimes the instrumental value (and thus quality) of life, and sometimes the patient-led, self-determined value of life. By plotting these three points, the law takes a position on the ethical boundaries within which clinicians and families must operate.

These boundaries look defensible: as I argued in Chapter 5, there are sound arguments for not allowing any one of these three positions to dominate and thus deny its rivals any dominion. Indeed, law might reasonably be tasked with holding the line and thus ensuring that the overall compromise persists.[36] Three examples should help to clarify this idea. First, the instrumental value of life could continue to feature in decisions to withdraw life-support from the critically ill, but legal and policy officials might reasonably resist any proposals

---

30 James 2008: 68.
31 See Chapter 5 section 5.1.
32 Keown 1997b; Sheldon and Wilkinson 1997; see also Chapter 5 section 5.2.
33 Huxtable 2000b, 2001, 2002a.
34 Miola 2007.
35 cf Doyal 1990; Doyal 2001: 145–46.
36 In the words of Hedley J, in *Trust A, Trust B, Dr V v Mr M* [2005] EWHC 807, the judges can 'stand sentry at the fence', which separates the permissible from the impermissible (para 12: see Chapter 3 section 3.2.1).

to embrace neonaticide, of the sort practised under the Groningen protocol in the Netherlands.[37] Secondly, precedent autonomy might rightly retain a role in relation to advance decision-making, albeit constrained by a prohibition on honouring patients' demands and on requests for interventions like assisted dying.[38] Finally, the sanctity of life, and its associated bundle of ideas, can still furnish the law with its primary preoccupation with preserving life – but, again, within limits, such as (for example) that there be no greater restriction like that sought by MP Ann Winterton in her Medical Treatment (Prevention of Euthanasia) Bill, which would have reversed *Bland*.[39]

Within the middle ground between these principles there is bound to be ample scope for choosing an answer which best suits the individual case. But how are we to decide which *particular* answer is best? Here our attention should shift from the *substance* of the compromise achieved in English law back to the *procedures* – and thus the ground rules – for achieving principled compromise and thus principled resolution. In the absence of agreement, negotiation is vital – even if we believe that a middle ground position exists, which splits the difference between the disputants. For example, I have suggested that a specific offence (and partial defence) of 'assisted dying', could be made available as an excuse rather than a justification, as this can split the difference between ethical arguments for and against the practice.[40] However, I have also acknowledged that the proposal needs further debate before we could expect to see any agreement on the matter.[41] The need for discussion is possibly even more pressing in the present context, where the 'right' mixture of values appears to be beyond our grasp.[42] In such cases, the ground rules for principled compromise will help guarantee that the various arguments are heard.

Importantly, there might be no 'one-size-fits-all' outfit in the pluralistic wardrobe: different mixtures of values might be appropriate according to the individual case and the parties around the compromise table. This conclusion is in keeping with the ontic uncertainty underlying the case for compromise.[43] It may be, then, that the outcome in an individual case more closely resembles or rests on one principle rather than another. As May put it, cited in Chapter 6, we are looking to establish when a principle has reached its 'territorial limit [and thus] must yield to another principle'.[44] Such 'yielding' will be appropriate if all of the valid contenders have reached the table and they have all

37 Manninen 2006.
38 See further Huxtable 2007.
39 Morris 2000.
40 Huxtable 2007.
41 ibid 172.
42 Benditt 1979: 34; van Willigenburg 2000: 399.
43 Van Willigenburg 2000: 399.
44 May 2003; see Chapter 6 section 6.3.

been scrutinised according to the ground rules. The legal picture as a whole will need to be depicted on a sufficiently broad canvas to accommodate a plurality of perspectives. Provided that such space is provided, then individual cases might in theory feature anywhere on that canvas.

Of course, law can help to determine where on the canvas the particular case should feature. On this account, law not only provides space for compromise, but also has the requisite authority for imposing an outcome. In doing so, law still needs to ensure that the overall compromise obtains. But it also needs help in securing the requisite ethical oversight, apparently now more than ever. Writing about America, Dan Callahan suspects that

> . . . there has come to be some enormous moral vacuum in this country, which for lack of better institutional candidates has been left to the law to fill. The churches are either too sectarian or too morally bland, the universities too caught up in professionalism or culture wars, the journals of opinion tiresomely focused on the religious right (the left) or assaulting politically correct liberals (the right), and political life reduced . . . to nasty negative attacks on anything and everyone. That leaves the law. It is relatively free of scandal, still generally respected, national and relatively uniform in its scope, and ready to take on ethics if that is what gets served up to it for the making of decisions. It may be the best institution we have, but it is a poor substitute for moral consensus and public debate on ethics.[45]

His comments also resonate closer to home. Montgomery certainly feels that English law is an increasingly 'poor substitute' to ethical evaluation: he bemoans the 'demoralisation' of contemporary medical law, from which ethical dimensions are being squeezed out, with health professionals' morale correspondingly being undermined.[46] Citing Morgan and Lee's reference to 'stigmata cases',[47] Montgomery suggests that

> . . . litigation provides a context in which the values of a society can be expressed and also a mechanism whereby clashes of competing values can be resolved. However, a new type of case is emerging that actually obscures such value conflicts and in which the translation of conflict into the discourse of law excludes moral debate rather than enables it to be addressed.[48]

45 Callahan 1996: 34.
46 Montgomery 2006.
47 Lee and Morgan 2001; see Chapter 4 section 4.5.
48 Montgomery 2006: 190.

Delegation to doctors in a ruling like *Re A* is a case in point. In such cases, formal issues take priority over substantive moral arguments; in short, legal positivism – in which legal discourse is divorced from its moral spouse – reigns, with the result that 'the stigmata of our value system will no longer appear on the bodies of our judgments. The morality will be sucked out of them'.[49] Medical law, now in the hands of judges like Munby J, becomes more law-like but correspondingly less ethics-alert. We could try to insist that the judges have open regard and give due weight to the ethical parameters of the cases before them, but (as the judges' earlier comments imply) our chances of success would seem to be slim. Perhaps, then, we are better off looking elsewhere for the missing ethical scrutiny.

7.3 Viewing values in clinical ethics support

Resolving conflict is not only a matter for the courts: amongst the alternative mechanisms for dispute resolution are mediators and tribunals, which need not be as costly (in all senses) as recourse to law.[50] Use of these mechanisms may well shed light on the ethical roots of a given dispute.[51] However, I want to focus upon a forum which, as its name implies, has ethical scrutiny at the core of its endeavour: the clinical ethics committee (CEC).[52] I will argue that this committee has the credentials necessary for achieving principled compromise, since it is capable of encouraging reliable, reflective and reciprocal negotiations, in which the interests of different participants are acknowledged. It can thereby do some of the work of a mediator – 'moral mediation', if you will – and some of the work of the court. Indeed, a committee can also operate within the limits of principled compromise, bounded – and thus led – by the law. Work undoubtedly needs to be done to ensure that such committees deliver on their potential; before considering (in the next chapter) what this work will involve, we need first to appreciate why there is value in expending such effort.

7.3.1 *For the ethics support of clinical ethics support*

Clinical ethics support is on the rise in the UK: in 2000 there were 20 CECs, but the number had risen to 75 in 2007.[53] Although support is sometimes available from individuals and the small but growing number of academic departments dedicated to ethics in medicine, committees tend to dominate

---

49 Montgomery 2006: 192.
50 See eg Ward Platt and Ward Platt 2005; Allen 2005; Mulcahy 2006; Meller and Barclay 2011.
51 See Meller and Barclay 2011; cf Nuffield Council on Bioethics 2006: 145–47.
52 Other labels are sometimes used eg clinical ethics advisory group.
53 Larcher, Slowther and Watson 2010: 30.

the field.[54] Such committees typically have consultative, supportive and educational functions, advising on individual cases and on policy in the local area, whilst also enlightening professionals about the ethical dimensions of their practice. Although there is no formal framework governing such work in the UK, the UK Clinical Ethics Network (UK CEN) has facilitated correspondence between committees and has taken the lead in setting standards (and, to some extent, standard operating procedures),[55] spurred on by reports from the Royal College of Physicians[56] and the Nuffield Council on Bioethics.[57]

There are three features of clinical ethics support – especially as conducted by committee – which suggest that it has the capacity to craft compromise. These concentrate respectively upon its goals, ethos and expertise. First, despite worldwide variations in the delivery of clinical ethics support, the endeavour is uniformly directed towards action, and important similarities can be detected in its *goals* and associated core competencies, many of which chime with principled compromise.[58] Writing in the US in the early 1990s, Fletcher and Siegler described the central goals of clinical ethics support as: facilitating the resolution of conflicts by identifying the interests, rights and duties of those involved; helping to generate policies and practices consistent with ethical standards; and helping individuals to address ethical dilemmas through the provision of ethics education.[59] In response, Andre saw the goals as being: ethical resolution of a contested issue; communication; and education, by which the parties are empowered to work through future dilemmas unaided and the institution is able to detect problematic patterns.[60] For Fox and Arnold, meanwhile, ethics support sought to achieve outcomes in four broad domains: ethicality; satisfaction; resolution of conflict; and education.[61]

A 1998 report on core competencies, issued by the American Society of Bioethics and Humanities (ASBH) and revised in 2010 took forward many of these ideas, in promoting the need to 'improve the provision of health care and its outcome through the identification, analysis and resolution of ethical issues as they emerge in clinical cases in health care institutions'.[62] Amongst

---

54 Slowther, Bunch, Woolnough and Hope 2001.
55 See Slowther, Johnston, Goodall and Hope 2004a; Slowther, Johnston, Goodall and Hope 2004b; Larcher, Slowther and Watson 2010.
56 Royal College of Physicians 2005.
57 Nuffield Council on Bioethics 2006.
58 See Paola and Walker 2006. There are tools which enable international comparison eg Pedersen 2010.
59 Fletcher and Siegler 1996.
60 Andre 1997.
61 Fox and Arnold 1996. Williamson (2007b: 359) warns against relying too heavily on empirical measures (like 'satisfaction') as proxies for ethicality: see further section 7.4.3.
62 See American Society for Bioethics and Humanities 1998; Aulisio, Arnold and Youngner 2000; American Society for Bioethics and Humanities 2010.

the goals listed in the report were the obligations to 'identify and analyze the nature of the value uncertainty or conflict that underlies the consultation' and 'facilitate resolution of conflicts in a respectful atmosphere with attention to the interests, rights, and responsibilities of those involved'.[63]

The question of core competencies is also now on the UK agenda.[64] Building on previous work published by the Ethox Centre and the Royal College of Physicians,[65] in 2010 the UK CEN proposed (but did not impose) a governance framework, with a call for further discussion of the issues.[66] The framework sets out collective requirements, to which a group as a whole – rather than any individual member – should aspire. Like their American predecessors, the requirements closely resemble the virtues of principled compromise. Committees are thus advised, through appropriate training, to: develop skills in ethical assessment, communication, facilitation, mediation and negotiation; possess knowledge of clinical terms, professional codes, law and basic concepts in ethical theory and principle; and appoint members who exhibit personal virtues such as integrity, honesty and reflection.[67]

Provided it is appropriately composed, skilled and knowledgeable, a CEC therefore looks like an ideal forum for securing principled compromise. Its orientation towards action should not be under-emphasised: no mere talking shop, the committee appears capable of providing the sort of conflict resolution apparently sought by clinicians.[68] A committee might, in other words, be able to take on some 'law-jobs',[69] and there are precedents – such as in Belgium – for explicitly empowering these bodies.[70] A committee might also enjoy certain advantages over the courts, because: it can, in principle, respond swiftly to an unfolding dilemma;[71] it can provide a practical answer in the face of legal and ethical indeterminacy;[72] and its answers can be both responsive to local needs and also consistent. As Doyal puts it, clinical ethics support may be 'necessary for any coherent approach to the formulation and implementation of good ethicolegal policy in a modern hospital setting'.[73]

Where CECs are secondly advantageous is in their *supportive* outlook. Notwithstanding concerns to the contrary,[74] clinicians appear to welcome this

63 American Society for Bioethics and Humanities 2010: section II.1.1.
64 cf Terry and Sanders 2011.
65 Slowther, Johnston, Goodall and Hope 2004b; Royal College of Physicians 2005.
66 Larcher, Slowther and Watson 2010.
67 ibid 31–32.
68 McLean 2008: 100.
69 See Llewellyn 1940.
70 McLean 2008: 100.
71 Royal College of Physicians 2005: 12; McLean 2008: 99.
72 Doyal 1990; Doyal 2001: i45–i46.
73 Doyal 2001: i44; cf Ravenscroft and Bell 2000: 440.
74 McCall Smith 1990: 138.

support,[75] apparently finding nothing to fear from these groups, since their advice is precisely that – and hence there is no threat to clinical autonomy.[76] The relative informality of CECs also calls to mind some of the advantages, identified in the Leggatt report, associated with the use of tribunals, as opposed to courts:

> Choosing a tribunal to decide disputes should bring two distinctive advantages for users. First, tribunal decisions are often made jointly by a panel of people who pool legal and other expert knowledge, and are the better for that range of skills. Secondly, tribunals' procedures and approach to overseeing the preparation of cases and their hearing can be simpler and more informal than the courts, even after the civil justice reforms. Most users ought therefore to be capable of preparing and presenting their cases to the tribunal themselves, providing they have the right kind of help. Enabling that kind of direct participation is an important justification for establishing tribunals at all.[77]

In keeping with the compromising spirit, communication and negotiation seem likely to be enhanced in such a framework, in which an assistive, rather than adversarial, model operates. Indeed, an ethics committee's inability conclusively to decide between adversaries might prove beneficial. Margot Brazier felt that Hedley J, presiding over the Charlotte Wyatt litigation, 'was in a sense undertaking in part the role of mediator. Yet as a mediator he cannot command total confidence because ultimately he *decides*';[78] by way of contrast, a committee might be better equipped to forge an alliance between the parties, in the manner of a mediator or conciliator.[79]

The third – and probably most important – advantage of using CECs is that 'mature reflection' on *ethical* matters is neither absent nor hidden but is instead the very point of the enterprise.[80] The open examination of any ethical obstacles that inhibit agreement or progress towards resolution is therefore encouraged. Such communication, which is essential to principled compromising, is facilitated because, according to Reiter-Theil, 'the language of ethics can serve as a common language in which conflicting viewpoints can be discussed'.[81] 'One of the important tasks of institutional ethics committees is

75 See eg Larcher, Lask and McCarthy 1997; Slowther, Bunch, Woolnough and Hope 2001: i4; Ravenscroft and Bell 2000: 438–39; Racine and Hayes 2006; Larcher, Slowther and Watson 2010: 30.
76 Slowther, Bunch, Woolnough and Hope 2001: 14; Ravenscroft and Bell 2000: 438–39.
77 Leggatt 2001: para 1.2.
78 Brazier 2005: 417, emphasis in original.
79 See further Allen 2005; Meller and Barclay 2011.
80 McLean 2009a: 76.
81 Reiter-Theil 2001: 22; cf Melley 1992: 239, 245–46; Zoloth-Dorfman and Rubin 1997: 428.

to provide a setting in which the moral language of health care can be rebuilt', say Winslow and Winslow, emphasising the pluralistic terminology available to such groups.[82] Law, meanwhile, fails to capture the plurality of languages and interests of its subjects.[83] A principled compromise will not overstep the boundaries of legality set by the law, but this still leaves ample 'room' in which the compromise can be sought.[84] As such, a CEC working within such limits will be able to hear diverse ideas uttered by a variety of voices – perhaps even the resource arguments avoided by the courts.[85] And whilst the court might want to separate disputants into winner or loser, and thus disputed claims into right or wrong, CECs can acknowledge the merits of each respective claimant and set of claims.[86]

Such open regard for the ethical landscape means that there can be equally open reflection on, and scrutiny of, the merits of the respective arguments, in keeping with the ground rules of principled compromise. The CEC can provide

> . . . an environment in which deeply divergent moral beliefs and perspectives can be given a forum, in which responding to moral distress becomes a communal and not individual responsibility, in which conflict is expected and open discussion of its sources is welcomed, in which the decision-making process is marked by a high degree of both thoughtful reflection and engagement.[87]

In short, the CEC can develop and exercise a type of ethical expertise.[88] UK CEN notes that committees in the UK tend to comprise doctors, nurses and other health care professionals, alongside lay members, a lawyer, an ethicist/philosopher, a chaplain and a patient.[89] Commenting on the US experience, Roger Dworkin commends widely-composed groups since 'they combine a high level of all relevant kinds of expertise with an element of popular representation',[90] and Jonsen confirms that committees are capable of developing 'the competence to respond in an informed and orderly manner'.[91] Accounts of core competencies (like those described earlier) abound, as do increasingly sophisticated methodological models, at least in countries with a long history

---

82 Winslow and Winslow 1991: 317.
83 Schneider 1994: 21.
84 See Benditt 1979: 34, discussed in Chapter 6 section 6.3.
85 See Doyal 2001: i48; Hope, Hicks, Reynolds, Crisp and Griffiths 1998.
86 cf Dworkin 1996: 7, 165.
87 Zoloth-Dorfman and Rubin 1997: 428.
88 The 'type' I have in mind will be explored in Chapter 8 section 8.4.
89 Slowther, Johnston, Goodall and Hope 2004b: 20.
90 Dworkin 1996: 168.
91 Jonsen 1998: 364.

of ethics consultation.[92] Once so equipped, as McCall Smith intimates, 'compromise may be achieved through public elucidation and debate about the issues involved and through the weighing of the relevant interests'.[93]

Support for such groups can be found in some seemingly unlikely places: even members of the judiciary appear receptive. Although the English judges have yet to comment directly on the work of clinical ethics committees,[94] it can be no coincidence that judges worldwide have found moral comfort in the deliberations of committees in cases where the removal or denial of life-support is in issue, that is – precisely those cases under consideration here. *In re Quinlan* (1976) NJ 355 A 2d 647 – the American authority that initiated the new era of medical jurisprudence – the court accepted that 'it would be more appropriate to provide a regular forum for more input and dialogue in individual situations and to allow the responsibility of these judgments to be shared'.[95] Another American judge, Terry J, opined to similar effect in the quotation with which this chapter opened.[96]

The judges have not only been optimistic about ethics support in principle, but also positive about its contribution in practice. In another American case, *In re Conservatorship of Torres*, 357 NW 2d 332 (Minn 1984), the court noted that three ethics committees had supported the proposal to remove artificial ventilation from a comatose patient, commenting that 'these committees are uniquely suited to provide guidance to physicians, families and guardians when ethical dilemmas arise'.[97] Similar evidence can be found elsewhere, such as in New Zealand. In *Re G* [1996] NZFLR 362, Fraser J pointed to seven

---

92 See eg Reiter-Theil 2009.

93 McCall Smith 1990: 125; cf Doyal 2001: i45–i46.

94 A search of Westlaw (27 January 2012) revealed 43 cases in which the phrase 'ethics committee' featured. Only five of these were cases that have featured in this book. Of those, three made reference to the BMA's ethics committee (*Airedale NHS Trust v Bland* [1993] 2 WLR 316; *NHS Trust A v M; NHS Trust B v H* [2001] 2 WLR 942; *R (on the application of Burke) v General Medical Council* [2005] 2 WLR 431), and another mentioned in passing the fact that the surgical separation of conjoined twins was considered by ethics committees in the USA (*Re A (children) (conjoined twins: medical treatment)* [2000] 4 All ER 961). Only *Re B (adult: refusal of medical treatment)* [2002] 2 All ER 449 included a reference (in a clinician's evidence) to the possible role a UK clinical ethics committee might play in a case of treatment refusal. Butler-Sloss P did not explicitly deal with this suggestion, although, in her closing recommendations, she stated: 'If the hospital is faced with a dilemma which the doctors do not know how to resolve, it must be recognised and further steps taken as a matter of priority. Those in charge must not allow a situation of deadlock or drift to occur' (para 100(vii)). She has repeated the need for timely responses in her other judgments (eg *NHS Trust A v H* [2001] 2 FLR 501, discussed in Chapter 3 section 3.2.1).

95 *In re Quinlan*, 355 A 2d 647, 668 (NJ 1976). The court cited a proposal by Teel (1975), an academic lawyer. See also *Re Colyer*, 660 P 2d 738 (1983).

96 *Re AC*, 573 A 2d 1235 (DC 1990) at 1237.

97 *In re Conservatorship of Torres*, 357 NW 2d 332 (Minn 1984) at 336.

'relevant, and in combination strongly persuasive' reasons why treatment should be withdrawn from an incapacitated patient, many of which cited with approval the deliberations (on four occasions) of an ethics committee.[98] Indeed, in another New Zealand case in which a committee had supported the withdrawal of ventilation from a patient with an extreme case of Guillain-Barré syndrome, the court phrased its three-part declaration conditionally, including the stipulation that this only occur if the committee concurred, in the specific circumstances that ultimately prevailed.[99] The judges in these cases therefore appear to believe that committees can develop not only a general ethical expertise but also a particular set of skills in relation to the possible termination of life-support.[100]

7.3.2 *Against the ethics support of clinical ethics support*

Despite the positive potential inherent in their goals, ethos and expertise, CECs also have their drawbacks, which render them not entirely fit for the task of principled compromising. Indeed, Sheila McLean in particular doubts that these committees are wholly 'fit for purpose' – assuming, that is, that their purpose can be fully discerned.[101] Amongst the problems (some of which, like the question of standards, have long dogged the endeavour[102]) are three particular areas of controversy, concerning function, product and process.

First, there is reason to question the *function*, and by extension the domain and the expertise, of an ethics committee. I suggested above that an ethics committee has ethics at its core, but it is not entirely obvious that any such committee (at least as currently composed) has the 'ethical' expertise we might expect. For its recommendations to be so labelled, an ethics committee must surely be capable of providing ethics advice.[103] The UK CEN requires 'ethical assessment skills' but is silent as to what these are and who possesses them.[104] There are no membership rules as such.[105] Research by McLean and colleagues found that 'a number' of chairpersons of UK committees were satisfied with the expertise of their committee – despite the majority of their members being qualified in medicine and lacking any particular expertise in ethics (or, for that matter, law).[106] But mere interest in ethical matters, whilst

---

98 *Re G* [1996] NZFLR 362 at 370. See Peart and Gillett 1998.

99 *Auckland Area Health Board v Attorney-General* [1993] 1 NZLR 235.

100 cf McCall Smith 1990: 132, 133, 137; Doyal 2001: i46; Hendrick 2001: i52; McLean 2007b: 498.

101 McLean 2009a: 77.

102 cf Melley 1992: 249.

103 McLean 2009a: 76–77.

104 Larcher, Slowther and Watson 2010: 31.

105 McLean 2009a: 77.

106 ibid 78.

important,[107] is surely insufficient, particularly if the committee's opinions are to have any authority.[108] Nevertheless, many committees appear only to have one obvious expert, who is usually drawn from an academic bioethics setting.[109] The apparent dearth of expertise is potentially troubling, since research from Norway by Pedersen et al (unsurprisingly) indicates that committee composition influences the outcomes of deliberations.[110] If the deliberators lack the skills and knowledge they purport to possess, then how safe are their conclusions?

This concern connects with wider fears about the dilution of the 'ethics' component in the field of bioethics, from which philosophical rigour is allegedly being crowded out by competing claims from other disciplines.[111] On this account, philosophers must put up resistance by continuing to bring their distinctive skills to bear in the clinical ethics context. Dawson and Wilkinson give an indication of what might be needed, when they describe philosophical practical ethics as comprising: 'appraisal of ethical arguments using the techniques of analytic philosophy'; 'conceptual analysis, which seeks to clarify and explain the role of particular ethical concepts and terms'; and 'the formulation and critical assessment of ethical principles or normative theories about how we should behave'.[112] McLean would surely be sceptical about the extent to which these activities feature in current clinical ethics work. Indeed, she doubts that committees are really being approached because they possess these sorts of skills. Instead, she argues, the reasons tend to be administrative, practical or professional, and the outcome sought tends to be one more legitimately associated with the legal process.[113] In truth, says McLean, a committee is approached as if it were an inferior court, tasked with dispute-resolution – but with none of the usual safeguards usually associated therewith.[114]

These concerns about the function of committees lead onto a second set of problems, regarding the *products* they supply. Committees might seek to distinguish their activities from those of the courts, by insisting that their decisions are specific to particular cases (in particular, local contexts) and are (in any event) only advisory in nature. But neither defence seems entirely satisfactory. First, the advice issued by ethics committees in individual consultations might be even less consistent and reflective than the rulings issued by courts.[115] The *ad hoc*, sporadic origins of UK committees suggest that the

107 Larcher, Slowther and Watson 2010: 32.
108 McLean 2009a: 86; Williamson 2007b: 357.
109 McLean 2009a: 81.
110 Pedersen, Akre and Førde 2009: 151.
111 Benatar 2006; Williamson 2007b: 357.
112 Dawson and Wilkinson 2009: 36.
113 McLean 2009a: 79; cf Bateman 1994: 256.
114 McLean 2007b: 497–98.
115 McLean 2008: 102; McLean 2009a: 82.

Royal College of Physicians is right to recommend that decisions be audited for consistency.[116] There is also the question of consistency between committees: the Norwegian study found significant variations in the conclusions reached, and even the factors considered, by nine committees presented with a common vignette, which concerned a DNAR order.[117]

Secondly, it does not suffice to say that committees offer no more than advice and that we therefore need not be overly concerned with what their advice is in individual cases, since they do not make the final decision. Certainly, there are reasons for keeping their deliberations (merely) advisory, since this will help to preserve both clinical autonomy and the professional-patient relationship.[118] Indeed, according to Wolf:

> Ethics committees should remain advisory. They have no warrant for pre-empting the decisional authority of patients or their surrogates. Ethics committees also should not substitute for courts. Committees have neither the personnel nor expertise to adjudicate legal claims. Indeed, committees vary enormously in quality, are bound by no commonly accepted rules of reasoning or system of precedent, and in any case lack the necessary independence of a court.[119]

McLean nevertheless fears that committee advice is, in practice, likely to be more than this and that it will potentially exert substantial influence.[120] The deference to 'responsible medical opinion' inherent in the *Bolam* standard might be one route by which this power is acquired,[121] which inevitably prompts questions about the legal status of committee recommendations.[122] Underlying McLean's reservations about the quality of the products on offer are substantial qualms about the quality of the processes by which they are made.[123]

Process is therefore the third area in which CECs can fail to satisfy the requirements of principled compromise. The extent and appropriateness of existing operational procedures in the UK is unclear: McLean's research unearthed some policies, although their transparency and the associated lines of accountability remained uncertain.[124] It is striking that the aforementioned Norwegian study bears out McLean's suspicion that deliberations are not

---

116 McLean 2007b: 499; McLean 2008: 101.
117 See Pedersen, Akre and Førde 2009: 150–51.
118 McCall Smith 1990: 126–27; Doyal 2001: i45, i48.
119 Wolf 1992: 94.
120 McLean 2007b; McLean 2008: 99, 101.
121 McLean 2008: 102. *Bolam v Friern Hospital Management Committee* [1957] 1 WLR 582.
122 Hendrick 2001; McLean 2008: 102.
123 McLean 2008: 99.
124 ibid 102.

sufficiently systematic, although the authors did find that deliberations became more systematic and transparent when a deliberation procedure was used.[125] McLean is not alone in thinking that these fundamental issues require attention.[126] Even the American system, in which committees are more powerful and experienced than in the UK, has been described as a 'due process wasteland'.[127] Returning to the UK, McLean demands that such concerns be addressed because

> ... it is not just the internal quality of decision-making that is important; what might be called external ethicality is also of considerable significance ... This requires a degree of sophistication in practice, as it suggests that an 'ethical' decision is one that not only gives informed consideration to the issue itself but also is reached in an "ethical" manner.[128]

The links with the virtues of principled compromise are evident: committees need to be able to reflect appropriately, and thereby give difficult cases their informed consideration, but their deliberations need also to be reliable and respectful – which is where process takes priority. Moreover, McLean adds that due process also has a significant legal dimension, since committee deliberations might fall within the purview of Article 6 of the Human Rights Act 1998, the right to a fair trial.[129] This implies that committees must demonstrate independence and impartiality, and may require rights of audience to be granted to patients and family members. Indeed, even without any such legal obligation, there is arguably an ethical requirement to involve and inform those who will be directly affected by the adoption of any committee recommendation.[130] Despite this, Ainsley Newson's research reveals that patient participation in clinical ethics consultation is currently low and appears unlikely to rise in the near future.[131]

Given all of these perceived procedural problems, it is unsurprising that McLean feels that CECs cannot and should not usurp the courts.[132] Calls for committees to assume a decisive role in the UK are rare, but they can be

125 Pedersen, Akre and Førde 2009: 147, 148.
126 Doyal 2001: i44. See also McCall Smith 1990: 130; McLean 2007b: 499; McLean 2008: 102.
127 McLean 2009a: 83.
128 ibid 81.
129 McLean 2008: 102; see also McLean 2009a: 82.
130 McLean 2007b: 499; McLean 2008: 102; McLean 2009a: 80–81; Pedersen, Akre and Førde 2009: 150, 151. Here we should recall the need to be alert to the relative interests of participants in principled compromise: see Chapter 6 section 6.5.
131 Newson 2009.
132 McLean 2008: 100.

glimpsed.[133] Annas, writing about the American context, suspects that 'encouraging a group of lay people to attempt to practice law makes no more sense than encouraging a group of lawyers to attempt to perform surgery . . . Good ethics committees begin where the law ends'.[134] Some judges in this jurisdiction would appear to agree: 'Deciding disputed matters of life and death is surely and pre-eminently a matter for a court of law to judge'.[135] However, both McLean and Annas also argue that if such committees are to play any role in dispute-resolution, then they must be equipped not only with relevant knowledge of the law but also with appropriate processes.[136] Clearly there is something of a tightrope to be walked here, since the committee needs to balance its commitment to legalistic concerns against the needs of its core business – 'doing ethics'.[137]

7.4 Conclusion: compromise in court or clinical ethics committee?

We have been pulled in different directions throughout this discussion: on the one side, CECs are ethics-led, supportive and capable of guiding those who find themselves in dispute, such that they appear competent to achieve principled compromise; but on the other side are legitimate concerns about their function (and purported expertise), the status and content of their decisions in individual cases, and their procedural rigour. These pros and cons seem to mirror, respectively, the cons and pros of using the courts as vehicles for values-based compromise: courts may be more process-heavy but they are ethics-light.

How to proceed? To my mind, the way forward surely lies in combining the strengths of each forum. Some of the deficiencies of the courts can be addressed by ensuring suitable ethical appraisal, which can come from CECs; in turn, these committees should, in particular, heed the calls for more robust processes. As Wolf has commented, if committees are to have 'influence over the fate of real patients', then 'they must do so responsibly, accountably, and with some guiding rules'.[138] McLean believes that adequate answers have so far been lacking in this area and that the onus now lies on defenders of clinical

---

133 Slowther has implied as much: see McLean 2008: 101.
134 Annas 1991: 21.
135 *Re A (children) (conjoined twins: medical treatment)* [2000] 4 All ER 961 at 987J (Ward LJ),. cf Hedley J's observation, in *Trust A, Trust B, Dr V v Mr M* [2005] EWHC 807, that the court, 'as a publicly accountable body', is best able to 'stand sentry at the fence', which separates 'natural consequences from deliberately brought-about death' (paras 11, 12: see Chapter 3 section 3.2.1).
136 Annas 1991; McLean 2008: 101, 102.
137 Annas 1991: 19; McLean 2008: 103; McLean 2009a: 82, 84.
138 Wolf 1992: 94.

ethics work.[139] At the same time, we need to heed Montgomery's concerns about the 'de-moralisation' of medical law.[140] In the final chapter, I will therefore propose ways of reconstructing clinical ethics support, so that it becomes more law-like, and can therefore better function alongside the courts, whose work is correspondingly 're-moralised'. By working alongside one another in this way, each forum should be able to contribute to the principled resolution of those conflicts in the clinic we have been examining throughout this book.

139 McLean 2009a: 84.
140 Montgomery 2006.

8 Committees, courts and compromise at the limits of life

> It is nearly always a matter of regret when the debate relating to the treatment of a seriously disabled or sick child, which frequently involves issues of life and death, needs to be conducted in a courtroom, rather than a hospital or a consulting room.
>
> *Portsmouth NHS Trust v Wyatt* [2005] EWCA Civ 1181
> para 86 (Wall LJ)

8.1 Reconstructing clinical ethics support

In the previous chapter we saw that there is a place in the hospital, to which the ethical 'issues of life and death' can be attended: the clinical ethics committee (CEC). However, we also encountered a number of objections to this group, particularly concerning its procedures for dealing with cases in which such issues arise. Meanwhile, the law courts, in which process reigns supreme, tend not to want to explore these difficult ethical dimensions. Each forum has the potential to facilitate the process of principled compromise but neither quite succeeds in realising that potential, since each appears to lack what the other possesses. The way forward, therefore, consists in their combination. However, fruitful combination of the respective expertise of the ethics committee and the judicial chamber will necessitate the reconstruction of clinical ethics support. Such reconstruction should ensure that the CEC can best deliver on its promise of ethical appraisal, whilst also meeting the demands of due process.

The task of reconstruction is not easy; even McLean, the main critic of these groups as they are currently conceived, concedes that she has no blueprint.[1] However, it is worth remembering what we seek: the resolution of conflict over whether or not to treat an incapacitated patient. Here, Dubler's work on principled resolution usefully complements our thinking about principled compromise, not least as she is often interested in the very same cases as us.[2]

---

1 McLean 2009a: 87.
2 Dubler 2011: 185.

For Dubler, principled resolution 'combines the strengths of a mediative process that levels the playing field with legal norms and ethical conventions, and uses both as support for forging a consensus'.[3] Principled resolution thus involves the search 'for consensus in chaos', in which 'the process is part of the product'.[4] That search occurs within recognised normative boundaries, such as those imposed by the law.[5]

Dubler argues that there is a role for a clinical ethics consultant here: despite a connection to the hospital or other healthcare institution, she believes (unlike some[6]) that such a consultant can engage in mediation in a sufficiently independent fashion, given his or her separation from decisions to date and ability to hear each side.[7] Others have also acknowledged the need for a dual outsider/insider status,[8] in which there is critical distance alongside direct involvement, that is, 'ethicists who are both strangers to and participants in the clinical process'.[9] Dubler advocates recourse to a single ethicist,[10] trained in 'bioethics mediation',[11] although she recognises the need occasionally to pool expertise (combining, say, lawyers and nurses) and to invite outside input.[12] Her analysis, coupled with the arguments considered in the previous chapter, suggests that there are three main areas to address when reconstructing clinical ethics support, which concerns its products, processes and expertise.

8.2 The products of clinical ethics consultation: issuing consistent guidance

We start with the products of CECs' deliberations, in particular their advice in individual case consultations. Throughout this book our focus has been on the question: to treat or not to treat? The question has been asked in numerous cases, spanning patients young and old. Built into the very concept of law is an aspiration to consistency, arising from its basic function of guiding action through a set of rules. Yet English law fails to meet the standard in these cases, since it often has more than one answer available – even in one and the

---

3 ibid 179.
4 ibid 187.
5 ibid 188–89; see similarly Chapter 6 section 6.2.
6 Meller and Barclay 2011.
7 Dubler 2011: 184.
8 Melley 1992: 237–38.
9 Zoloth-Dorfman and Rubin 1997: 428.
10 cf Sokol 2005.
11 Dubler 2011: 185. This may be distinguished from 'bioethics consultation'. Bioethics consultation involves a substantive, directive process for resolving conflicts, whereas bioethics mediation is more empowering and inclusive: Dubler and Liebman 2004. My proposal, which follows, arguably has elements of both.
12 Dubler 2011: 188.

same case. This failure to issue clear edicts appears to be linked to the nature of the dilemma from which the question arose, and in particular its status as an ethical dilemma. It is in the nature of an ethical dilemma that there will be arguments on either side. We might initially presume that one set of arguments will prove stronger than the other but scrutiny of the ethical arguments for and against a response in one direction or the other has failed to yield a clear way forward.

It should be no surprise, then, that CECs also struggle to meet the standard: they too differ, as a matter of fact, in their answers to the fundamental question. But we have explored how this need not be a problem as a matter of principle. In short, not only is ethical plurality present *in fact* but ethical pluralism is also defensible *in principle*. And pluralism propels the case for principled compromise – at least, where particular conditions are present and certain ground rules are observed. Attending to these ground rules, which require respectful, reliable and reflective negotiations, should then maximise consistency in at least a procedural sense. Substantive answers to individual dilemmas may still differ; after all, pluralism instructs us that sometimes there may be different, equally legitimate answers available. However, even here the aspiration to consistency is not entirely abandoned, as ensuring consistency in the *procedures* which reflect the virtues of compromising should help to ensure that the *products* of those procedures are also as consistent as possible.[13]

Others too believe that an appropriate balance can be struck between responding to the particularities of the individual case and striving for consistency. Reflecting on the policy-work dimension of clinical ethics consultancy, Doyal advocates translating national guidance into 'locally agreed language', as this 'should create a feeling of ownership of moral and legal principles that have been agreed nationally'.[14] Inherent in this argument is the assumption that some regional variation will be inevitable and even desirable. Variation is also present in different case consultations, as the Norwegian study attests.[15] Yet, such fluctuations have been treated with suspicion. Researchers exploring this issue in the research ethics context have noted how 'inconsistencies have traditionally been treated primarily as evidence of the incompetent, vexatious or capricious nature of the process'.[16] But, for their part, these researchers feel the pull of pluralism: they acknowledge that differently composed committees will decide differently and they argue that some moral diversity will be inevitable, in the absence of any single correct answer.[17] This does

13 At least, as I noted in Chapter 1 section 1.3.2, so far as the nature of the subject admits: Aristotle 1954: 3; cf Frith 2009.
14 Doyal 2001: i46.
15 See Pedersen, Akre and Førde 2009: 151 (and references therein).
16 Angell et al 2007: 97.
17 ibid 98.

not mean that they abandon all hope of defensible answers: 'Although the exercise of judgement may be inherently fallible, it is not merely arbitrary power and caprice; in this respect it is analogous to judicial decision-making'.[18] Their solution comes close to the ground rules of principled compromise, when they insist that research ethics committees should arrive at answers, in good faith, which will be agreeable to reasonable people. Pedersen et al (who conducted the Norwegian study) come even closer, in their discussion of CECs, when they advocate 'multidisciplinary, systematic, transparent discussions'.[19]

Clearly, for these various authors at least, good processes provide the key to promoting coherent and defensible answers. CECs should therefore adopt common approaches with, as Campbell urges, defined goals.[20] At a minimum, the goal of case deliberation is to advise on what should (not) happen in a particular case. Pedersen et al suggest that a deliberation procedure can help to maximise consistency here.[21] The provision of a procedure alone will not suffice: the group will also need to practise its application:[22] 'Good routines in clinical ethics deliberations are important to include key elements, such as identification of the main ethical problems, scrutinising key concepts and legal regulations and exploring analogous clinical situations'.[23] Pedersen et al therefore provide a useful starting place. However, given their central role in maximising consistency, we need to consider further the sorts of routines and processes that are to be encouraged.

8.3 The processes of clinical ethics consultation: observing due process

Although some perceive the merits of 'eclectic pragmatism',[24] we do need to take seriously McLean's calls for due process and for the certainty and consistency required by 'formal justice'.[25] Amongst the most important requirements will be those pertaining to a committee's skill set, composition, training, transparency, resourcing, monitoring and accountability (the latter of which may be linked to its potential liability). For convenience these can be organised into three groups, concerning the members, meetings and monitoring of clinical ethics support.

---

18 ibid.
19 Pedersen, Akre and Førde 2009: 151.
20 Campbell 2001.
21 Pedersen, Akre and Førde 2009: 148; Doyal suggests that fair procedures should also minimise the possible domination of certain vested interests: Doyal 2001: i46.
22 Pedersen, Akre and Førde 2009: 151; cf Singer 1972: 117; Bowman 2010.
23 Pedersen, Akre and Førde 2009: 151.
24 Hurst, Chevrolet and Loew 2006.
25 McLean 2009a: 82. See also Chapter 1 section 1.2.3.

First, there should be uniform, minimum expectations in terms of the group's *members*. Some basic skills are likely to be required across the committee: communication skills are one obvious example, as are facilitation skills (at least for the chairperson).[26] These will entail the provision of appropriate training where needed.[27] But the work of a CEC involves more than just these skills, since it is a multi-disciplinary endeavour,[28] which depends on the presence of diverse expertise.[29] The core competencies outlined by the UK CEN exemplifies this need, as it lists a wide range of required skills and knowledge.[30] Indeed, the benefits of diversity seem sufficient to outweigh calls for alternative models, like the lone clinical ethicist promoted by Dubler.[31] Even she acknowledges the virtues of occasionally pooling expertise and I would argue that a committee can best deliver on this – provided that it is appropriately composed.

At a minimum, a committee would seem to require clinical, legal, ethical and lay representation.[32] Clinicians – medical, non-medical and from the allied health professions – should help to provide the clinical boundaries surrounding a difficult case;[33] indeed, there may be questions of professional obligation (or even 'internal morality') on which their input will be crucial.[34] Although their perspective (no more than anyone else's) should not dominate deliberations,[35] a legal representative should be able to identify situations where the legal steer is clear, as well as those where matters are 'fuzzy' or 'indeterminate'.[36] The legal representative can therefore provide the legal limits,[37] within which a principled compromise is sought, and, again, there may be some questions on which a legal opinion will be decisive.[38] Of course, in keeping with the pluralistic premise, we should not expect representatives

---

26 Pedersen, Akre and Førde 2009: 148, 150, 151.
27 ibid 151.
28 See Zoloth-Dorfman and Rubin 1997: 423, 426.
29 McCall Smith 1990: 130; Doyal 2001: i47; Campbell 2001: i56; Williamson 2007b: 358; McLean 2009a: 87.
30 Larcher, Slowther and Watson 2010: 31–32.
31 Dubler 2011; cf Sokol 2005.
32 More than one representative is likely to be needed from the clinical realm, to ensure different specialities feature. The other groups might also benefit from having more than one representative, although (in what follows) I will refer to a single such member. The group's expertise could also be expanded through eg inclusion of a representative from the healthcare institution (hospital etc), a chaplain, and so on. These are details that can be filled in another time; my main intention here is to consider the main areas of expertise that should be covered if the committee is to succeed in its function.
33 Pedersen, Akre and Førde 2009: 149–50.
34 Paola and Walker 2006.
35 McLean 2009a: 82.
36 See Pedersen, Akre and Førde 2009: 150; Doyal 1990; Doyal 2001: i45–46.
37 Melley 1992: 243.
38 Paola and Walker 2006.

of either of these groups (clinicians and lawyers) to converge on 'the' single right answer. Contrary to some clinicians' expectations, lawyers will disagree in their respective readings of the law. This is undoubtedly inevitable, not least in an adversarial system. However, we surely can expect these experts to represent to the best of their abilities the (defensible) positions available in their particular realm of expertise, somewhat akin to the role of experts providing evidence in court proceedings.[39] We will return to the 'ethicist' and what we might expect of him or her shortly. The layperson, meanwhile, cannot be expected to represent the total plurality of views available outside the clinic or courtroom. The role of the layperson on the committee is arguably somewhat different, however, as McCall Smith has noted: 'Although it is possible that professional interests may set and control the agenda, lay presence is an important safeguard of patient as opposed to institutional interest (which, of course, may not always coincide)'.[40] While the involvement of laypersons will entail risks and benefits (both for them and for the committee),[41] McCall Smith makes a good case for (better) securing their participation.[42]

Secondly, there should be some common requirements in relation to the group's *meetings*. Different models are available,[43] but at the very least meetings should be regular,[44] adequately resourced and supported, with minutes kept and deliberations communicated as appropriate. Procedures for responding to emergencies (such as the establishment of a sub-group) should be in place.[45] Although confidentiality must be maintained,[46] committee proceedings should be open – both to hearing from and to disseminating to those parties likely to be affected by the advice issued. Suitably anonymised annual reports will do some of this work,[47] but committees will probably need to widen their rights of audience. As McCall Smith says:

39 eg General Medical Council 2008: para 9; cf the *Bolam* standard (*Bolam v Friern Hospital Management Committee* [1957] 1 WLR 582).
40 McCall Smith 1990: 130. Indeed, lay presence might help to ensure there is the due recognition of agent-relativity, which is required by principled compromise: see Chapter 6 section 6.5.
41 Updale 2006.
42 Newson 2009; see for a comparative perspective Fournier, Rari, Førde, Neitzke, Pegoraro and Newson 2009.
43 eg sub-groups might be convened where appropriate: see Slowther, Johnston, Goodall and Hope 2004b.
44 The volume of work, which should be monitored, might dictate the frequency of meetings – although research suggests that the number of cases considered by UK committees is currently low: Whitehead, Sokol, Bowman and Sedgwick 2009.
45 See McCall Smith 1990: 129–30; Doyal 2001: i47. In this regard, note that the courts should retain their role as the ultimate arbiter: see section 8.5.
46 Doyal 2001: i47.
47 Slowther, Bunch, Woolnough and Hope 2001: i6.

If there is to be a hospital policy on a matter which concerns patients or their families, then surely the most appropriate way of developing that policy is in the open, and once the policy is made, then surely there is no justification for not explaining it to those affected by it.[48]

His comment seems no less (and is arguably even more) applicable to individual case referrals.[49]

Related to such openness is accountability,[50] which occupies the third group of procedural concerns, *monitoring*. If CECs are to attain – and be seen to attain – suitable consultancy standards,[51] then audit and evaluation will be essential.[52] Where appropriate, measures will be needed to remedy defective processes, which may require the provision of an appeals process,[53] plus thinking (in advance of anything going wrong) about the potential liability of the committee. Perhaps there is little need to worry: Judith Hendrick suspects that legal actions in judicial review or negligence would fail, particularly if the committee is tasked only with issuing advice, which the responsible clinician is therefore free to reject.[54] Put more positively, the committee will be required to work within legal boundaries,[55] so we might expect the margin of (legal) error to be small.[56] Yet, provision should still be made for managing malpractice within these margins and the healthcare institution should be prepared to assume vicarious liability. Unanswerable groups are otherwise sure to be seen with suspicion.

None of this should mean that the committee ought to be associated with 'risk management' or 'liability control'. The legal dimension to its work should not crowd out the overriding ethical dimension.[57] However, the committee should be associated with appropriate clinical governance. As Alastair Campbell says, 'The demand for clinical governance combines a quest for values with a pressing need to make everyone feel part of the endeavour'.[58] As a component of such governance and accordingly this 'quest for values', a CEC should be prepared to defend the values-based advice it has issued, including in a court. Of course, this inevitably raises one of the most significant questions attending the work of CECs: what sorts of 'values-based

---

48 McCall Smith 1990: 130.
49 cf *Re OT* [2009] EWHC 633; see Chapter 2 section 2.2.2.
50 cf Slowther, Bunch, Woolnough and Hope 2001: i2.
51 Campbell 2001: i56.
52 Doyal 2001: i48; Williamson 2007a.
53 McLean 2009a: 88.
54 Hendrick 2001: i52–53.
55 cf Chapter 6 section 6.2.
56 See Doyal 2001: i47; Hendrick 2001: i51. McCall Smith (1990: 126) also feels that the existence of a CEC might mean there are fewer aggrieved persons.
57 Hendrick 2001: i51.
58 Campbell 2001: i55.

advice' can legitimately be expected from them? This leads us into our closing discussion, about ethical pluralism and the need for a particular sort of ethical expertise.

8.4 Expertise in clinical ethics consultation: exhibiting ethical expertise

The clinical ethics endeavour depends, for its success, upon careful engagement with each of its key words. The 'ethics' component must surely take priority: it is the core element of the endeavour.[59] That element must then latch onto the 'clinical' dimension, for which clinical insight is undoubtedly needed (although – as I noted earlier – care must also be taken to ensure that clinical ethics work is not too closely allied with clinical practice).[60] A sturdy bridge must then be erected between the two, so that occupants of each domain can understand the other's language, and ethical analysis can be translated into action in clinical practice.[61] All of this depends, of course, on the initial ethical analysis, for which particular ethical skills, expertise and training are needed.[62]

As we noted earlier, a framework for thinking through moral problems can help committees to fulfil their analytical function. There is a myriad of contenders, as was found in the Norwegian study, in which none of the nine committees investigated used only one moral theory – instead, 'pluralistic approaches dominated'.[63] Popular contenders from the USA include the four principles approach, from Beauchamp and Childress, and the four quadrants approach from Jonsen, Siegler and Winslade.[64] Beauchamp and Childress describe respect for autonomy, beneficence (providing that which is beneficial), non-maleficence (avoiding that which is harmful) and justice (particularly in a distributive sense) as the four principles of biomedical ethics.[65] They admit that the principles need further specification and balancing in particular moral contexts, which they argue should be regulated by a process of 'reflective equilibrium', in which the deliberator tacks between various moral beliefs, judgments, principles and background theories, in the pursuit of coherence.[66] As Beauchamp and Childress explain, approached in this way, the 'four clusters of principles do not constitute a general moral theory. They

---

59 Notice some of the alternative labels used, eg moral deliberation: see Pedersen, Hurst, Schildmann, Schuster and Molewijk 2010: 137.
60 Contrast La Puma, cited in Zoloth-Dorfman and Rubin 1997: 423.
61 Melley 1992: 246; Williamson 2007b: 358.
62 See Williamson 2007b: 358.
63 Pedersen, Akre and Førde 2009: 148.
64 Beauchamp and Childress 2001; Jonsen, Siegler and Winslade 2006.
65 See also Gillon 2003.
66 We encountered this idea in Chapter 1 section 1.3.2.

provide only a framework for identifying and reflecting on moral problems'.[67] Jonsen, Siegler and Winslade, meanwhile, describe four broad topics – medical indications, patient preferences, quality of life and contextual features – each of which gives rise to more specific questions, which may help when thinking through an ethical dilemma.

Both of these approaches have their merits in bringing ethically salient features to light, so (in theory) either may aid the work of the CEC.[68] Indeed, whichever approach is chosen (including some other), it must allow for ethical pluralism, and thus openness to a variety of viewpoints. However, not just any alleged moral perspective will necessarily pass muster: there must be, as principled compromising requires, appropriate critical attention to the values under the 'ethical stethoscope'.[69] This should not collapse into abstract theorising – the link with practice must be maintained.[70] However, critical bite is important, as McLean's colleague Williamson explains:

> It must be constantly borne in mind that committees are not just a forum for discussing the facts of a particular case and the normative values that surround it but must also have critical teeth to allow them to dissect flawed reasoning that may be used (perhaps inadvertently) either to support bad practice or to prevent much-needed developments within clinical practice. To fulfil these tasks, ethical, and not only empirical, training is required.[71]

Indeed, the application of empirical measures such as user-satisfaction will not (alone) guarantee that an 'ethical' outcome has been secured.[72] Distinctive philosophical skills will be needed to help steer the committee towards such an outcome:

> To secure a more consistent commitment to ethics specialisation, it is important for ethicists to clearly articulate that the role of ethical analysis is to test the consistency of arguments and identify flawed logic or dubious premises as part of its pursuit to determine the right or best way for humans to live.[73]

---

67 Beauchamp and Childress 2001: 15.
68 eg Hurst, Chevrolet and Loew 2006 (four principles approach); Sokol 2008 (four quadrants approach).
69 Sokol 2008: 516.
70 Melley 1992: 246–47; Williamson 2007b: 359.
71 Williamson 2007b: 359.
72 Williamson 2007b: 359.
73 ibid. Notice the echoes of Regan and Pollock's criteria, described in Chapter 1 section 1.3.2.

In short, if it is to function well, the CEC needs not only the skills of a philosopher but also a sort of ethical expertise. The committee members should therefore be trained accordingly by a suitably qualified (moral) philosopher (or 'ethicist', in Williamson's terminology);[74] and such a philosopher will also need to be present on the committee, since he or she will have an important role to play.

The role of philosophy (and specifically the philosopher) on CECs has been captured in various metaphors, of which the best is provided by Zoloth-Dorfman and Rubin. They describe the responsible clinician as the captain of the ship, with the philosopher as the navigator:

> . . . knowing the map, being familiar with the terrain and its complexities, calling attention to how the desired or expected course might be changed by the immediacy, temporality or particularity of a given case, and above all, guiding, but not controlling, the course.[75]

On this account, philosophers have the training required to reveal and read the map, as they possess a particular expertise. One such philosopher who is closely associated with bioethics, Peter Singer, has gone so far as to argue that moral philosophers can be 'experts in matters of morals'.[76] Singer argues that, in order to think through moral conflicts, one needs information, from which salient data is selected, which is combined with a moral position, from which bias has been eliminated. He maintains that practice makes perfect (or, at least, approaches perfection): the more often one does this, the more often one will reach sound conclusions.[77] Yet many other philosophers have rejected this conclusion, and the issue has recently arisen again amongst bioethicists who have been contemplating philosophers' roles on (for example) national bioethics commissions.[78] As Holm puts it, it is 'always nice when non-ethicists suggest the creation of work for the boys and girls in the ethics field', but, he says, this does not mean these 'boys and girls' can resolve matters like where the best interests of an incapacitated patient 'really' lie.[79]

Non-philosophers might be surprised by these philosophers' opposition to calls on (and defence of) their purported expertise. However, the resistance looks like it is directed at *moralism* (dictating right and wrong), rather than the sort of expertise to which I am referring. Clinical ethics 'is a discipline that functions not by offering declarative normative judgments,

---

74 Zoloth-Dorfman and Rubin 1997: 427; Williamson 2007b: 359; cf Melley 1992: 245.
75 Zoloth-Dorfman and Rubin 1997: 429; cf Campbell 2001: i55.
76 Singer 1972: 117.
77 ibid 116–117.
78 eg Gesang 2010; Kovacs 2010 Archard 2011; Cowley 2011.
79 Holm 2008: 254.

but rather by raising critical questions and focussing upon conversation and deliberation'.[80] Here the philosopher – as navigator – can undoubtedly help. Indeed, as Melley recognises, the philosopher's usefulness will be limited if he were to lapse into the moralistic role: 'Those who express pedantry and omniscience with those unfamiliar to philosophy will soon lose the hard won credibility for the entire profession'.[81]

Melley helpfully spells out the distinctive skills the philosopher can draw on in clinical ethics consultation, in particular his skills in 'clarification and critical review'.[82] Philosophers can, therefore, 'act as cognitive go-betweens, clarifiers, intellectual sounding boards for conflicting beliefs',[83] by supplying the language to discuss and resolve differences.

> The accurate articulation of mutual, and possibly conflicting duties is part of what philosophy does tolerably well. Although the philosopher would not be in any decision-making position, he or she could describe the conflicts, the opposing theories, and the arguments underlying them.[84]

To maintain credibility, the philosopher needs a degree of distance, remaining a 'critical observer'.[85] However, he or she must work effectively with others on the committee: the pooling of expertise is central to its success.[86] The philosopher also needs knowledge of both theoretical and practical domains,[87] to the latter of which the clinicians can surely contribute. These clinicians, alongside the lawyer, will further help to specify the boundaries of the terrain to be searched (ie within which the advice must be located);[88] as navigator, the philosopher can clarify the features of that landscape.[89] Indeed, clarification – notably of normative terms and distinctions – is a task shared by the lawyer and the philosopher, although the latter is not constrained, unlike the former, by the dictates of *stare decisis* or (perhaps) the demands of the client.[90] Although

---

80 Zoloth-Dorfman and Rubin 1997: 430. Recall the 'debate' element of principled compromise: see Chapter 6 section 6.5.

81 Melley 1992: 250.

82 ibid 249. Like others to whom I have referred here, Melley focuses upon the individual philosopher as a consultant, yet many of his arguments apply equally well to work on committees.

83 ibid 239.

84 ibid 240.

85 ibid 247.

86 ibid 248.

87 ibid 251–52. Indeed, Melley resists the notion of 'ethical technicians', preferring instead the scientist who is also qualified in philosophy.

88 Recall the discussion of boundaries in section 8.3 above.

89 See Melley 1992: 244.

90 The lawyer in question may feel particularly constrained if he or she represents the healthcare institution (eg as trust solicitor).

the committee should aspire to consistency in its advice,[91] the philosopher can exercise his or her critical imagination when helping the committee to arrive at and articulate its advice on an individual case. As 'moral historian',[92] the philosopher should have a wealth of traditions and thought-experiments on which to draw.[93] Such knowledge and skills enable the philosopher to engage in the 'active reflection' on the moral dimensions of medicine for which (as Singer implied) clinicians sometimes lack the time.[94] The philosopher may not utter the last word on a given case but he or she can help to ensure that the words used are suitably careful, clear and critical.

Philosophers can therefore play a vital role in exhibiting and educating the committee in ethical expertise – which does not mean that they can exhibit or inculcate such mastery of morals that they (or the committees they train) can be expected to pronounce definitively on matters of right and wrong. This is not to say that a certain expertise cannot be developed on particular types of dilemmas, such as those we have explored throughout this book. Indeed, it may be thought appropriate that certain cases be referred to sub-groups or specialist panels, which possess extensive knowledge of dilemmas arising at the limits of life.[95] This idea has its merits, and it could fit alongside calls for a suitable national body.[96] Meanwhile, back at the local level, we should also not overlook the merits of mediation.[97] Yet, notwithstanding the benefits offered by these different models of addressing ethical conflict, my intention here – given the relative inadequacy of the courts' dealings with moral matters – was to explore the main model for addressing such issues: the CEC. Many such committees already exist, and there is evidence that they are already addressing the sorts of dilemmas with which we have been concerned. I believe there is much to be said for their capacity to craft principled compromise, and now is the time to say such things, given calls to formalise the system we currently have in this jurisdiction. The UK CEN has laid the groundwork, on which we should now build: whether through legislation or further local effort,[98] suitable standards of clinical ethics consultancy should be set and maintained.[99]

---

91 See section 8.2 above.

92 Melley 1992: 243.

93 eg like Rachels's thought experiment involving the drowning cousins, described in Chapter 5 section 5.3.2.

94 Melley 1992: 244.

95 cf McLean 2009a: 81. I am grateful to Ainsley Newson for suggesting this possibility.

96 eg Miola 2007.

97 See Nuffield Council on Bioethics 2006: 145–47.

98 Models include the framework governing the creation, constitution and conduct of research ethics committees; see eg McLean 2008: 103.

99 Doyal 2001; Campbell 2001; McLean 2008: 103.

8.5 Conclusion: clinical ethics committees, courts and compromise

The CEC has its merits as a location for scrutinising the values embroiled in a particular conflict in the clinic and for issuing guidance thereon. This forum should therefore be ideally equipped to tackle the 'tiresome' problem, which Ian Kennedy mentioned, of 'resolving conflicts between clashing principles and dealing rationally with argument and counter-argument'.[100] Like the courts, the committee aims to guide action; however, unlike the legal system, its outlook is supportive and its decisions merely advisory. Moreover, as the name implies, ethics is central to the clinical ethics endeavour, as opposed to being hidden away in the margins of judges' rulings. CECs are not problem-free, however. Their function, and accordingly their domain and purported expertise, can be questioned. Whether they are adequately qualified in ethical analysis and advice is open to doubt; in truth, they might be more accurately viewed as (very) inferior courts. But, if that is so, then their procedures and the advice they issue appear to need urgent attention, since they seem to lack the clarity and consistency we might legitimately expect of courts.

CECs therefore require some reconstruction. I have tendered a design based on the blueprint of principled compromise, drawing on the school of ethical pluralism. This reconstruction has three central features. First, there must be attention to the *product* issued by CECs: the advice issued in individual cases can vary according to the particularities of the cases, but substantive consistency may be improved with the development of consistent processes. Secondly, then, suitable *processes* must be in place, which seek to ensure that there is: a pluralistic membership, equipped with diverse expertise; regular and (appropriately) open meetings; and monitoring, evaluation and accountability. Thirdly, the committee must possess the *ethical expertise* essential to its endeavour. The committee should accordingly employ a pluralistic ethical framework, in which different values can be identified, which are then subject to critical attention. Here, a philosopher can contribute to the group as both a member and an educator, helping it to navigate through concepts and arguments, before the group as a whole decides on the advice it will issue.

Ideally, the advice issued by the CEC will serve to resolve the conflict. The interested parties, both professional and lay, could well agree to follow the steer, and the conflict might therefore dissipate. However, where this does not occur – say, where one or other party continues to contest the course proposed – then recourse to the courts must remain an option. Contrary to the view expressed in *In re Quinlan* (1976) NJ 355 A 2d 647, from which McLean also recoiled, I do not believe that a CEC can wholly supplant a court in cases like those we have considered throughout this book. Indeed, law will undoubtedly need to take some sort of stand in cases of life or death. Law will

---

100 Kennedy 1991: 158; see Chapter 4 section 4.5.

also provide some of the boundaries within which a principled compromise can be sought (and others will be provided by, for example, what medical science can realistically achieve). Of course, the courts are not entirely suited to principled compromising: they often fail to issue consistent guidance, and they are typically resistant to examining the ethics of the case before them, which is too often cast in an adversarial mould that seems ill-suited to the clinical encounter. However, courts also have their advantages: the legal lexicon of best interests and precedent autonomy is sufficiently flexible to accommodate some values-talk; the courts possess procedural rigour; and judges, backed by sanctions, can *decide* – not merely advise. Given these virtues, a court can therefore plug the gaps of the CEC, and it should be obliged to receive and consider carefully the advice of such a group.[101] As Annas put it earlier: 'Good ethics committees begin where the law ends';[102] however, it should also be the case that where the ethics committee reaches its limits, then the courts should be expected to step in, albeit without ignoring the committee's appraisal of the values it tends to overlook.[103]

What would this interplay between CEC and court look like in practice? In particular, how might the principled compromise process work in a case in which the fundamental question has been posed, that is, to treat or not to treat? Recall the scenario with which this book began, the case of Mr W, the patient with end-stage multiple sclerosis, whose GP – fearful of legal reprisal if he failed to 'force-feed' his patient – had admitted Mr W to hospital for the insertion of a feeding tube. Mr W's family felt the tube should not be sited, claiming 'He's had enough'; one of the nurses, meanwhile, argued that 'You can't just let him starve to death'.[104]

Ideally the parties will discuss their differences and reach agreement. But if they fail to achieve this, then the stage may be set for the principled compromise process. In cases like this it is conceivable that some middle ground can be found, and perhaps even a compromise reached. Evidence from the clinics and the courts supports this suggestion. The BBC Radio 4 programme *Inside the Ethics Committee*, in which a panel considers ethical dilemmas arising in

---

101 My aim here was to explore the principles involved, rather than specify the ensuing detail: further work will be needed eg to determine the weight such advice should carry and to clarify when cases should go before a committee and a court respectively. In this regard, we might query whether it is strictly necessary for PVS cases (and perhaps even MCS cases) which involve the removal of CANH to go before the judges. Some scrutiny of such cases seems advisable, but whether this needs to be provided by the courts in all such cases is open to question.

102 Annas 1991: 21.

103 The court therefore has the benefit of the committee's expertise in ethical matters, while the committee's deliberations occur in the shadow of the court. In Shapiro's terms, 'negotiation under threat of litigation lies along the continuum . . . between mediation and litigation': Shapiro 1979: 173.

104 See introduction; National Council for Palliative Care 2007: 19.

health care, has featured a (real) case involving a woman with severe anorexia who sought palliation rather than active treatment following an overdose; in the event, both this panel and its real-life predecessor 'rejected her request for palliative care and suggested a compromise solution'.[105] As I observed in Chapter 6, similar solutions can be detected in some of the rulings, like those directed at baby MB[106] – 'a paradigm case'[107] according to Lyons – and minimally conscious Ms M,[108] who the judge decided was to continue receiving clinically assisted nutrition and hydration (CANH) but was not to be resuscitated in the event of cardiac arrest. These three cases are not isolated examples of compromise in action: like Verhagen et al before her,[109] Moratti's research into practices in Dutch neonatal intensive care units found that, in 'cases of persistent disagreement', doctors 'are inclined to seek a compromise between their own professional judgment and the parents' preferences'.[110]

Of course, not every purported 'compromise between the various interests at stake' to which Moratti refers will be all that it appears.[111] The so-called 'slow code', which Lantos and Meadow believe should be 'resuscitated', may be a case in point.[112] These authors argue that, where CPR is likely to be ineffective but a patient's family cannot bring themselves to consent or even assent to a DNAR order against attempting resuscitation, then doctors should have 'a carefully ambiguous discussion about end-of-life options' and provide 'resuscitation efforts that are less vigorous or prolonged than usual'.[113] This initially looks like a compromise. However, on reflection, we should doubt whether it is sufficiently *principled*. The authors claim to denounce deception but this seems to be intrinsic to their proposal, which is thus contrary to the reliability – and arguably even the respectful and reflective behaviour – required by principled compromise.

If unprincipled compromises are not to be mistaken for principled resolutions in the cases with which we are concerned, then it seems sensible to invest in a process in which there is due attention to the ground rules of principled compromise, such that the negotiation is respectful, reliable and reflective. Indeed, this is doubly advised because, in many cases, a compromise solution will be difficult – perhaps impossible – to stipulate in advance of this sort of discussion and deliberation. Consider Mr W again: there are options that might involve compromise – like inserting the feeding tube but remaining

---

105 Sokol 2008: 568.
106 *An NHS Trust v MB* [2006] EWHC 507.
107 Lyons 2010: 193.
108 *W v M and S and A NHS Primary Care Trust* [2011] EWHC 2443.
109 Verhagen et al 2009.
110 Moratti 2010: 292.
111 ibid 299; cf Dubler 2011: 194.
112 Lantos and Meadow 2011: 8.
113 ibid.

open to its removal, or inserting the tube but otherwise declining to intervene in the event of infection or cardiac arrest – but we cannot be sure how best to proceed without more considered contemplation. As I suggested earlier, provided that there is room for considering a plurality of ethical perspectives, then the decision reached in a particular case may come close to one value or another. The point is that we will not necessarily discern which value or combination of values is most appropriate in the individual case, and therefore for the parties involved, without converging around the compromise table.

Let us assume that no consensus has been reached between the professionals and family members concerned with Mr W's care. Either group should be entitled to approach a CEC for advice on how to proceed.[114] Drawing on its diverse expertise, the committee can identify the boundaries within which an answer should be sought. The clinicians can help to illuminate the clinical issues, such as Mr W's symptoms and his likely prognosis, both with and without tube feeding;[115] they can also point out pertinent professional guidance, such as that issued by the General Medical Council, in which (for example) a distinction is drawn between basic care and CANH.[116] A legal representative can further fill in the normative picture, by clarifying as best she can when there is – and is not – a legal duty to feed or to treat an incapacitated individual. In a case like Mr W's, the lawyer(s) should be particularly alert to the import of the Mental Capacity Act 2005: where, as the National Council for Palliative Care suggests,[117] a patient like Mr W lacks an advance decision to refuse treatment, a lasting power of attorney or a court-appointed deputy, then (legally) everything will turn on the patient's best interests, which will require consultation with the patient's family. Attention to these sorts of issues, both clinical and legal, should improve understanding amongst the parties (the GP, for example, should be clearer about the proper scope of 'force-feeding') and may facilitate further communication between them.

But merely attending to the clinical and legal dimensions of a contested case may be insufficient if the underlying ethical dilemma remains. The conflict over Mr W's care surely rested on more than misunderstanding – it arose from the different values espoused by the competing parties, to which the CEC should accordingly attend. A pluralistic ethical framework can help in ensuring that salient values are given due consideration. Amongst the values engaged in Mr W's case are those underpinning the nurse's comment, 'You can't just let him starve to death'. This nurse appeared to prioritise the intrinsic value of life; the committee can explore this idea, its associated

---

114 I will presently leave to one side the practicalities pertaining to who may approach the committee (eg any member of the family or team?) and how they may do so.
115 See National Council for Palliative Care 2007: 19–20.
116 General Medical Council 2010.
117 National Council for Palliative Care 2007: 19–20.

precepts and concepts, like 'futility', and how these ought or ought not to apply in Mr W's case. Mr W's family, meanwhile, felt that 'He's had enough'. They might have had in mind either an instrumental account of the value of Mr W's life, such that they believe he has endured 'enough', or a self-determined account, according to which they believe that, if he was competent now, Mr W would decline the imposition of a tube. These ideas and their potential impact on Mr W's care would also be scrutinised by the committee.

In so exploring the ethics of the case, the committee can ensure that the values are not reduced to their counterparts in law or professional guidance: for example, even in the absence of a robustly executed advance decision to refuse treatment, there may still be persuasive evidence of Mr W's wishes, which at least carries ethical weight.[118] With the aid of a philosopher, the committee can scrutinise the different arguments – looking for clarity, consistency and the like – and thereby weigh up the merits of opposing judgments, and associated principles and even theories, before arriving at their advice.[119] That advice should then be communicated clearly to all of the interested parties. These parties may feel that a principled resolution has been reached; where one or other does not feel able to accept the advice, and conflict persists, then the court can be called on to issue decisive guidance. If it is to qualify as law, then the court decision should indeed do this, that is, it should be decisive and capable of guiding action; and if it is to be appropriately alert to the essential ethical dimensions of such decisions, then it should be appropriately informed by the deliberations of the ethics committee.

In the end, then, we have a plea for process – although we started with a desire for a decision, specifically about whether or not life-supporting treatment ought to be offered to an incapacitated patient. It might therefore appear that the endeavour has failed, since we still lack a single solution. If that be so, then the failure is surely a noble one, because we have come to appreciate the importance of principled compromising, according to which we should be open to diverse defensible solutions to dilemmas at the limits of life. Such solutions are urgently needed, not just in the UK in which difficult cases like those of David Glass and Charlotte Wyatt continue to arise, but also internationally, as cases like those of Terri Schiavo and Eluana Englaro vividly illustrate.[120] Law can only go so far in such cases, particularly as the judges appear

---

118 Contrast this approach with that apparently taken in *W v M and S and A NHS Primary Care Trust* [2011] EWHC 2443. In that case, the judge adopted a rather narrow legalistic focus, in which Ms M's failure to execute an advance directive of the type specified in law (albeit at a point beyond which she had already lost capacity) meant that the case turned on her best interests: see Huxtable 2012b.

119 Again, the detail of the decision-method needs to be specified, eg whether decisions should be reached by consensus, majority rule etc: see Frith 2009.

120 See for discussion of Englaro's case Luchetti 2010.

increasingly inclined to strip away the ethical dimensions of their judgments.[121] Clinical ethics committees have the potential to plug this growing gap, although they correspondingly need to become more law-like in their attention to due process. I think that the way forward involves a process of principled compromise, in which a plurality of plausible perspectives is available for resolving conflict in the clinic at the limits of life. Principled compromise can combine the best of law with the best of ethics support: to paraphrase Kant, law without ethics is empty, but ethics without law is blind – only through their unison can knowledge arise.

121 Montgomery 2006.

Bibliography

A Children's Physician (1979) 'Non-treatment of defective newborn babies', *The Lancet*, 2: 1123–24.

Adams, J. and Brownsword, R. (1995) *Key Issues in Contract*, London: Butterworths.

Adams, J.N. and Brownsword, R. (1992) *Understanding Law*, London: Fontana Press.

Alldridge, P. and Morgan, D. (1992) 'Ending Life' *New Law Journal*, 142: 1536.

Allen, M.T. (2005) 'A new way to settle old disputes: Mediation and healthcare', *Medico-Legal Journal*, 73: 93–110.

Amarasekara, K. and Mirko, B. (2004) 'Moving from voluntary euthanasia to non-voluntary euthanasia: Equality and compassion', *Ratio Juris*, 17(3): 398–423.

American Society for Bioethics and Humanities (1998) *Core competencies for health care ethics consultation*, Glenview, IL: American Society for Bioethics and Humanities.

— (2010) *Core competencies for health care ethics consultation* (2nd edn), Glenview, IL: American Society for Bioethics and Humanities.

Andre, J. (1997) 'Goals of ethics consultation: Toward clarity, utility and fidelity', *Journal of Clinical Ethics*, 8: 193–98.

Andrews, K. (1993a) 'Recovery of patients after four months or more in the persistent vegetative state', *British Medical Journal*, 306: 1597–600.

— (1993b) 'Patients in the persistent vegetative state: Problems in their long term management', *British Medical Journal*, 306: 1600–1602.

Andrews, K. and Hinchliffe, M. (1993) 'Airedale NHS Trust v Bland', *Family Law*, 137–40.

Angell, E.L., Jackson, C.J., Ashcroft, R.E., Bryman, A., Windridge, K. and Dixon-Woods, M. (2007) 'Is "inconsistency" in research ethics committee decision-making really a problem? An empirical investigation and reflection', *Clinical Ethics*, 2: 92–99.

Annas, G.J. (1991) 'Ethics committees: From ethical comfort to ethical cover', *Hastings Center Report*, 21: 18–21.

— (2001) 'Conjoined twins: The limits of law at the limits of life', *New England Journal of Medicine*, 344: 1104–08.

Archard, D. (2011) 'Why moral philosophers are not and should not be moral experts', *Bioethics*, 25(3): 119–27.

Aristotle (1962) *The Politics* (T.A. Sinclair, translator), London: Penguin.

Ashcroft, R.E. (2005) 'Making sense of dignity', *Journal of Medical Ethics*, 31: 679–82.

Atkins, K. (2000) 'Autonomy and the subjective character of experience', *Journal of Applied Philosophy*, 17(1): 71–79.

Aulisio, M.P., Arnold, R.M. and Youngner, S.J. (2000) 'Health care ethics consultation: nature, goals, and competencies. A position paper from the Society for Health and Human Values-Society for Bioethics Consultation Task Force on Standards for Bioethics Consultation', *Annals of Internal Medicine*, 133(1): 59–69.

Bailey, R. (2000) 'The pursuit of happiness, Peter Singer interviewed by Ronald Bailey', *Reason*, December 2000 available at http://reason.com/archives/2000/12/01/the-pursuit-of-happiness-peter (accessed 11 December 2011).

Baines, P. (2008) 'Death and *best* interests', *Clinical Ethics*, 3, 171–75.

— (2010) 'Death and *best* interests: a response to the legal challenge', *Clinical Ethics*, 5, 195–200.

Balkin, J. (1992) '(A) just rhetoric?', *Modern Law Review*, 55: 746–53.

Bateman, R.B. (1994) 'Attorneys on bioethics committees: Unwelcome menace or valuable asset?', *Journal of Health Law*, 9(2): 247–72.

Battin, M.P. (2005) *Ending Life: Ethics and the Way We Die*, Oxford: Oxford University Press.

Beale, J.H. (1935) 'The nature of law', in L.L. Fuller (ed), *The Problems of Jurisprudence: A Selection of Readings Supplemented by Comments Prepared by the Editor* (temporary edn), 346–55, Brooklyn: The Foundation Press.

Beauchamp, T.L. and Childress, J.F. (2001) *Principles of Biomedical Ethics*, 5th edn, Oxford: Oxford University Press.

Benatar, D. (2006) 'Bioethics and health and human rights: a critical view', *Journal of Medical Ethics*, 32: 17–20.

Benditt, T.M. (1979) 'Compromising interests and principles', in J.R. Pennock and J.W. Chapman (eds) *Compromise in Ethics, Law and Politics, Nomos, XXI*, 26–37, New York: New York University Press.

Benjamin, M. (1990a) *Splitting the Difference: Compromise and Integrity in Ethics and Politics*, Lawrence, Kansas: University Press of Kansas.

— (1990b) 'Philosophical integrity and policy development in bioethics', *The Journal of Medicine and Philosophy*, 15(4): 375–89.

— (1994) 'Conflict, compromise, and moral integrity', in C.S. Campbell and B.A. Lustig (eds) *Duties to Others*, 261–78, Dordrecht: Kluwer Academic Publishers.

— (2003) *Philosophy and this Actual World*, Maryland: Rowman and Littlefield.

Berlin, I. (1968) *Four Essays on Liberty*, Oxford: Oxford University Press.

— (1991) *The Crooked Timber of Humanity*, New York: Knopf.

Beyleveld, D. and Brownsword, R. (1991) 'Privity, transitivity and rationality', *The Modern Law Review*, 54: 48–71.

— (1994) *Law as a Moral Judgment*, Sheffield: Sheffield Academic Press.

— (2001) *Human Dignity in Bioethics and Biolaw*, Oxford: Oxford University Press.

Beynon, H. (1982) 'Doctors as murderers', *Criminal Law Review*, 17–28.

Biggs, H. (2006) 'In whose best interests: who knows?', *Clinical Ethics*, 1(2): 90–93.

Biggs, H.M. (2003) 'A Pretty fine line: life, death, autonomy and letting it B', *Feminist Legal Studies*, 11(3): 291–301.

Birks, P. (2000) 'Rights, wrongs, and remedies', *Oxford Journal of Legal Studies*, 20(1): 1–37.

Blom-Cooper, L. and Drewry, G. (1976) *Law and Morality*, London: Duckworth.

Bowman, D. (2010) 'An exception to the rule? Practising ethics in practice' available at http://www.intellectualdisability.info/changing-values/an-exception-to-the-rule-practising-ethics-in-practice (accessed 30 December 2011).

Boyle, R.J., Salter, R. and Arnander M.W. (2004) 'Ethics of refusing parental request to withhold or withdraw treatment from their premature baby', *Journal of Medical Ethics* 30: 402–405.

Brahams, D. and Brahams, M. (1983) 'Symposium 1: The Arthur case – a proposal for legislation', *Journal of Medical Ethics*, 9: 12–15.

Brazier, M. (2005) 'An intractable dispute: when parents and professionals disagree', *Medical Law Review*, 13: 412–418.

Brazier, M. and Cave, E. (2007) *Medicine, Patients and the Law*, 4th edn, London: Penguin.

Breen, C. (2002) *The Standard of the Best Interests of the Child: A Western Tradition in International and Comparative Law*. Dordrecht: Martinus Nijhoff.

Bridgeman, J. (1995) 'Declared innocent?', *Medical Law Review*, 3: 117–41.

— (2009) 'A response to "Death and *best* interests" ', *Clinical Ethics*, 4, 15–18.

— (2010) 'Editorial: Critically ill children and best interests', *Clinical Ethics*, 5, 184–87.

British Medical Association (2007) *Withholding and Withdrawing Life-Prolonging Treatment: Guidance for Decision Making*, 3rd edn, London: British Medical Association.

British Medical Association, the Resuscitation Council (UK) and the Royal College of Nursing. (2007) *Decisions Relating to Cardiopulmonary Resuscitation*, London: British Medical Association.

Brock, D.W. (1993) *Life and Death: Philosophical Essays in Biomedical Essays* Cambridge: Cambridge University Press.

Brownsword, R. (1993) 'Towards a rational law of contract', in T. Wilhelmsson (ed), *Perspectives of Critical Contract Law*, 241–72, Aldershot: Dartmouth.

— (1997) 'From co-operative contracting to a contract of co-operation', in D. Campbell and P. Vincent-Jones (eds), *Contract and Economic Organisation*, 14–39, Aldershot: Dartmouth.

— (2008) 'Bioethics: bridging from morality to law?' in M. Freeman (ed), *Law and Bioethics: Current Legal Issues 2008, Volume 11*, 12–30, Oxford: Oxford University Press.

Burnet, D. (2001) 'Re A (Conjoined Twins: Medical Treatment): conjoined twins, sanctity and quality of life, and invention the mother of necessity', *Child and Family Law Quarterly*, 13(1): 91–99.

Burt, R.A. (2005) 'The end of autonomy', *Improving End of Life Care: Why Has It Been So Difficult? Hastings Center Report Special Report*, 35(6): s9–s13.

Butler-Sloss, Dame E. (2006) 'Legal aspects of medical ethics', *Web Journal of Current Legal Issues* 2 available at http://webjcli.ncl.ac.uk/2006/issue2/butlersloss2a.html (accessed 19 January 2012).

Callahan, D. (1996) 'Escaping from legalism: is it possible?', *Hastings Center Report*, 26(6): 34–35.

Campbell, A.V. (2001) 'Clinical governance: watchword or buzzword?', *Journal of Medical Ethics*, 27 Suppl. I: i54–i56.

Choudhry, S. (2008) 'Best interests in the MCA 2005: what can healthcare law learn from family law?', *Health Care Analysis*, 16, 240–51.

Clauss, R. and Nel, W. (2006) 'Drug induced arousal from the permanent vegetative state', *NeuroRehabilitation*, 21: 23–28.

Coggon, J. (2006) 'Could the right to die with dignity represent a new right to die in English law?', *Medical Law Review*, 14(2): 219–37.

— (2007a) 'Ignoring the moral and intellectual shape of the law after Bland: the unintended side-effect of a sorry compromise', *Legal Studies*, 27(1): 110–25.

— (2007b) 'Varied and principled understandings of autonomy in English law: justifiable inconsistency or blinkered moralism?', *Health Care Analysis* 15: 235–55.

— (2008) 'Best interests, public interest and the power of the medical profession', *Health Care Analysis*, 16, 219–32.

— (2010a) 'Assisted dying and the context of debate: "medical law" versus "end-of-life law" ', *Medical Law Review*, 18: 541–63.

— (2010b) 'Doctors and assisted suicide', *British Medical Journal* 340: 1394.

Cohen-Almagor, R. (2006) 'On compromise and coercion', *Ratio Juris*, 19: 434–55.

Commission on Assisted Dying (2011) *'The current legal status of assisted dying is inadequate and incoherent . . .'*, London: Demos.

Cowley, C. (2011) 'Expertise, wisdom and moral philosophers: a response to Gesang', *Bioethics*, doi: 10.1111/j.1467-8519.2010.01860.x.

Cox, D., La Caze, M. and Levine, M. (2008) 'Integrity', *The Stanford Encyclopedia of Philosophy (Fall 2008 Edition)*, E.N. Zalta (ed) available at http://plato.stanford.edu/archives/fall2008/entries/integrity/ (accessed 6 December 2011).

Craig, P. (1997) 'Formal and substantive conceptions of the rule of Law: an analytical Framework'. *Public Law*, 467–87.

Crane, D. (1977) *The sanctity of social life: Physicians' treatment of critically ill patients*, New Brunswick: Transaction.

Cuttini M., Rebgliato M., Bortilo P. and Hansen G. (1999) 'Parental visiting, communication, and participation in ethical decisions: a comparison of neonatal unit policies in Europe', *Archives of Disease in Childhood Fetal Neonatal Ed*, 81: 84–91.

Daily Telegraph (1998) 'The coma girl who refused to die', *The Daily Telegraph*, 11 June.

Daniels, N. and Sabin, J.E. (1997) 'Limits to health care: fair procedures, democratic deliberation and the legitimacy problem for insurers', *Philosophy and Public Affairs*, 26(4): 303–50.

Dawson, A. and Wilkinson, S. (2009) 'Philosophical clinical ethics', *Clinical Ethics*, 4: 36–37.

DeGrazia, D. (1995) 'Value theory and the best interests standard', *Bioethics*, 9, 50–61.

De Haan, J. (2002) 'The ethics of euthanasia: advocates perspectives', *Bioethics*, 16(2): 154–72.

Department for Constitutional Affairs (2007) *Mental Capacity Act 2005: Code of Practice*, London: The Stationery Office.

Department of Health (2008) *End of life care strategy: Promoting high quality care for all adults at the end of life*, London: Department of Health.

Devlin, P. (1965) *The Enforcement of Morals*, Oxford: Oxford University Press.

Dickenson, D., Huxtable, R. and Parker, M. (2010) *The Cambridge Medical Ethics Workbook*, 2nd edn, Cambridge: Cambridge University Press.

Director of Public Prosecutions. (2010) *Policy for Prosecutors in Respect of Cases of Encouraging or Assisting Suicide*, London: Crown Prosecution Service, February 2010.

Donchin, A. (2000) 'Autonomy, interdependence, and assisted suicide: respecting boundaries/crossing lines', *Bioethics*, 14(3):187–204.

Donnelly, M. (2009) 'Best interests, patient participation and the Mental Capacity Act 2005', *Medical Law Review*, 17(1): 1–29.

Douglas, G. (2004) *An Introduction to Family Law*, Oxford: Oxford University Press.

Doyal, L. (1990) 'Medical ethics and moral indeterminacy', *Journal of Law and Society*, 17(1): 1–16.

— (2001) 'Clinical ethics committees and the formulation of health care policy', *Journal of Medical Ethics*, 27 (Suppl. I): i44–i49.

— (2006) 'Dignity in dying should include the legalisation of non-voluntary euthanasia', *Clinical Ethics*, 1: 65–67.

Dubler, N.N. (2011) 'A "principled resolution": The fulcrum for bioethics mediation', *Law and Contemporary Problems*, 74: 177–200.

Dubler, N.N. and Liebman, C.B. (2004) *Bioethics Mediation: A guide to shaping shared solutions*, New York: United Hospital Fund of New York.

Duff, R.S. and Campbell, A.G.M. (1973) 'Moral and ethical dilemmas in the special-care nursery', *New England Journal of Medicine*, 289: 890–94.

— (1980) 'Moral and ethical dilemmas: Seven years into the debate about human ambiguity', *Annals of the American Academy of Political and Social Science* 447: 19–28.

Duffy, D. and Reynolds, P. (2011) 'Babies born at the threshold of viability: attitudes of paediatric consultants and trainees in South East England', *Acta Paediatrica*, 100(1): 42–46.

Dunn, M. and Foster, C. (2010) 'Autonomy and welfare as *amici curiae*', *Medical Law Review*, 18(1): 86–95.

Dunphy, K., Finlay, I., Rathbone, G., Gilbert, J. and Hicks, F. (1995) 'Rehydration in palliative and terminal care: if not – why not?', *Palliative Medicine*, 9(3): 221–28.

Dyer, C. (1995) 'Judge rules doctors can withhold food from PVS victim', *The Guardian*, 18 November.

Dworkin, G. (1988) *The theory and practice of autonomy*, Cambridge: Cambridge University Press.

Dworkin, R. (1975) 'Hard cases', *Harvard Law Review*, 88, 1057–1109.

— (1985) *A Matter of Principle*, Cambridge: Harvard University Press.

Dworkin, R.B. (1996) *Limits: The Role of Law in Bioethical Decision Making*, Bloomington and Indianapolis: Indiana University Press.

Elliston, S. (2007) *The Best Interests of the Child in Health Care*, London: Routledge-Cavendish.

d'Entreves, A.P. (1970) *Natural Law: An Introduction to Legal Philosophy*, London: Hutchinson University Library.

Fagerlin, A. and Schneider, C.E. (2004) 'Enough: the failure of the living will', *Hastings Center Report*, 34(2): 30–42.

Falmagne, R.J. and Marjori, H. (eds.) (2002) *Representing Reason: Feminist Theory and Formal Logic*, Lanham: Rowman and Littlefield.

Fenton, B. (1995) 'Doctor admits "mercy killing" of two babies', *The Daily Telegraph*, 15 February.

Finnis, J. (1986) *Natural Law and Natural Rights*, Oxford: Clarendon Press.

— (1993) 'Bland: crossing the Rubicon?' *Law Quarterly Review*, 109: 329–37.

Fletcher, G.P. (1969) 'Prolonging life: some legal considerations', in A.B. Downing (ed.) *Euthanasia and the Right to Death: The Case for Voluntary Euthanasia*, 71–84, London: Peter Owen.

Fletcher, J. and Siegler, M. (1996) 'What are the goals of ethics consultation? A consensus statement', *Journal of Clinical Ethics*, 7: 122–26.

Forbes, K. (1998) 'Response to euthanasia and the principle of justice', in R. Gill (ed.) *Euthanasia and the Churches*, 98–103, London: Cassell.

Foster, C. (2005) 'Baby Charlotte: the end of intolerability', *Solicitors Journal*, 1240–41.

—— (2009) *Choosing Life, Choosing Death: The Tyranny of Autonomy in Medical Ethics and Law*, Oxford: Hart.

—— (2011) *Human Dignity in Bioethics and Law*, Oxford: Hart.

Fournier, V., Rari, E., Førde, R., Neitzke, G., Pegoraro, R. and Newson, A.J. (2009) 'Clinical ethics consultation in Europe: a comparative and ethical review of the role of patients', *Clinical Ethics*, 4: 131–38.

Fox, E. and Arnold, R.M. (1996) 'Evaluating outcomes in ethics consultation research', *Journal of Clinical Ethics*, 7: 127–38.

Frankfurt, H. G. (1971) 'Freedom of the will and the concept of a person', *Journal of Philosophy*, 68(1): 5–20.

Frith, L. (2009) 'Process and consensus: Ethical decision-making in the infertility clinic – a qualitative study', *Journal of Medical Ethics*, 35: 662–67.

Fuller, L.L. (1967) *Legal Fictions*, Stanford: Stanford University Press.

—— (1968) *Anatomy of the Law*, London: Frederick A. Praeger.

—— (1969) *The Morality of Law* (revised edn), New Haven: Yale University Press.

General Medical Council (2002) *Withholding and Withdrawing Life-prolonging Treatments: Good Practice in Decision-making*, London: General Medical Council.

—— (2008) *Acting as an expert witness*, London: General Medical Council.

—— (2010) *Treatment and care towards the end of life: Good practice in decision making*, London: General Medical Council.

Gesang, B. (2010) 'Are moral philosophers moral experts?', *Bioethics*, 24: 153–59.

Gewirth, A. (1978) *Reason and Morality*, Chicago: University of Chicago Press.

Giacino, J.T., Ashwal, S., Childs, N., Cranford, R., Jennett, B., Katz, D.I., Kelly, J.P., Rosenberg, J.H., Whyte, J., Zafonte, R.D. and Zasler, N.D. (2002) 'The minimally conscious state: definition and diagnostic criteria', *Neurology*, 58(3): 349–53.

Gillon, R. (1997) ' "Futility" – too ambiguous and pejorative a term?', *Journal of Medical Ethics*, 23: 339–40.

—— (2003) 'Ethics needs principles – four can encompass the rest – and respect for autonomy should be "first among equals" ', *Journal of Medical Ethics*, 29: 307–312.

Glasson, J. and Irwin, S. (1997) 'Declaration of life and death', *New Law Journal*, 147: 1389–90, 1432–33.

Golding, M.P. (1979) 'The nature of compromise: a preliminary inquiry', in J.R. Pennock and J.W. Chapman (eds) *Compromise in Ethics, Law and Politics, Nomos, XXI*, 3–25, New York: New York University Press.

Goodstein, J.D. (2000) 'Moral compromise and personal integrity: exploring the ethical issues of deciding together in organizations', *Business Ethics Quarterly*, 10(4): 805–19.

Gordijn, B. (2001) 'Regulating moral dissent in an open society: the Dutch experience with pragmatic tolerance', *Journal of Medicine and Philosophy* 26(3): 225–44.

Gormally, A.J.L. (1978a) 'Prolongation of life: the principle of respect for human life', *Linacre Centre Papers*, 1: 1–28.

— (1978b) 'Prolongation of life: is there a morally significant difference between killing and letting die?' *Linacre Centre Papers*, 2: 1–20.

Gouldner, A.W. 'Anti-minotaur: the myth of a value-free sociology', *Social Problems*, 9(3): 199–213.

Grubb, A. (1995) 'Incompetent patient in PVS: views of relatives and "best interests" ', *Medical Law Review*, 3: 80–84.

Guardian (1978) 'Murder inquiry into patient's death', *The Guardian*, 10 January.

— (1997a) 'Judge extends law by allowing patient's death', *The Guardian*, 22 March.

— (1997b) 'Hillsborough victim "awakes" ', *The Guardian*, 26 March.

— (2000) 'Euthanasia claim MP clear', *The Guardian*, 25 August.

Gunn, M. (1994) 'The meaning of incapacity', *Medical Law Review*, 2: 8–29.

Gunn, M.J. and Smith, J.C. (1985) 'Arthur's case and the right to life of a Down's syndrome child', *Criminal Law Review*, 705–715.

Habermas, J. (1990) *Moral Consciousness and Communicative Action*, Cambridge: MIT Press.

Halliday, R. (1997) 'Medical futility and the social context', *Journal of Medical Ethics*, 23: 148–53.

Hardwig, J. (1997) 'Is there a duty to die?', *Hastings Center Report*, 27(2): 34–42.

Hare, R.M. (1973) 'Survival of the weakest', in S. Gorovitz, A.L. Jameton, R. Macklin, J.M. O'Connor, E.V. Perrin, B.P. St. Clair and S. Sherwin (eds) (1976) *Moral Problems in Medicine*, 364–69, New Jersey: Prentice-Hall.

Harmon, L. (1990) 'Falling off the vine: legal fictions and the doctrine of informed consent', *Yale Law Journal*, 100: 1–71.

Harrington, J. (2003) 'Deciding best interests: medical progress, clinical judgment and the "good family" ', *Web Journal of Current Legal Issues* 3 available at http://webjcli.ncl.ac.uk/2003/issue3/harrington3.html (accessed 19 January 2012).

Harrington, J.A. (1996) 'Privileging the medical norm: liberalism, self-determination and refusal of treatment', *Legal Studies*, 16: 348–67.

Harris, J. (1985) *The Value of Life: An Introduction to Medical Ethics*, London: Routledge and Kegan Paul.

— (1997) 'The philosophical case against the philosophical case against euthanasia', in J. Keown (ed) *Euthanasia Examined: Ethical, Clinical and Legal Perspectives*, 36–45, Cambridge: Cambridge University Press.

Hart, H.L.A. (1963) *Law, Liberty and Morality*, Oxford: Oxford University Press.

— (1965) 'Review: Lon L. Fuller, The morality of law', *Harvard Law Review*, 78: 1281–1296.

Hendrick, J. (2001) 'Legal aspects of clinical ethics committees', *Journal of Medical Ethics*, 27 (Suppl. I): i50–53.

Henry, C. and Seymour, J. (2008) *Advance Care Planning: A Guide for Health and Social Care Staff*, London: Department of Health.

Herring, J. (2005) 'Farewell welfare?', *Journal of Social Welfare and Family Law*, 27, 159–71

Hill Jr., T.E. (1991) *Autonomy and Self-Respect*, Cambridge: Cambridge University Press.

Hinchliffe, M. (1996) 'Vegetative state patients', *New Law Journal*, 146: 1579–80, 1585.

Hollis, M. (1970) 'The limits of irrationality', in B.R. Wilson, (ed), *Rationality*, 214–20, Oxford: Basil Blackwell.

Holm, S. (2008) 'Best interests: what problems in family law should health care law avoid?', *Health Care Analysis*, 16: 252–54.

— (2010) 'Euthanasia: agreeing to disagree?', *Medicine Health Care and Philosophy*, 13: 399–402.

Hope, T., Hicks, N., Reynolds, D.J.M., Crisp, R. and Griffiths, S. (1998) 'Rationing and the health authority', *British Medical Journal*, 317: 1067–69.

House of Lords Select Committee (1994) *Report of the Select Committee on Medical Ethics*, HL Paper 21, London: Her Majesty's Stationery Office.

Hurst, S.A., Chevrolet, J. and Loew, F. (2006) 'Methods in clinical ethics: a time for eclectic pragmatism?', *Clinical Ethics* 1: 159–64.

Huxtable, R. (1999) 'Withholding and withdrawing nutrition/hydration: the continuing (mis)adventures of the law', *Journal of Social Welfare and Family Law*, 21(4): 339–56.

— (2000a) 'Re M (Medical Treatment: Consent): time to remove the "flak jacket"?', *Child and Family Law Quarterly*, 12(1): 83–88.

— (2000b) 'The Court of Appeal and conjoined twins: condemning the unworthy life?', *Bulletin of Medical Ethics*, 162: 13–18.

— (2001) 'Logical separation? Conjoined twins, slippery slopes and resource allocation', *Journal of Social Welfare and Family Law*, 23(4): 459–71.

— (2002a) 'Separation of conjoined twins: where next for English law?', *Criminal Law Review*, 459–70.

— (2002b) 'Re B (Consent to Treatment: Capacity): a right to die or is it right to die?', *Child and Family Law Quarterly*, 14(3): 341–55.

— (2007) *Euthanasia, Ethics and the Law: From Conflict to Compromise*, London: Routledge-Cavendish.

— (2008) 'Whatever you want? Beyond the patient in medical law', *Health Care Analysis*, 16(3): 288–301.

— (2012a) 'Law at the limits at the limits of life?', in C. Cowley (ed) *Reconceiving Medical Ethics*, 175–88, London: Continuum.

— (2012b) 'Treating the minimally conscious patient: life before choice?', *Journal of Bioethical Inquiry*, 9: 9–12.

— (2012c) 'Dealing with uncertainty: compromise, clinical ethics and disorders of consciousness', in R.J. Jox, K. Kuehlmeyer, G. Marckmann and E. Racine (eds) *Vegetative State: A Paradigmatic Problem of Modern Societies*, 185–199, Münster: Lit.

— (2012d) 'Euthanasia excused: between prohibition and permission', in A. Alghrani, R. Bennett and S. Ost (eds) *The Criminal Law and Bioethical Conflict: Walking the Tightrope*, Cambridge: Cambridge University Press (forthcoming).

Huxtable, R. and Forbes, K. (2004) 'Glass v UK: maternal instinct vs. medical opinion', *Child and Family Law Quarterly*, 16(3): 339–54.

Huxtable, R. and Möller, M. (2007) ' "Setting a principled boundary"? Euthanasia as a response to "life fatigue" ', *Bioethics*, 21(3): 117–26.

James, T. (2008) 'The appeal to law to provide public answers to bioethical questions: it all depends what sort of answers you want', *Health Care Analysis*, 16: 65–76.

Jenkins, R. (2005) 'Staff were right to let boy die, mother told', *The Times*, 10 May.

Jonsen, A., Siegler, M. and Winslade, W. (2006) *Clinical Ethics*, 6th edn, New York: McGraw-Hill.

Jonsen, A.R. (1998) *The Birth of Bioethics*, Oxford: Oxford University Press.

Jox, R.J. (2011) 'End-of-life decision making concerning patients with disorders of consciousness', *Res Cogitans*, 8(1): 43–61.

Judiciary of England and Wales (2011) *Court of Protection Report 2010* available at http://www.judiciary.gov.uk/publications-and-reports/reports/family/court-of-protection/court-of-protection-report-2010 (accessed 22 January 2012).

Kant, I. (1991) *The Moral Law: Groundwork of the Metaphysic of Morals*, translated and analysed by H.J. Paton, London: Hutchinson and Co.

Kennedy, I. (1977) 'Switching off life support machines: the legal implications', *Criminal Law Review*, 443–52.

— (1981) *The Unmasking of Medicine*, London: Allen and Unwin.

— (1991) *Treat Me Right: Essays in Medical Law and Ethics*, Oxford: Clarendon Press.

— (1997) 'Child: discontinuation of treatment', *Medical Law Review*, 5: 102–104.

Kennedy, I. and Grubb, A. (1993) 'Withdrawal of artificial hydration and nutrition: incompetent adult', *Medical Law Review*, 1: 359–70.

Keown, J. (ed) (1997a) *Euthanasia Examined: Ethical, Clinical and Legal Perspectives*, Cambridge: Cambridge University Press.

— (1997b) 'Restoring moral and intellectual shape to the law after *Bland*', *The Law Quarterly Review*, 113: 481–503.

— (2000) 'Beyond Bland: a critique of the BMA guidance on withholding and withdrawing medical treatment', *Legal Studies*, 20(1): 66–84.

— (2002a) *Euthanasia, Ethics and Public Policy: An Argument Against Legalisation*, Cambridge: Cambridge University Press.

— (2002b) 'The case of Ms B: suicide's slippery slope?', *Journal of Medical Ethics*, 28(4): 238–39.

Keown, J. and Gormally, L. (1999) 'Human dignity, autonomy and mentally incapacitated patients: a critique of *Who Decides?*', *Web Journal of Current Legal Issues*, 4 available at http://webjcli.ncl.ac.uk/1999/issue4/keown4.html (accessed 11 December 2011).

Kovács, J. (2010) 'The transformation of (bio)ethics expertise in a world of ethical pluralism', *Journal of Medical Ethics*, 36(12): 767–70.

Kramer, M. (1998) 'Scrupulousness without scruples: a critique of Lon Fuller and his defenders', *Oxford Journal of Legal Studies*, 18: 235–63.

Kuflik, A. (1979) 'Morality and compromise', in J.R. Pennock and J.W. Chapman (eds) *Compromise in Ethics, Law and Politics, Nomos*, XXI, 38–65, New York: New York University Press.

Kuhse, H. (1987) *The Sanctity-of-Life Doctrine in Medicine: A Critique*, Oxford: Clarendon Press.

Kutner, L. (1969) 'The living will: a proposal', *Indiana Law Journal*, 44(1): 539–54.

Lamb, D. (2006) 'Reversibility and death: a reply to David J. Cole', *Journal of Medical Ethics*, 33: 146–49.

Lantos, J.D. and Meadow, W.L. (2011) 'Should the "slow code" be resuscitated?', *The American Journal of Bioethics*, 11(11): 8–12.

Larcher, V., Slowther, A. and Watson, A.R. (2010) 'Core competencies for clinical ethics committees', *Clinical Medicine*, 10(1): 30–33.

Larcher, V.F., Lask, B. and McCarthy, J.M. (1997) 'Paediatrics at the cutting edge: do we need clinical ethics committees?', *Journal of Medical Ethics*, 23(4): 245–49.

Laureys, S., Celesia, G.G., Cohadon, F., Lavrijsen, J., León-Carrión, J., Sannita, W.G., Sazbon, L., Schmutzhard, E., von Wild, K.R., Zeman, A., Dolce, G. and the European Task Force on Disorders of Consciousness (2010) 'Unresponsive wakefulness syndrome: a new name for the vegetative state or apallic syndrome', *BMC Medicine* 2010: 68

Lee, R. and Morgan, D. (2001) 'Regulating risk society: stigmata cases, scientific citizenship and biomedical diplomacy', *Sydney Law Review*, 23(3): 297–318.

Leggatt, A. (2001) *Tribunals for Users: One System, One Service*, London: Department for Constitutional Affairs.

Leng, R. (1982) 'Death and the criminal law', *Modern Law Review*, 45: 206–211.

Leonard, E. (2000) *Be Cool*, London: Penguin.

Lewis, P. (2002) 'Procedures that are against the medical interests of incompetent adults', *Oxford Journal of Legal Studies*, 22(4): 575–618.

Levin, A. (2009) '80 lawyers refused to help save Baby OT, leaving the parents to fend for themselves', *The Daily Mail*, 22 March.

Linacre Centre (The Linacre Centre for Health Care Ethics) (1982) 'Euthanasia and clinical practice: trends, principles and alternatives. a Working Party report', in L. Gormally (ed.) (1994) *Euthanasia, Clinical Practice and the Law*, 1–107, London: The Linacre Centre for Health Care Ethics.

— (1993) 'Submission to the Select Committee of the House of Lords on Medical Ethics', in L. Gormally (ed.) (1994) *Euthanasia, Clinical Practice and the Law*, 111–65, London: The Linacre Centre for Health Care Ethics.

Llewellyn, K. (1940) 'The normative, the legal, and the law-jobs theory: the problem of juristic method, *Yale Law Journal*, 49: 1355–1400.

Luchetti, M. (2010) 'Eluana Englaro, chronicle of a death foretold: ethical considerations on the recent right-to-die case in Italy', *Journal of Medical Ethics* 36: 333–35.

Lukes, S. (1970) 'Some problems about rationality', in B.R. Wilson (ed.), *Rationality*, 194–213, Oxford. Basil Blackwell.

Lyons, B. (2010) 'Children, best interests and the courts: a response to Bridgeman', *Clinical Ethics*, 5, 188–94.

MacIntyre, A. (2007) *After Virtue*, 3rd edn, Notre Dame, IN: University of Notre Dame Press.

Maclean, A.R. (2006) 'Advance directives, future selves and decision-making', *Medical Law Review*, 14(3): 291–320.

— (2008) 'Advance directives and the rocky waters of anticipatory decision-making', *Medical Law Review*, 16(1): 1–22.

Manninen, B.A. (2006) 'A case for justified non-voluntary active euthanasia: exploring the ethics of the Groningen Protocol', *Journal of Medical Ethics*, 32: 643–51.

Margalit, A. (2010) *On Compromise and Rotten Compromises*, Princeton: Princeton University Press.

May, W.F. (2003) 'Oral evidence to President's Council on Bioethics' available at http://bioethics.gov/transcripts/oct03/oct17full.html (accessed 28 March 2007).

McCall Smith, A. (1990) 'Committee ethics? Clinical ethics committees and their introduction in the United Kingdom', *Journal of Law and Society*, 17(1): 124–39.

McHaffie H.E., Laing I.A., Parker M. and McMillan J. (2001) 'Deciding for imperilled newborns: medical authority or parental autonomy?', *Journal of Medical Ethics* 27: 104–109.

McLean, S. (1994) 'Letting die or assisting death: how should the law respond to the patient in persistent vegetative state?', in K. Peterson (ed.) *Law and Medicine: A Special Issue of Law in Context (Volume 11(2) 1993)*, 3–16, La Trobe University: La Trobe University Press.

— (1996) 'End-of-life decisions and the law', *Journal of Medical Ethics*, 22, 261–62.

McLean, S.A.M. (2007a) 'Law, ethics and health care', in R. Ashcroft, A. Dawson, H. Draper and J. McMillan (eds), *Principles of Health Care Ethics* (2nd edn), 193–98, Chichester: John Wiley and Sons.

— (2007b) 'What and who are clinical ethics committees for?' *Journal of Medical Ethics*, 33: 497–500.

— (2008) 'Clinical ethics committees: a due process wasteland?' *Clinical Ethics*, 3: 99–104.

— (2009a) 'Clinical ethics consultation in the United Kingdom', *Diametros*, 22: 76–89.

— (2009b) 'Live and let die', *British Medical Journal*, 339: 4112.

Meller, S. and Barclay, S. (2011) 'Mediation: an approach to intractable disputes between parents and paediatricians', *Archives of Disease in Childhood*, 96: 619–21.

Melley, C.D. (1992) 'The philosopher in the health care setting: objections and replies', *HEC Forum*, 4(4): 237–54.

Michalowski, S. (1997) 'Is it in the best interests of a child to have a life-saving liver transplantation? *Re T (Wardship: Medical Treatment)*', *Child and Family Law Quarterly*, 9: 179–89.

— (2005) 'Advance refusals of life-sustaining medical treatment: the relativity of an absolute right', *Modern Law Review*, 68(6): 958–82.

Mill, J.S. (1962) 'Utilitarianism', in M. Warnock (ed.) *Utilitarianism, On Liberty, Essay on Bentham (by John Stuart Mill), together with selected writings of Jeremy Bentham and John Austin*, 251–321, London: Collins, The Fontana Library.

Miola, J. (2007) *Medical Ethics and Medical Law: A Symbiotic Relationship*, Oxford: Hart.

Montgomery, J. (2000) 'Time for a paradigm shift? Medical law in transition', *Current Legal Problems*, 53(1): 363–408.

— (2006) 'Law and the demoralisation of medicine', *Legal Studies*, 26(2): 185–210.

Monti, M.M., Vanhaudenhuyse, A., Coleman, M.R., Boly, M., Pickard, J. D., Tshibanda, L., Owen, A.M. and Laureys, S., (2010) 'Wilful modulation of brain activity in disorders of consciousness', *New England Journal of Medicine*, 362: 579–89.

Moratti, S. (2010) 'Management of conflicts with the parents over administration of life-prolonging treatment in Dutch NICUs', *Medicine and Law*, 29: 289–301.

Moreno, J.D. (1995) *Deciding Together: Bioethics and Moral Consensus*, New York: Oxford University Press.

Morgan, D. (1994) 'Odysseus and the binding directive: only a cautionary tale?', *Legal Studies*, 14(3): 411–42.

Morris, A. (2000) 'Easing the passing: end of life decisions and the Medical Treatment (Prevention of Euthanasia) Bill', *Medical Law Review*, 8: 300–315.

— (2009) 'Selective treatment of irreversibly impaired infants: decision-making at the threshold', *Medical Law Review*, 17: 347–76.

Morrison, W. (1997) *Jurisprudence: From the Greeks to Post-Modernism*, London: Cavendish.

Mulcahy, L. (2006) *Mediating Medical Negligence Claims: An Option for the Future?*, Norwich: The Stationary Office.

Nachi, M. (2004) 'The morality in/of compromise: some theoretical reflections', *Social Science Information*, 43: 291–305.

Nagasawa, Y. (2004) 'Subjective character of experience in medical ethics: a reply to Atkins', *Journal of Applied Philosophy*, 21(2): 219–23.

Nagel, T. (1986) *The View from Nowhere*, Oxford: Oxford University Press.

National Council for Palliative Care (2007) *Artificial Nutrition and Hydration: Guidance in End of Life Care for Adults*, London: National Council for Palliative Care.

National Health and Medical Research Council (2004) *Post-coma Unresponsiveness (Vegetative State): A Clinical Framework for Diagnosis: An Information Paper*, Canberra: NHMRC.

Newson, A.J. (2009) 'The role of patients in clinical ethics support: a snapshot of practices and attitudes in the United Kingdom', *Clinical Ethics*, 4(3): 139–45.

NICE (2008) *Social Value Judgements: Principles for the Development of NICE Guidance* (2nd edn) Available at http://www.nice.org.uk/aboutnice/howwework/socialvaluejudgements/socialvaluejudgements.jsp (accessed 17 February 2012).

Norrie, A. (1993) *Crime, Reason and History: A Critical Introduction to Criminal Law*, London: Weidenfeld and Nicolson.

Nozick, R. (1993) *The Nature of Rationality*, Princeton, New Jersey: Princeton University Press.

Nuffield Council on Bioethics (2006) *Critical Care Decisions in Fetal and Neonatal Medicine: Ethical Issues*, London: Nuffield Council on Bioethics.

O'Neill, O. (2002) *Autonomy and Trust in Bioethics*, Cambridge: Cambridge University Press.

— (2003) 'Some limits of informed consent', *Journal of Medical Ethics*, 29: 4–7.

Olivier, P.J.J. (1975) *Legal Fictions in Practice and Legal Science*, Rotterdam: Rotterdam University Press.

Osman, A., Ferriman, A. and Timmins, N. (1981) 'Women cry "Thank God" as Dr Arthur is cleared', *The Times*, 6 November.

Owen, A.M., Coleman, M.R., Boly, M., Davis, M.H., Laureys, S. and Pickard, J.D. (2006) 'Detecting awareness in the vegetative state', *Science*, 313: 1402.

Paola, F.A. and Walker, R. (2006) 'Ethicians, ethicists and the goals of clinical ethics consultation', *Intern Emerg Med*, 1(1): 5–14.

Pearson, G. and Salter, M. (1999) 'Getting public law back into a critical condition: the rule of law as a source for immanent critique', *Social and Legal Studies*, 8(4): 483–508.

Peart, N. and Gillett, G. (1998) 'Re G: a life worth living?' *Journal of Law and Medicine*, 5(3): 239–51.

Pedersen, R., Akre, V. and Førde, R. (2009) 'What is happening during case deliberations in clinical ethics committees? A pilot study', *Journal of Medical Ethics*, 35(3): 147–52.

Pedersen, R., Hurst, S.A., Schildmann, J., Schuster, S. and Molewijk, B. (2010) 'The development of a descriptive evaluation tool for clinical ethics case consultations', *Clinical Ethics*, 5: 136–41.

Pollock, L. (1988) 'Evaluating moral theories', *American Philosophical Quarterly*, 25(3): 229–40.

Price, D. (2001) 'Fairly Bland: an alternative view of a supposed new "death ethic" and the BMA guidelines', *Legal Studies*, 21: 618–43.

— (2007) 'My view of the sanctity of life: a rebuttal of John Keown's critique', *Legal Studies*, 27(4), 549–65.

Quigley, M. (2008) 'Best interests, the power of the medical profession, and the power of the judiciary', *Health Care Analysis*, 16, 233–39.

Rachels, J. (1979) 'Euthanasia, killing, and letting die', in J. Ladd (ed.) *Ethical Issues Relating to Life and Death*, 146–63, Oxford: Oxford University Press.

— (1986) *The End of Life: Euthanasia and Morality*, Oxford: Oxford University Press.

— (1993) 'Euthanasia', In T. Regan (ed.) *Matters of Life and Death: New Introductory Essays in Moral Philosophy*, 30–68, New York: McGraw Hill.

Racine, E. and Hayes, K. (2006) 'The need for a clinical ethics service and its goals in a community healthcare service centre: a survey', *Journal of Medical Ethics*, 32: 564–66.

Radin, M.J. (1989) 'Reconsidering the rule of law', *Boston University Law Review*, 69(4): 781–819.

Ravenscroft, A.J. and Bell, M.D.D. (2000) ' "End-of-life" decision making within intensive care: objective, consistent, defensible?', *Journal of Medical Ethics*, 26: 435–40.

Rawls, J. (1972) *A Theory of Justice*, Oxford: Oxford University Press.

Raz, J. (1977) 'The rule of law and its virtue', *The Law Quarterly Review*, 93: 195–211.

— (1990) 'The politics of the rule of law', in J. Raz (1994), *Ethics in the Public Domain: Essays in the Morality of Law and Politics*. Oxford: Clarendon Press, 354–62.

Read, J. and Clements, L. (2004) 'Demonstrably awful: the right to life and the selective non-treatment of disabled babies and young children', *Journal of Law and Society*, 31(4): 482–509.

Regan, T. (2004) *The Case for Animal Rights* (2nd edn), Berkeley: University of California Press.

Reiter-Theil S. (2001) 'The Freiburg approach to ethics consultation: process, outcome and competencies', *Journal of Medical Ethics*, 27 Suppl I: i21–23.

— (2009) 'Dealing with the normative dimension in clinical ethics consultation', *Cambridge Quarterly of Healthcare Ethics*, 18(4): 347–59.

Roberts, S.E. (1990) 'When not to prolong life', *The Law Quarterly Review*, 106: 218–22.

Ross, W.D. (1930) *The Right and the Good*, Oxford: Oxford University Press.

Royal College of Paediatrics and Child Health (1997) *Withholding or Withdrawing Life Saving Treatment in Children: A Framework for Practice*, London: Royal College of Paediatrics and Child Health.

— (2004) *Withholding or Withdrawing Life Saving Treatment in Children: A Framework for Practice* (2nd edn) London: Royal College of Paediatrics and Child Health.

Royal College of Physicians (2003) *The Vegetative State: Guidance on Diagnosis and Management*, London: Royal College of Physicians.

— (2005) *Ethics in Practice: Background and Recommendations for Enhanced Support*, London: Royal College of Physicians.

Samanta, J. (2009) 'Lasting powers of attorney for healthcare under the Mental Capacity Act 2005: enhanced prospective self-determination for future incapacity or a simulacrum?', *Medical Law Review*, 17: 377–409.

Sawyer, C. (1997) 'Under the eye of God: the cultural inheritance of family law', Presentation delivered at Socio-Legal Studies Association annual conference, Cardiff, April 1997.

Schneider, C.E. (1994) 'Bioethics in the language of the law', *Hastings Center Report*, 24(4): 16–22.

Scruton, R. (2001) 'Armchair moralising', *New Statesman* 22 January 2001 available at http://www.newstatesman.com/200101220048.htm (accessed 11 December 2011).

Seale, C. (2010) 'The role of doctors' religious faith and ethnicity in taking ethically controversial decisions during end-of-life care', *Journal of Medical Ethics*, 36: 677–82.

Shapiro, M. (1979) 'Compromise and litigation', in J.R. Pennock and J.W. Chapman (eds) *Compromise in Ethics, Law and Politics, Nomos*, XXI, 163–75, New York: New York University Press.

Sheldon, S. and Wilkinson, S. (1997) 'Conjoined twins: the legality and ethics of sacrifice', *Medical Law Review*, 5: 149–71.

Simmonds, N.E. (2007) *Law as a Moral Idea*, Oxford: Oxford University Press.

Singer, P. (1993) *Practical Ethics*, 2nd edn, Cambridge: Cambridge University Press.

—— (1994) *Rethinking Life and Death: The Collapse of Our Traditional Ethics*, New York: St Martin's Press.

—— (1995) 'Presidential address: is the sanctity of life ethic terminally ill?', *Bioethics*, 9: 327–43.

Skegg, P.D.G. (1974) 'A justification for medical procedures performed without consent', *The Law Quarterly Review*, 90: 517–30.

—— (1988) *Law, Ethics and Medicine: Studies in Medical Law*, revised edn, Oxford: Clarendon Press.

Skene, L. and Parker, M. (2002) 'The role of the church in developing the law', *Journal of Medical Ethics*, 28: 215–218.

Slowther, A., Bunch, C., Woolnough, B. and Hope T. (2001) 'Clinical ethics support services in the UK: an investigation of current provision of ethics support to health professionals in the UK', *Journal of Medical Ethics*, 27: 2–8.

Slowther, A., Johnston, C., Goodall, J. and Hope, T. (2004a) 'Development of a national clinical ethics network', *British Medical Journal* 328: 950–52.

—— (2004b) *A Practical Guide for Clinical Ethics Support*, Oxford: The ETHOX Centre.

Smajdor, A., Ives, J., Baldock, E. and Langlois, A. (2008) 'Editorial: Getting from the ethical to the empirical and back again: the danger of getting it wrong, and the possibilities for getting it right', *Health Care Analysis*, 16(1): 7–16.

Smith, T.V. (1942) 'Compromise: its context and limits', *Ethics*, 53(1): 1–13.

Smyth, C. (2009) 'Parents split on whether disabled son should live or die', *The Times*, 3 November.

Sokol, D.K. (2005) 'Meeting the ethical needs of doctors: we need clinical ethicists in addition to other measures', *British Medical Journal*, 330: 741–42.

—— (2008) 'The "four quadrants" approach to clinical ethics case analysis: an application and review', *Journal of Medical Ethics*, 34: 513–516.

Summers, R.S. (1982) *Instrumentalism and American Legal Theory*, Ithaca: Cornell University Press.

—— (1984) *Lon L. Fuller*, London: Edward Arnold.

Tännsjö, T. (2007) 'Why no compromise is possible', *Metaphilosophy*, 38: 330–43.

Teel, K. (1975) 'The physician's dilemma: a doctor's view: what the law should be', *Baylor Law Review*, 27: 6–9.

Terry, L.M. and Sanders, K. (2011) 'Best practices in clinical ethics consultation and decision-making', *Clinical Ethics*, 6: 103–108.

Thompson, T., Barbour, R. and Schwartz, L. (2003) 'Adherence to advance directives in critical care decision making: vignette study', *British Medical Journal*, 327: 1011–14.

Thorpe, L.J. (1997) 'The Caesarean section debate', *Family Law*, 663–64.

Times (1997) 'Woman in coma allowed to die', *The Times*, 12 November.
— (1998) 'Mother wins legal right to let son die', *The Times*, 17 June.
Timmins, N. (1981) 'Dr Jolly is not to be prosecuted', *The Times*, 6 October.
Twining, W. and Miers, D.R. (1991) *How to do Things with Rules*, 3rd edn, London: Butterworths.
Updale, E. (2006) 'The challenge of lay membership of clinical ethics committees', *Clinical Ethics*, 1(1): 60–62.
Veatch, R.M. and Miller, F.G. (eds) (2001) 'The internal morality of medicine', *Journal of Medicine and Philosophy*, 26(6).
Veitch, K. (2007) *The Jurisdiction of Medical Law*, London: Ashgate.
Velleman, J.D. (2004) 'Against the right to die' available at https://files.nyu.edu/jrs477/public/Velleman%20-%20Against%20the%20Right%20to%20Die.pdf (accessed 17 February 2012).
Verhagen, A.A.E., De Vos, M., Dorscheidt, J.H.H.M., Engels, B., Hubben, J.H. and Sauer, P.J. (2009) 'Conflicts about end-of-life decisions in NICUs in the Netherlands', *Pediatrics*, 124: e112–e119.
Ward Platt, M. and Ward Platt, A. (2005) 'Conflicts of care', *Archives of Disease in Childhood*, 90: 331.
Weber, W. (1968) *Economy and Society: An Outline of Interpretive Sociology*, G. Roth and C. Wittich, eds.; E. Fischoff (et al), translators, New York: Bedminster Press.
Whitehead, J.M., Sokol, D.K., Bowman, D. and Sedgwick, P. (2009) 'Consultation activities of clinical ethics committees in the United Kingdom: an empirical study and wake-up call', *Postgraduate Medical Journal*, 85: 451–54.
Wilkinson, D. (2006) 'Is it in the best interests of an intellectually disabled infant to die?', *Journal of Medical Ethics*, 32: 454–59.
Williams, G. (1973) 'Euthanasia', *Medico-Legal Journal*, 41: 14–34.
— (1977) 'Letters to the Editor: Switching off life support machines', *Criminal Law Review*, 635.
— (1981) 'Letter: Life of a Child', *The Times*, 13 August.
Williamson, L. (2007a) 'Empirical assessments of clinical ethics services: implications for clinical ethics committees', *Clinical Ethics*, 2: 187–92.
— (2007b) 'The quality of bioethics debate: implications for clinical ethics committees', *Journal of Medical Ethics*, 34: 357–60.
Willigenburg, T. van (2000) 'Moral compromises, moral integrity and the indeterminacy of value rankings', *Ethical Theory and Moral Practice*, 3: 385–404.
Winslow, B.J. and Winslow, G.R. (1991) 'Integrity and compromise in nursing ethics', *The Journal of Medicine and Philosophy*, 16: 307–23.
Wolf, S.M. (1992) 'Due process in ethics committee case review', *HEC Forum*, 4: 83–96.
Woodcock, T. and Wheeler, R. (2010) 'Law and medical ethics in organ transplantation surgery', *Annals of the Royal College of Surgeons of England*, 92(4): 282–85.
Zoloth-Dorfman, L. and Rubin, S.B. (1997) 'Navigators and captains: expertise in clinical ethics consultation', *Theoretical Medicine and Bioethics*, 18(4): 421–32.

Index

absolute value of life, 109
accountability, 171
actus reus ('physical' element of offence), 56
Adams, J., 21
adults, incapacitated, 4, 51–74; advance directives, 52, 55, 65–71, 90, 91, 92; autonomy or welfare, 72–4; best interests, 55–65; clinically assisted nutrition and hydration decisions, 52, 55, 56, 57, 60, 61, 63, 64, 69, 73; lasting powers of attorney in relation to, 71–2; minimally conscious state, 53, 59, 63, 64, 73; persistent vegetative state in, 55–62, 86; *see also* children, welfare of
advance care plans, 94
advance directives, 52, 55, 65–71; autonomy, respecting, 90, 91, 92; *see also* refusal of treatment, advance
Alzheimer's disease, 116
American Society of Bioethics and Humanities (ASBH), 154
amici curiae, 147
amputation, refusal, 66, 93
analytic philosophy, 160
Andre, J., 154
Andrews, Keith, 61, 64
Annas, George J., 75, 148, 149, 163, 178
Aquinas, St. Thomas, 15
Aristotle, 15, 19, 27
Arnold, R.M., 154
Arthur, Leonard, 38–9, 49–50, 78–9, 89, 96
artificial nutrition and hydration (ANH) *see* clinically assisted nutrition and hydration (CANH)

artificial ventilation: refusal of, 66; withdrawal or denial in adults, 158, 159; withholding/withdrawing in adults, 54, 67, 93, 103; withholding/withdrawing in children, 33, 34, 42, 43–4, 46, 47, 49; *see also* intubation; oxygen dependence
assisted dying, resistance to, 91; *see also* euthanasia
Association for Children's Palliative Care (ACT), 2
Attard twins ('Jodie and Mary'), separation of, 44–5, 97, 106, 111, 123, 150
Austin, John, 15
autonomy: best desire, 117–18, 120, 121; current desire, 117, 118, 120, 121–2; ideal desire, 118, 121; or welfare, 72–4; precedent, 4, 55, 64, 92, 119, 145, 178; principled, 118; whether respecting, 67, 90–5, 116, 117, 120; right to, under ECHR, 58; and sanctity of life, 108; and value of life, 116–19
awareness, low, 42, 62, 83

Baines, P., 84, 85, 101
Baker, J, 64, 65, 94, 124
balancing of interests, child cases, 35, 47
Barclay, S., 147
Beauchamp, T.L., 114, 116, 172–3
Benditt, T.M., 127, 131, 134, 136, 137, 138, 139
beneficence, 116
Benjamin, M., 126, 127, 132, 133, 134, 139
Bentham, Jeremy, 15, 116–17, 120

Berlin, Isaiah, 131–2
Berlusconi, Silvio, 55
best desire autonomy, 117–18, 120, 121
best interests, 5; of adults, 55–65; beyond persistent vegetative state, 62–5; *Bolam* test, 56, 78, 100; of children, 33, 34, 35, 36–50, 107; in English law, 145; and persistent vegetative state, 55–65; and subjective judgments, 120; substituted judgment test, 42, 87–8; treatment decisions, 80–90, 99; welfare and the law, 36–49
Beyleveld, Deryck, 15, 16
Bingham, Sir Thomas (MR), 57, 77, 83
bioethics, 84, 117, 120, 160, 174; US, 149
Birks, P., 148
Bland, Anthony, 55–7, 58, 64; treatment decisions, 77, 78, 79, 82, 83, 87; and value of life, 105, 107, 108, 111, 113, 114, 115
blood transfusions, refusal, 67, 69, 90
Bodey, J., 44
Bolam test: best interests, 56, 78, 100; responsible medical opinion, 161
Bradney, Anthony, 24–5
Brady, Ian, 92
brain damage cases, 41, 42, 59
Brazier, Margot, 156
Bridgeman, J., 84
British Medical Association (BMA), 2, 63, 100
Brooke, L.J., 45
Brown, Sir Stephen (P.), 43, 57, 58, 62
Browne-Wilkinson, Lord, 78
Brownsword, Roger, 3, 15, 16–18, 19, 21–2, 24, 79, 82, 149
Burke, Leslie, 69, 70, 91, 93
Bush, Jeb, 53
Bush, President George W., 54
business law, 22
Butler-Sloss, P., 46, 58, 59, 61, 81, 88, 122, 158

Callahan, Dan, 152
Campbell, A.G.M., 37
Campbell, A.V. (Alastair), 168, 171
CANH *see* clinically assisted nutrition and hydration (CANH)
cardiac massage, 46

cardiopulmonary resuscitation (CPR), 47, 61, 62, 112, 124, 134
Cazalet, J., 44, 106
cerebral palsy cases, 40
Chapman, J.W., 126
children, welfare of, 4, 33–50; balancing of interests, 35, 43; best interests, 33, 34, 35, 36–50, 107; civil court cases, 39–49; duty of care, 38–9, 76; murder charges for failure to fulfil duty of care, 38–9; non-treatment, selective, 39; open-ended declarations relating to, 35, 36; oxygen dependence, 33, 46; palliative care, 44, 48, 49; severely disabled infants, treatment routinely being withdrawn/withheld from, 37–8, 40; specific issue orders, 40; treatment decisions, 81–4; Wyatt case, 33–6; *see also* adults, incapacitated; artificial ventilation; minors
Children Act 1989, 40–1, 50; treatment decisions, 83, 86
Childress, J.F., 114, 116, 172–3
Choudhry, S., 84, 98
civil court cases, 5, 79; children, 39–49
clinical ethics committees (CECs), 6, 165; advantages of use, 155–8; concerns, 159–63, 177; courts and compromise, 177–82; as ethics-heavy but process-light, 7, 161–163; numbers of, 7, 153; and philosophy, 174, 175, 176; questions, 171–2; recommendations for, 7–8, 168, 177; in UK, 160–1, 162–3
clinical ethics consultation: accountability, 171; and English law, 166–7; expertise, 172–6; meetings, 170; monitoring, 171; processes, 168–72; products, 166–8
clinical ethics, discipline of, 174–5
clinical ethics support: consistent guidance, issuing, 166–8; crafting of compromise, 154; for ethics support of, 153–9; against ethics support of, 159–63; goals, 154; process, 161–2; reconstructing, 165–6; in US, 163; values, viewing in, 153–63
clinically assisted nutrition and hydration (CANH), 179; duty to provide, 70; as form of medical treatment, 56, 77–8; treatment

decisions, 91; value of life, 104;
withdrawal or denial in adults, 52,
55, 56, 57, 60, 61, 63, 64, 69, 73,
77, 111, 178; withdrawal or denial
in children, 44–5; *see also* feeding
tubes
Clough, A.H., 110
Coe, Daniel, 57
Coggon, John, 3, 85–6, 90, 93, 95–6,
117, 118, 121, 124
Cohen-Almagor, R., 129
Coleridge, J., 48–9, 61, 145, 146
communication, and compromise,
138, 146
competence issues, 66, 87, 93; core
competencies, 154, 155, 157, 169
complexity, 134, 135, 149
compromise: case for, at limits of life,
123–41; complexity, 134, 135;
confusion objection, 129;
contemplation of, 125–7; in courts
or clinical ethics committees, 163–4;
crafting, 143–64; criticism of,
127–32; English law leaning
towards, 123–5; integrity, 127,
128, 129, 136, 140; and intrinsic
value of life, 124, 132–3, 150; and
morality, 136; mutual respect,
137–8, 140; necessity, 133, 135;
negotiation, 137–8; peaceful
coexistence, 133–4, 135, 145;
principled *see* principled
compromise; prudence, 132–3,
135; reasons for, 132–5; resource
scarcity, 133; surrender objection,
127, 128; in theory and practice,
140–1; three virtues of
compromising, 135–40;
treatment decisions, 143–4;
uncertainty, 134, 135
conflicts: case of Alexandra (B.), 38, 39,
79, 81; case of Charlotte Wyatt *see*
Wyatt, Charlotte: case of; case of
David Glass *see* Glass, David: case of;
case of John Pearson, 39, 49–50, 78,
79; case of Karen Ann Quinlan,
54–5; case of Luke Winston-Jones,
45–6, 87, 98; case of Terri Schiavo
see Schiavo, Terri: case of; principled,
125, 144; treatment decision,
75–6; value of life, 122; of
values, 129
confusion objection, 129
congenital myotonic dystrophy, 48

conjoined twins ('Jodie' and 'Mary'),
separation of, 44–5, 97, 106, 111,
123, 150
Connell, J., 43, 81
consent to treatment, refusal, 43, 44
consequentialism, 113, 114
constitutional constraints, 137
consultancy standards, 171
continuous positive airway pressure
(CPAP), 34
convulsions, 41
Court of Protection, 60, 64, 71, 72
courts: authority of, 145–6; civil court
cases, 39–49, 79; compromise in,
163–4, 177–82; ethics-resistant, 7,
146; High Court jurisdiction, 86;
judicial role, 145–6; law and ethics
in, 148–53; procedural rigour of,
146, 178; as process-heavy but
ethics-light, 7, 148–153; rules, 146,
149; viewing values in, 144–53
courts as vehicle of values: arguments
for, 145–6; arguments against, 146–7
Craig, P., 19, 21
criminal law: children, involving, 38–9;
gross negligence, 77; intentionality,
76, 77; *mens rea* or *actus reus*, 56,
76–7; *see also* homicide law; murder
charges
Cruzan, Nancy, 55
current desire autonomy, 117, 118, 120,
121–2

Daniels, N., 140
Darling, J., 76
Dawson, A., 160
DeGrazia, David, 120, 121
dementia, 116
desire: best, 117–18, 120, 121; current,
117, 118, 120, 121–2; first-order
desires, 117; ideal, 118, 121
Devlin, P., 149
dialysis, 62–3
diamorphine use, 12, 45
Dicey, Albert V., 18
dihydrocodeine (appetite suppressant), 38
discrimination, freedom from (Article
14 ECHR), 13
distributive question, 25
'Do Not Attempt Resuscitation'
(DNAR) orders *see* 'Do Not
Resuscitate' (DNR) orders
'Do Not Resuscitate' (DNR) orders,
12, 52, 62, 161

doctors, legal duties, 56
Donaldson, Lord (MR), 41, 42, 66, 67, 105
Donnelly, M., 88
dosage of medications, 12
double effect doctrine, value of life, 109–10
Douglas, Gillian, 85
Down's syndrome, 38, 39, 79, 81
Doyal, L., 155, 167
drug treatment, 110
Dubler, N.N., 165–6
due process, 19, 168–72
Duff, R.S., 37
Dunn, L.J., 87
duty of care, murder charges for failure to fulfil, 38–9
duty to treat issues, 76–80
Dworkin, Ronald, 18, 19, 20, 117, 118, 157
dying, assisted, 91; *see also* euthanasia

eclectic pragmatism, 168
Edward's syndrome (trisomy 18), 45–6
embryo, status of, 134
End of Life Care Strategy (DoH), 94
enduring power of attorney, 71
Englaro, Eluana, 55, 181
English law: adults, incapacitated, 73; best interests in, 145; and clinical ethics consultation, 166–7; and compromise, 123–5, 144; and immanent critique, 24, 104; substituted judgment test, best interests, 42, 87–8; treatment of incapacitated adults, 51; value of life in, 104–8, 123; values, looking for, 103–4
ethical pluralism, 6, 167
ethics: in and beyond the courts, 148–53; judging *see* judging of ethics; language of, 156; theories, choosing between, 27–8; *see also* morality
Ethics Advisory Committee of the Royal College of Paediatrics and Child Health, 2, 43, 48, 100
Ethox Centre, 155
eunomics, 19
European Convention on Human Rights (ECHR): discrimination, freedom from (Article 14), 13; fair trial, right to (Article 6), 13, 162; inhuman or degrading treatment, right to be free of (Article 3), 44, 59, 69; life, right to (Article 2), 13, 44, 49, 58, 69; private and family life, right to respect for (Article 8), 13, 14, 49, 58, 69
European Court of Human Rights, Strasbourg, 13, 45, 70, 90
euthanasia, 12, 52, 60, 126, 129; in Netherlands, 130; non-voluntary, 114, 115; voluntary, 105; *see also* dying, assisted; assisted dying, resistance to
Euthanasia Examined (Keown), 130
Ewbank, J., 38
expertise: clinical ethics consultation, 172–6; treatment decisions, 98–9, 100

Fagerlin, A., 118–19
fair trial, right to (Article 6 ECHR), 13, 162
Family Procedure Rules 2010, 40
Farquharson, J., 39
feeding tubes, use or withdrawal, 68, 93, 178, 179–80; adults, incapacitated, 1, 51, 52, 53, 54, 58, 59, 64–5; dislodged tubes, 57; *see also* clinically assisted nutrition and hydration (CANH)
Finnis, John, 15, 18, 20, 82, 130
first-order desires, 117
Fletcher, J., 154
formal justice, 168
formal rationality, 3, 16–17, 21, 24, 30
Foster, C., 94–5, 99
Fox, E., 154
Frankfurt, H.G., 117, 118
Fraser, J., 158–9
Fuller, Lon L., 15, 16, 17, 21, 22, 24, 29, 136; legal fiction, 88; Rule of Law, 19–20; treatment decisions, 84, 85, 86
functional magnetic resonance imaging (fMRI), 54, 61
futility concerns, 181; persistent vegetative state, treatment in case of, 56, 62, 64, 78; value of life, 111–13; withholding of treatment, in children, 34, 50

gastrostomy tubes *see* feeding tubes
General Medical Council (GMC), 2, 63, 65, 69, 100, 145, 180
Gewirth, Alan, 18, 25
Gillon, Raanan, 113, 116

Glass, David: case of, 3, 4, 37, 43, 50, 75, 181; diamorphine administration, 12, 45; judging of law and ethics, 11–14, 15, 17, 18, 27, 30; principles of Court of Appeal, 22; treatment decisions, 89, 90, 98, 143
Goff, Lord, 51, 55, 77, 78
Golding, M.P., 126, 130, 131, 136, 137, 138, 139
good faith, bargaining in, 139
Greer, J., 53, 54
grievous bodily harm, intention to cause, 76
Groningen protocol, Netherlands, 151
Grubb, A., 78
Guillain-Barré syndrome, withdrawal of ventilation, 159
Gunn, M.J., 79

haemophagocytic lymphohistiocytosis, 47
Hailsham, Lord, 25
Halliday, R., 112
Harrington, J., 100
Harris, J., 114, 130
Hart, H.L.A., 15, 19–20, 149
Hedley, J., 33–4, 35, 36, 45, 46, 59–60
Hendrick, Judith, 171
Herring, J., 85, 89
High Court jurisdiction, 86
Hillsborough football stadium disaster, 55
Hinchliffe, M., 57
Hitler, Adolf, 129
Hoffmann, L.J., 103
holding operations, 79
Holm, S., 128, 129–30, 174
Holman, J., 47, 81, 82, 87, 97, 100, 124
homicide law, 39, 76; and value of life, 104, 105
Hughes, J., 67
Human Rights Act 1998, 44, 45, 58, 61, 69, 105, 162
hydrocephalus cases, 11, 40
hypoxia, 51

ideal desire autonomy, 118, 121
immanent critique, 5, 23–4, 30, 104
in loco parentis, 76, 79
independent mental capacity advocate (IMCA), 71–2
informed consent, 120

inhuman or degrading treatment, right to be free of (Article 3 ECHR), 44, 59, 69
Inside the Ethics Committee (Radio 4), 178–9
instrumental rationality, 3, 16, 17, 21, 22, 30
instrumental value of life, 105, 106, 107, 114–16, 121; *see also* value of life
integrity, 14, 127, 128, 129, 136, 140
intellectual milestones, 80–1, 84
intentionality, 109; criminal law, 76, 77
interest groups, 38
internal morality, 8, 29, 136, 169
intolerability, 35, 46, 50, 62, 80, 87, 107
intrinsic value of life, 105, 107, 109–13, 114, 144; acting vs omitting, 110, 115; and compromise, 124, 132–3, 150; *see also* value of life
intubation, 12, 33, 36, 46, 48, 51; *see also* artificial ventilation
ischiopagus tetrapus conjoined twins *see* conjoined twins ('Jodie' and 'Mary'), separation of
Islam, 63, 67, 128

James, T., 148, 149–50
Jehovah's Witnesses, 67, 90, 128
Jennings, Ivor, 18
Johnson, J., 44–5, 111
Jonsen, A.R., 157, 172, 173
Judaism/Judeo-Christian thinking, 43, 105, 109
'judge knows best' model, 101
judging of ethics: immanent critique of law, 6, 23–4, 30; judgments, principles and theories distinguished, 4, 26, 30; from within law, 22–5; from outside the law, 25–9
judging of law: from within, 14–16; criteria for, 16–18, 21–2, 30; legal fictions, avoiding, 22, 88; rational law, criteria for, 16–18, 30; Rule of Law, 18–20, 21
justice, 116, 168

Kant, Immanuel, 28, 116, 117, 118, 182
Kelsen, Hans, 15

Kennedy, Ian, 42, 78, 96–7, 177
Keown, John, 78, 105, 106, 108, 150;
    Euthanasia Examined, 130; value of
    life, 110–13, 114, 121
Kirkwood, J., 63
'know-ability,' 21, 86–9
Kramer, M., 15, 20
Kuflik, A., 126, 128, 133–4, 135, 136,
    137, 139
Kuhse, H., 113
Kutner, Luis, 65

Lamb, D., 28
Lane, L.J., 77
language of ethics, 156
Lantos, J.D., 179
lasting power of attorney (LPA), 71–2;
    treatment decisions, 87, 90, 93, 97
law: action-guiding function, 75; in and
    beyond the courts, 148–53;
    conceptual sense, 15; immanent
    critique, 23–4, 30; inner morality of,
    17; judging *see* judging of law;
    judging of ethics from within, 22–5;
    whether a moral enterprise, 15, 149;
    rational, criteria for, 16–18, 30
Lee, R., 101, 152
legal fictions, 22, 88
legal positivism, 15, 149
Leggatt report, 156
Leonard, Elmore, 26
liability control, 171
liberty, 116–17
life, right to (Article 2 ECHR), 13, 44,
    49, 58, 69
life-sustaining measures, 5, 97; in
    adults, 52, 54, 55, 56, 60, 62, 65, 66,
    71, 72; in children, 36–7, 44;
    withholding/withdrawing, 4, 76,
    106, 141; *see also* artificial
    ventilation; cardiopulmonary
    resuscitation (CPR); clinically
    assisted nutrition and hydration
    (CANH)
like cases, treating alike: as formal
    principle of justice, 26; treatment
    decisions, 80–4
liver transplant, withholding of, 43,
    50, 81
living wills *see* advance directives
locked-in state, 53
logonomocentrism, 24
low awareness states, 42, 62, 83
Lowry, Lord, 77

LPA *see* lasting power of attorney (LPA)
Lyons, B., 81, 84, 179

machine, body viewed as, 112; *see also*
    mind-body separation
MacIntyre, Alastair, 15, 138
Maclean, A.R., 92, 123–4
May, W.F., 132, 151
McCall Smith, A., 158, 170–1
McHaffie, H.E., 97
McLean, Sheila, 78, 148, 149, 168,
    177; and clinical ethics support,
    159, 160, 161, 162, 163–4, 165
Meadow, W.L., 179
medical law, 3, 22, 30, 120, 153;
    'de-moralisation,' 152, 164
medical treatment: CANH as form
    of, 56, 77–8; life-sustaining *see*
    life-sustaining measures;
    proportionate or disproportionate,
    106, 110; serious, removal of, 72;
    see also treatment decisions; *specific
    types of treatment*
Meller, S., 147
Melley, C.D., 175
mens rea ('mental' element of offence),
    56, 76–7
Mental Capacity Act 2005, 5, 60, 61,
    63, 64, 70, 180; treatment decisions,
    73, 82, 83, 87, 88, 91, 94, 95, 98;
    value of life, 108, 124
mental disorder, 66, 69
Mental Health Act 1983, 66
mental state welfare/mental statism, 120
mercy-killing *see* euthanasia
metabolic conditions, 48
Michalowski, S., 81
Miers, David, 84
Mill, John Stuart, 114, 116–17, 120
mind-body separation, 107; *see also*
    machine, body viewed as
minimally conscious state (MCS), 53,
    59, 63, 64, 73, 124; treatment
    decisions, 83, 93; *see also* persistent
    vegetative state (PVS)
minors, 62
Miola, J., 150
monitoring, 171
Montgomery, J., 152, 164
moral integrity, 129
moral philosophy, 25–6, 131, 148, 174
moralism, 174
morality: of aspiration, 20; and
    compromise, 136; ideal moral

judgment, 26; internal, 8, 29, 136, 169; of law, 15, 17; legal enforcement, 149; objective, 129; pre-reflective and reflective intuitions, 27; simplicity of moral theory, 28; *see also* ethics
Moratti, S., 179
Morgan, D., 5, 101, 152
morphine use, 11, 12
Morris, A., 87, 98
Morrow, Reverend, 39, 56
motor neurone disease, 67
multiple sclerosis, 68
Munby, J., 67, 68, 69, 90, 106, 107, 113, 152, 153
murder charges: ceasing of artificial feeding, 56, 76, 77; failure to fulfil duty of care, 38–9; separation of conjoined twins, 45
Mustill, Lord, 77, 78, 83
mutual accommodation, 139
mutual respect, 137–8, 140

Nachi, M., 136, 139
naso-gastric feeding, 40, 46, 55, 77; *see also* clinically assisted nutrition and hydration (CANH); feeding tubes
National Council for Palliative Care (NCPC), 1, 180
National Institute for Health and Clinical Excellence (NICE), 140
natural law, 15, 20
necessity, 133, 135
needle phobia, 118
negligence, 77
negotiation, 137–8, 141
Netherlands, 130; Groningen protocol in, 151
Newson, Ainsley, 162, 176
non-contradiction principle, 16–17, 26, 29
non-maleficence, 116
normative pluralism, 131–2
Nozick, R., 16
Nuffield Council on Bioethics, 154

objective judgments/rules: treatment decisions, 84–5; value of life, 120–2
objective morality, 129
objective welfare, 121
Odysseus, 5, 65, 95, 101, 119
Office of the Public Guardian, registration with, 72
O'Neill, O., 117, 118, 137

Ormerod, Mary, 65
oxygen dependence, 33, 46; *see also* artificial ventilation

palliative care, 62, 63, 179; children, 44, 48, 49
paranoid schizophrenia, 66
parental responsibility, 40
Parker, J., 49
peaceful coexistence, 133–4, 135, 145
Pearson, G., 23–4, 25
Pearson, John, 39, 49–50, 78, 79
Pedersen, R., 160, 168
Pennock, J.R., 126
percutaneous endoscopic gastrostomy (PEG) tubes *see* feeding tubes
'perform-ability,' 21, 93; treatment decisions, 86, 89
permanent vegetative state (PVS) *see* persistent vegetative state (PVS)
persistent vegetative state (PVS), 37, 53, 178; in adults, 55–62, 86; artificial nutrition and hydration, withdrawing, 44–5, 56; and best interests, 55–62; best interests beyond, 62–5; description, 52; futility concerns, 56, 62, 64, 78; Practice Notes, 57, 83; Royal College of Physicians, guidelines of, 58; treatment decisions, 78, 82, 83, 90, 97; *see also* minimally conscious state (MCS)
personal integrity, 129
personhood, 134
Pétrovici, 127
philosophy: analytic, 160; and clinical ethics committees, 174, 175, 176; moral, 25–6, 131, 148, 174
pluralism: ethical, 6, 167; normative, 131–2
Pollock, Lansing, 25–6, 28, 29, 137, 146
post-coma unresponsiveness *see* persistent vegetative state (PVS)
Potter, P., 48, 61
powers of attorney, lasting *see* lasting power of attorney (LPA)
precedent autonomy, 4, 55, 64, 92, 119, 145, 178
preference welfare, 120
Price, David, 112–13
principled autonomy, 118
principled compromise, 6, 124, 126, 141, 179; courts or clinical ethical committees, 7, 144, 146, 147, 157;

virtues of compromising, 136, 137, 139, 140; *see also* compromise
principled resolution, 125, 144, 165, 166, 181
private and family life, right to respect for (Article 8 ECHR), 13, 14, 49, 58, 69
professional misconduct, 64–5
prolonging of life, 78, 107, 119; in children, 42, 43–4, 45
proxy decision-making, 55
prudence, 132–3, 135
PVS *see* persistent vegetative state (PVS)

quadriplegia cases, 11, 41
quality of life, 41, 47, 63, 81, 116; intolerable, 35, 46, 50, 62, 80, 87, 107; *see also* sanctity of human life; value of life
Quigley, M., 101
Quinlan, Karen Ann, 54–5, 103

Rachels, James, 111, 115
Radin, M.J., 19, 21, 86
rationality: criteria for, 16–18, 30; formal, 3, 16–17, 21, 24, 30; instrumental, 3, 16, 17, 21, 22, 30; interpretation, 16; substantive, 3, 16, 22; treatment decisions, 80, 81
Rawls, John, 18, 20, 27
Raz, Joseph, 18, 19, 20, 21
refusal of treatment, advance, 65, 67, 69, 71, 73, 91, 94; amputation, 66, 93; *see also* advance directives
Regan, Tom, 26, 27–8, 29, 121, 137, 146
Reiter-Theil, S., 156
religion, influence of, 43, 63, 147; Jehovah's Witnesses, 67, 90, 128; Judeo-Christian thinking, 105, 109; Roman Catholicism, 52, 105, 109
resolution, principled, 125, 144, 165, 166, 181
resource scarcity, 133
resuscitation issues, 11, 12, 33, 41, 47; *see also* artificial ventilation, withholding/withdrawing; oxygen dependence
Ricœur, Paul, 126
risk management, 171
Roman Catholicism, 52, 105, 109
Royal College of Nursing (RCN), 2
Royal College of Paediatrics and Child Health (RCPCH), 2, 48; *see also* Ethics Advisory Committee of the

Royal College of Paediatrics and Child Health
Royal College of Physicians, 58, 154, 155, 161
Rubin, S.B., 174
Rule of Law, 18–20, 21
rule-handling, 16
Ryder, J., 61, 62

Sabin, J.E., 140
Salter, M., 23–4, 25
Samanta, J., 87–8
sanctity of human life, 124, 150, 151; adults, incapacitated, 51, 56; children, 41, 43; treatment decisions, 108, 113; *see also* value of life
Santayana, George, 127
Sawyer, Caroline, 83
Schiavo, Terri: case of, 4, 75, 143, 181; adults, incapacitated, 51–4, 55, 59, 67, 72; 'Terri's Law,' 53–4
Schneider, C.E., 118–19
Scott Baker, J., 13, 41
self-determination: right to, 51, 70, 90; self-determined value of life, 116–19; and value of life, 105, 108, 116–19
Shapiro, M., 147, 178
Sheldon, S., 150
Siegler, M., 154, 172, 173
Simmonds, N.E., 15, 20
Singer, Peter, 107, 114, 115, 116, 174
slow code, 179
Smith, J.C., 79
Society for the Protection of Unborn Children and Life, 38
spina bifida, 115
spinal muscular atrophy, 43, 46–7, 82
stare decisis doctrine, 175
Steyn, Lord, 28
stigmata cases, 101, 152
subjective judgments: treatment decisions, 95–101; value of life, 120–2
substantive question, 25
substantive rationality, 3, 16, 22
substituted judgment test, 42, 87–8
suicide, decriminalisation of, 108
surrender objection, 127, 128
system rationality, 16

Tännsjö, T., 129
Taylor, Dr, 64–5
Taylor, L.J., 41, 42

Templeman, L.J., 38, 80, 87
Terry, J., 143, 158
Thorpe, J., 66, 148
tolerability of life, 41; intolerability, 35, 46, 50, 62, 80, 87, 107
total parenteral nutrition (TPN), 48
treatment decisions, 75–101; best interests, 80–90; children, 81–4; compromise, 143–4; denial of treatment for severely disabled infants, 37–8, 40; duty to treat issues, 76–80; whether know-ability and perform-ability, 86–90; like cases, whether to treat alike, 80–4; non-treatment, selective, 39; whether objective rules, 84–5; refusal of treatment, advance, 65, 66, 67, 69, 71, 73, 91, 94; standards, guiding, 100; whether subjective judgments, 95–101; taking exception, 79; to treat or not to treat question, 1, 2, 8, 31, 50, 75–6, 89, 95, 120, 133, 143–4, 166, 178; withholding or withdrawing of treatment *see* artificial ventilation, withholding/withdrawing; clinically assisted nutrition and hydration (CANH); *see also* medical treatment
Twining, William, 84
twins, conjoined *see* conjoined twins ('Jodie' and 'Mary'), separation of

UK Clinical Ethics Network (UK CEN), 154, 155, 159, 169, 176
uncertainty, 134, 135
United States (US), 149, 152, 155, 158, 163, 172
unresponsive wakefulness syndrome *see* persistent vegetative state (PVS)
utilitarianism, 27, 114, 131

value enquiries, 145
value of life, 103–22; absolute, 109; and autonomy, 116–19; calculating, 109–19; and conflict, 122; double effect doctrine, 109–10; in English law, 104–8, 123; futility concerns, 111–13; instrumental,

105, 106, 107, 114–16, 121; intrinsic *see* intrinsic value of life; self-determination, 105, 108, 116–19; subjective or objective judgments, 120–2; *see also* sanctity of human life
values: conflicts of, 129; courts as vehicles of, 145–7; looking for, in English law, 103–4; viewing in clinical ethics support, 153–63; viewing in court, 144–53
vegetative state (VS), 64, 73, 82, 83; *see also* persistent vegetative state (PVS)
ventilation, artificial *see* artificial ventilation, withholding/withdrawing
Verhagen, A.A.E., 179
vitalism, 109, 113

Waite, J., 42
Wall, L.J., 35, 50, 165
Ward, L.J., 40, 45, 57, 97, 123
welfare: and children, 36–49; mental state/preference, 120; objective, 121; or autonomy, 72–4; principle, 40, 85
wholeness, 128; *see also* best interests
Wilkinson, D., 86–7
Wilkinson, S., 150, 160
Williams, Glanville, 38
Williamson, L., 173
Willigenburg, T. van, 128–9, 132, 134, 137, 139–40
Winslade, W., 172, 173
Winslow, B.J. and G.R., 134, 135, 138, 139, 157
Winston-Jones, Luke, 45–6, 87, 98
Winterton, Ann, 151
Wolf, S.M., 161, 163
Woolf, Lord (MR), 13, 23, 43, 75
Wooltorton, Kerrie, 91
worth, 109
Wyatt, Charlotte: case of, 4, 33–6, 37, 45, 46, 50, 75, 147, 156, 181; treatment decisions, 80–1, 86, 87, 98, 143

Zoloth-Dorfman, L., 174
Zolpidem (sleeping pill), 61

Taylor & Francis ———————————

eBooks

FOR LIBRARIES

ORDER YOUR
FREE 30 DAY
INSTITUTIONAL
TRIAL TODAY!

Over 23,000 eBook titles in the Humanities,
Social Sciences, STM and Law from some of the
world's leading imprints.

Choose from a range of subject packages or create your own!

Benefits for
you

▶ Free MARC records
▶ COUNTER-compliant usage statistics
▶ Flexible purchase and pricing options

Benefits
for your
user

▶ Off-site, anytime access via Athens or referring URL
▶ Print or copy pages or chapters
▶ Full content search
▶ Bookmark, highlight and annotate text
▶ Access to thousands of pages of quality research
   at the click of a button

For more information, pricing enquiries or to order
a free trial, contact your local online sales team.

UK and Rest of World: **online.sales@tandf.co.uk**

US, Canada and Latin America:
e-reference@taylorandfrancis.com

www.ebooksubscriptions.com

ALPSP Award for
BEST eBOOK
PUBLISHER
2009 Finalist

Taylor & Francis eBooks
Taylor & Francis Group

A flexible and dynamic resource for teaching, learning and research.